PHILOSOPHICAL AND SOCIOLOGICAL PERSPECTIVES IN EDUCATION

PHILOSOPHICAL AND SOCIOLOGICAL PERSPECTIVES IN EDUCATION

Dr. M.S. Talawar
M.A., M.Ed., Ph.D.
Professor in Education &
Director –UGC-Academic Staff College,
Bangalore University, Bangalore

Dr. V.A. Benakanal
M.A., M.Ed., M.Phil., Ph.D.

CENTRUM PRESS
NEW DELHI-110002 (INDIA)

CENTRUM PRESS
H.O.: 4360/4, Ansari Road, Daryaganj,
New Delhi-110 002 (India)
Ph.: 23278000, 23261597

B.O.: No. 1015, Ist Main Road, **BSK IIIrd Stage**
IIIrd Phase, IIIrd Block,
Bangalore - 560 085 (India)
Tel.: 080-41723429
Visit us at: www.centrumpress.com

Philosophical and Sociological Perspectives in Education

First Edition, 2009

PRINTED IN INDIA

Printed at Balaji Offset, Delhi

Contents

Preface

Educational processes are rooted in and are defined by, philosophical thoughts and social realities; it is therefore necessary for educators to do the better to comprehend the complexities which lie behind making education accessible for everybody. The sociology of education is the study of how public institutions and individual experiences affect education and its outcome. It is most concerned with the public schooling systems of modern industrial societies, including the expansion of higher, further, adult, and continuing education.

Education has always been seen as a fundamentally optimistic human endeavour characterised by aspirations for progress and betterment. It is understood by many to be a means of overcoming handicaps, achieving greater equality and acquiring wealth and status. Having a "philosophy of education," in this sense of the term, is simply a phrase for the process in which educational practitioners or reformers develop thoughtful, and to varying degrees systematic or coherent, justifications for their educational practices and commitments (something with which, not surprisingly, few academic philosophers have had very much experience or direct concern).

Education is perceived as a place where children can develop according to their unique needs and potential. It is also perceived as one of the best means of achieving greater social equality. Philosophy and sociology serve as highly resourceful subjects for understanding the mechanisms operating behind the prevalence of education, even as they draw from the educational field itself.

Author

Unit I

Fundamentals of Philosophy of Education

MEANING AND CONCEPT OF PHILOSOPHY OF EDUCATION

The first difficulty in tracing the development of the term "philosophy of education" is that throughout most of Western thought what might be regarded broadly as philosophical reflections on education were never regarded as constituting a distinct discipline or branch of philosophy. On the one hand, for most of the great writers in the philosophy of education pantheon (such as Plato, Aristotle, or Rousseau) such reflections were continuous with their accounts of epistemology, ethics, politics, or human nature. It would never have occurred to them that a philosophy of education could be developed that was not, at heart, an elaboration of such "purely" philosophical themes. (Though in some cases the ruminations of philosophers on education has had little or nothing to do with their actual philosophical positions and has merely expressed their own predilections.)

At the same time, and from what might be termed the opposite direction of the theory-practice dialectic, what today is called "philosophy of education" has also long been regarded as continuous with the serious reflections of practicing educators, curriculum theorists, and educational policymakers. Having a "philosophy of education," in this sense of the term, is simply a phrase for the process in which educational practitioners or reformers develop thoughtful, and to varying degrees systematic or coherent, justifications for their educational practices and commitments (something with which, not surprisingly, few academic philosophers have had very much experience or direct concern). Hence, while in the contemporary context a central tension within philosophy of education has been between its philosophical, disciplinary aspirations and its relevance to educational policy and practice, at earlier points in its development this dichotomy would not have been recognized, either from the perspective of the philosopher or from the perspective of the educationist.

These continuities are particularly striking when viewed in an international context, where philosophy of education has been a less professionalized and institutionalized endeavor and where, as a consequence, it has been less isolated from other educational concerns. In European thought, for example, education has consistently been considered in a broader context apart from schooling, and so a "philosophy of education" has usually been regarded as continuous with concerns about childrearing generally. In many non-European traditions, issues of intellectual development are frequently not regarded as separate from matters of spiritual, moral, or cultural development. Here, something that could be termed a "philosophy of education" would need to be also a philosophy of faith or duty to some larger source of identity and identification. The repeated use of quotation marks here is therefore necessary because in fact the phrase "philosophy of education" rarely comes up in such contexts: in many European contexts, for example, the phrase "pedagogical science" or "theory" encompasses many of the same activities that philosophers of education take as their domain.

This is revealing, first, in helping to introduce the question of what the very name "philosophy of education" assumes about the nature of philosophy and its relation to educational concerns and, second, in leading us to ask where the phrase does come from, and why it has gained the meanings, particularly in English-speaking contexts, that it has. This becomes a particularly delicate, even intractable, problem when attempting to offer an institutionalized perspective on a field, as in this chapter. In both contexts across nations and contexts across disciplines of practice, many people are involved in teaching and writing about issues that could be called, in the broadest sense, "philosophies of education" (rather like "philosophies of life," one might say). Yet only a portion of these are identified with the organizations, graduate programs, and journals that use this particular label and hence authorize what counts as official knowledge in this field.

Should a proposed account of philosophy of education be drawn broadly enough to encompass all activities that might be identified as such, or narrowly in terms of a label that has professional and institutional authorization? I have settled for the narrower, institutionalized account, largely because it is a story that deserves to be considered for its own sake, but also because documentation is more easily available to substantiate it. As a result, I am dealing with philosophy of education within the context of a particular history of concepts and debates, which is a subset of all the possible activities that might be classified as part of it. Others would certainly offer a different criterion of demarcation.

THE FORMATION OF PHILOSOPHY OF EDUCATION

The origins of philosophy of education as a distinct discipline arrived with the 19th century in English-speaking countries, most notably the United States. First of all, they accompanied the spread of an Enlightenment faith in the reasoned formulation of public policy, the attempt to ground policy on a systematic, consistent foundation of purposes and justifications. At the same time, they accompanied a growing institutionalization and professionalization of the teaching endeavor itself, especially as it was expressed in the ideals of public education and the common school. In this context, a philosophy of education was intimately linked with the argument for a conception of personal betterment and social perfectibility that would serve to initiate, guide, and inspire practitioners, and to justify this set of aims to a broader public that was being asked to support and fund educational programs on an unprecedented scale.

While still not described by the name "philosophy of education," such formulations of purpose and justification can be seen as the first explicit attempts to develop a reasoned, general account of the meaning and aims of education. And what is most significant about this development is the assumption, difficult for us to recognize today as it has become so widely accepted, that it is either possible or desirable to provide such a general account. Soon, having a philosophy of education was seen as an indispensable dimension of competent, responsible practice in education. Such a belief was centrally established on the educational agenda by the life's work of John Dewey. No one before him had so persistently argued for the need for educational practice to be grounded in sound philosophical principles (and, of equal importance to him, but often neglected by commentators, the corresponding need for philosophical reflection to be informed by educational practice). Certainly no philosopher writing about education has ever, before or since, been so prolific.

Dewey, through his voluminous publications and his many talks and articles as a public intellectual, had a singular effect on the theory and practice of education. His approach, broadly termed "Progressive education," but often conflated with the wider movement of Progressivism in the U.S. after the turn of the century, emphasized the independent motivations of the learner, the need for schools to be small-scale laboratories for experiments in democratic social reform, and the basis of authentic learning in inquiry and experience.

Yet the lasting legacy of Dewey must be traced, not only in terms of the shifting fortunes of Progressivism as an educational philosophy (about which even Dewey voiced skepticism as it took various shapes in U.S. schools), but in the establishment of the idea that practitioners must have an educational philosophy, and the relentless promotion of a particular one as the potential basis of *all* educational thought and practice. It is during this period that we see the first codified account of the phrase "philosophy of education" in Paul Monroe's *Cyclopedia of Education* in 1911-13. We see the beginnings of the argument for requiring courses in the preparation of educators that seek to promote the systematic, grounded formulation and justification of educational aims. And we see, significantly, the first professional organization dedicated to philosophical reflection on education, the John Dewey Society (JDS), in 1935.

The emergence of professional organizations is crucial for a variety of reasons. As these took shape across a range of academic disciplines in the U.S. just after the turn of the century, they were not simply the institutionalized embodiment of fields of intellectual practice, nor simply convocations of like-minded scholars seeking an opportunity to share their ideas. They had consistent effects in reshaping the fields they represented. As we will see, this is strikingly true in the case of philosophy of education. For this reason, it is not an exaggeration to consider "the possibility that the origins of educational philosophy were better attached to the organizations of its embodiment than to their annotated bibliographies".

This claim becomes even more plausible when one considers the shifting fortunes of the publications sponsored by these organizations – the publications that, by accepting and rejecting certain articles, determine what *can* be included on "annotated bibliographies". In the case of the John Dewey Society, as with other professional organizations in the social sciences and humanities, debates often centered around the degree and forms of social activism and advocacy that were appropriate to a professional organization, as such. Inspired by Dewey's own role as a public intellectual and his involvement across a range of political issues throughout his career, the members of JDS saw a close connection between their teaching, writing, and social commitments.

Yet within this shared understanding, there were strong disagreements over the substance of political issues and over the kinds of activism that were appropriate. Many of these debates revolved around the journal *The Social Frontier*, which, under the editorship of George S. Counts, expressed positions that rested uneasily with many members of JDS and, indeed, with Dewey himself. Over time, these concerns were manifested in the formation of a new, separate organization, the Philosophy of Education Society (PES), in 1941. In many respects, this event marks a crucial turn in the development of philosophy of education as a discipline (indeed, of its aspiration to regard itself as a distinct discipline). R. Bruce Raup and the other founders of PES were quite explicit about defining their organization, in contrast with JDS, as a professional society and not an advocacy group.

This insistence took the form of, first, beginning with a self-selected charter membership of 34 persons who explicitly distanced themselves from the policies and views of JDS; second, establishing strict criteria of membership, and levels of membership, that would insure that "professional" philosophers of education would always constitute a voting majority of the organization; and, third, proclaiming that philosophical method was the disciplinary core that provided the field with its substance and credibility.

It is important to see the fundamental interdependence of these three choices: of excluding activism and partisanship, of establishing strict "professional" criteria of membership, and of proclaiming a disciplinary method as the principle uniting PES's members. Choices about intellectual method or the scope of a discipline need to be seen, in this context, as implicated in decisions about the inclusion and exclusion of people and their points of view. Soon after this, in 1954, a select PES committee sought to formalize philosophy of education as a discrete discipline, based on suitable philosophical methods.

The formation of PES was followed, in Great Britain, by the formation of a similar society, the Philosophy of Education Society of Great Britain (1966), which was seen as heralding a "revolution in philosophy of education," involving a "greater consciousness of and involvement with the methods and results of philosophy as an academic discipline". Partly because of the dominance of the influence of R.S. Peters and P.H. Hirst, and their analytic conception of philosophy of education, Kaminsky (1993, 191) calls PESGB during this period a "profoundly conservative" organization, characterized by a narrow preoccupation with that analytic approach to philosophical method.

The force of this hegemony was so strong that a commentator such as Dearden could say, with no sense of self-contradiction, that "I do not myself think that philosophy of education stands in need of a single paradigm," then follow this by saying that whatever it is, philosophy of education must be concerned with "general concepts, principles, positions and practices"; that it should make "necessary distinctions to clarify meaning," should "explore conceptual possibilities," "identify what is necessary and what is contingent," "expose question-begging...and inconsistency," "draw implications," "reveal absurd consequences," "test assumptions," "probe the validity of justifications," and so forth – all activities which, whatever their merit, clearly express the orientations of a particular conception of philosophical method.

The prominence of R.S. Peters in Britain, his influence on contemporaries such as Hirst and Dearden, and his many students who carried forth his reputation and commitment to analytic philosophy make him a pivotal figure in the philosophy of education. His argument that the term "education" itself required analysis, and the results of his investigations – that the term refers to a process of "initiation" into a form of life, and that to call something "educational" is to valorize the means and ends of that process (as opposed to socialization into norms that may be instrumentally beneficial but not of intrinsic value) – defined an agenda of questions, and a method of inquiry, that helped shape the approach of a generation of philosophers of education throughout the English-speaking world.

At the same time, during the 1960s and 70s, the analytic approach gained predominance in the U.S. as well, especially through the influence of Israel Scheffler (although he was never active in PES). Scheffler, even more than Peters, focused on the justifiability of the means and ends of education from an epistemological point of view: Do the activities of teaching support the development of reason, both as a process of learning and as an educational aim itself? Where do relativism and activism in education threaten this ideal of rationality? How can the analysis of educational language detect the effects of slogans and ideologies of belief? In many respects, the faith in analytic methods in philosophy of education was stronger and more absolute in the U.S. than in Britain. Hence, although it is often assumed that the influence of the analytic school ran from the British side of the Atlantic toward the U.S., a good argument can be made that the main influences actually ran in the other direction.

Either way, in both contexts analytic work in philosophy came to dominate the articles found in the respective journals sponsored by PES and PESGB. *Educational Theory,* originally established by JDS in 1951 but soon co-sponsored by PES as well, came to represent what Kaminsky calls a "thoroughly professional version" of philosophy of education. The *Proceedings* of the PES meetings during these years show a similar convergence around specific issues and styles of philosophical argumentation. At the height of this analytic period, as Kaminsky (1993, 89) tells it, "At the 1971 meeting of the Philosophy of Education Society, Jonas Soltis declared that 'we are all analytical philosophers,' and no one laughed."

In yet another English-speaking context, Australia and New Zealand, the Philosophy of Education Society of Australasia (PESA) was formed in 1970. *Educational Philosophy and Theory,* which was to become its sponsored journal, actually preceded the formation of PESA by one year. While the influence of analytic work was felt strongly in these countries as well, in both Australia and New Zealand there was from the very beginning a more skeptical attitude toward the dominance of analytic philosophy (expressed most directly, perhaps, in the work of Kevin Harris, Michael Matthews, and Jim Walker) and, during the 70s, a much wider acceptance of Left scholarship as legitimate terrain for philosophers of education, although this perspective was also seen increasingly in work presented at PES (which came to see itself increasingly as an international organization, comprising not only scholars from the United States and Canada, but from around the world) and at PESGB.

THE METHODS OF PHILOSOPHY OF EDUCATION

This account reveals a particular consequence of the professionalization of philosophy of education, as it was expressed in the aspiration to ground itself on philosophical method. It meant, during the period being described here, a desire to establish standards of rigor and tough-mindedness that could help this emergent field attain academic credibility. The methods of philosophical analysis were ideally suited to a stance of clear-eyed skepticism in the face of educational claptrap; of reasoned, balanced objectivity in the face of highly contested educational disputes; and of providing a helpful, elucidative service that colleagues in education – whether in pedagogy, policy, or research – could find amenable to their concerns.

Without neglecting the philosophical arguments that were posed in favor of analytic method, to which I will turn in a moment, there can be little doubt that these stances also suited the professional self-interest of a discipline seeking academic credibility as philosophically rigorous, in part through stronger affiliations with professional associations in philosophy. They also reinforced a position of nonpartisanship in the constantly shifting arena of competing educational fads and trends. Analytic philosophy of education made substantial contributions in elucidating such concepts as "authority," "indoctrination," and even the terms "teaching" and "education" themselves.

This method specialized in offering fine-grained distinctions and typologies; diagnosing hidden equivocations or blurriness in the ordinary concepts found within educational slogans or clichés; and criticizing faulty logic or misleading uses of statistics or other evidence. In many cases, educators found such analyses salutary and helpful: this was philosophy in the service of plain speaking and no nonsense. This analytic movement within philosophy of education followed (though lagging by several years) developments within Anglo-American philosophy: notably the movement of logical positivism and various forms of linguistic philosophy. But the arguments raised in favor of analytic methods had the widespread appeal that they did within philosophy of education, in large part, because of their congruence with other imperatives within the field as an increasingly professionalized discipline.

First, as Maloney points out, there is a certain ambivalence that has often accompanied philosophy of education: on the one hand seeking credibility in relation to the traditions of philosophy; on the other seeking legitimacy within the often-utilitarian climate of schools of education. This tension tends to pull philosophy of education in competing, incompatible directions and helps to account for what she calls (1985, 252) the relentless need to *explain* and *justify* the discipline – hence the perennial business of negotiating and renegotiating just what philosophy of education is. Analytic method seemed to hold promise as the indisputably philosophical core that would uncontroversially link the discourses of philosophy of education with mainstream philosophy.

At the same time, its appeal to clarity and logic meant that philosophers of education would not have to endure the accusations of abstraction, obscurantism, and irrelevance they often heard within schools of education – here, finally, was something *useful* that philosophers could offer policymakers and practitioners. Second, the rise of analytic method clearly severed the chains joining philosophy of education, especially in the U.S., to the ghost of Dewey.

While the polymorphous Dewey continued, and continues, to be read and reread in light of shifting philosophical trends (so that topics such as "Dewey and Marxism," "Dewey and Karl Popper," "Dewey and Feminism," "Dewey and Foucault," and so on, remain a hardy staple of scholarship in the field), the analytic period established the independence of philosophy of education (and, in the U.S. and Canada, the Philosophy of Education Society) from Progressivism (and the John Dewey Society). Once again, there were both professional and philosophical reasons for this split.

Third, the analytic movement in philosophy of education took a particular shape in opposition to the movement that had preceded it, the so-called "isms" approach: the recounting of traditional philosophical positions – with varying degrees of philosophical depth and accuracy – then tracing their "implications" for education. One of the central tenets of the analytic school, repeated often, was that there were no direct implications of substantive philosophical positions for education: that a person may believe in Realism, for instance, but still favor any of a variety of educational aims and practices. The attempt to provide encapsulated summaries of complex, difficult philosophical positions, and then to read off from them neat implications for practice, was regarded as being philosophically sloppy, first of all, and as overpromising what philosophy could provide to education.

This debate and transition away from the "isms" approach can be traced across a series of NSSE Yearbooks devoted to philosophy of education, published in 1942, 1955, 1972, and 1981. Yet, not incidentally, this rejection of the "isms" approach and the attendant view that philosophies had implications for education also put at one more remove the concerns of professional philosophy of education from those of practitioners.

No longer would a required course for teachers, for example, promise to help students acquire or formulate their own "philosophy of education" – instead, these courses promised to help them "think philosophically" about their educational aims and practices, whatever they were. This transition to a philosophically grounded discipline reached its apotheosis in the subtitle of the 1981 NSSE Yearbook: "Philosophy *and* Education" (emphasis added). Similarly, the journal *Studies in Philosophy and Education*, which ran from 1960-1976, then lay dormant until 1989, was acquired by a commercial publisher and resuscitated as a journal with an emphasis on "clarity and excellence in philosophical argumentation" as its chief editorial criteria.

NEW PERSPECTIVES IN PHILOSOPHY OF EDUCATION

Yet this evolution had other, less intended, consequences.

Over time, the desire to seek a grounding for philosophy of education in philosophy meant that more and more scholars, including students studying for graduate degrees in the field, went into philosophy departments or the relevant aisles in libraries and bookstores and started reading (or, in some cases, returning again to) work in existentialism, phenomenology, and other "Continental" philosophies. It meant that many philosophers of education read or re-read primary sources in philosophy (from the pre-Socratics to Nietzsche, Heidegger, de Beauvoir, or Wittgenstein) and looked increasingly outside Anglo-American philosophy to more international sources. They also turned to texts on the margins of what had been counted as "philosophy" before: critical theory, feminism, and those (such as Foucault) who would later be termed "postmodern" writers.

Their scholarship made substantial contributions to understanding such topics as power and inequality in education, and the critique of cultural intolerance in both the tacit and the "hidden" curricula. In many ways returning to the older vision of philosophy of education as necessarily implicated in issues of politics, critique, and reform, these philosophers eschewed the methods of analysis but, even more profoundly, rejected its vision of philosophy of education as an exercise in rational or objective reconnaissance. Hence, no sooner did it happen that Jonas Soltis offered his widely accepted characterization of philosophy of education in 1971 than, within a year, essays were already appearing with titles like "Analytic philosophy of education at the crossroads".

Criticisms of analytic philosophy, some though not all from critical theory or feminist points of view, gained wider credibility during this decade. These criticisms included, chiefly, the question of *whose* concepts were being taken for granted; the criticism that the methods of analysis, ostensibly neutral and objective, in fact imported substantive value commitments; the argument that the view of language undergirding this method was culturally bounded and ahistorical; and the complaint that its focus on "merely verbal" concerns often made its results trivial and irrelevant. Even such sympathetic commentators as Barrow, Ericson, and Phillips give some weight to these criticisms, though they differ in their assessments of analytic philosophy of education today.

For Barrow, these criticisms are mostly "irrelevant" and the "objections can be met." For Phillips (1994, 4454), on the other hand, "antisepsis triumphed" as "analytic philosophy became more technical and more inward looking, directed at issues of interest to other philosophers of education to the neglect of issues of relevance to a broad range of educationists." For Ericson (1994), the criticisms held weight, but a "second generation" of analytic philosophy of education still survived. This second generation of analytic philosophers, including many of these selfsame authors made substantial contributions to understanding issues of critical thinking, the forms of knowledge, and philosophical problems in educational research, for example. What is unmistakable, however, is that by the end of the decade of the 70s, no one could say any longer "we are all analytical philosophers of education."

The philosophical work in education from critical theory or neo-Marxist, feminist, and postmodern perspectives, beginning during this period and expanding to the present day, brought not only a shift in philosophical perspectives and methods, but a more explicitly political commitment. The tone of speakers and writers changed. Issues of class, gender, race, and other dimensions of disadvantagement and exclusion became explicit topics of investigation and focal points of advocacy. As we will see in a moment, these issues were raised, reflexively, as points of critique against the field of philosophy of education itself. These shifts in philosophical outlook, in turn, shaped and were shaped by the articles published in the professional journals of the field, and in the papers presented at conferences. Such manifestations have a dual relation to the scope and content of a field: representing the work with which people are actually engaged, yet also reflecting back to the field what literatures, topics, and perspectives are of current interest or importance.

To the extent that scholars, especially younger scholars,

are influenced by what they read and by what they find is publishable, such shifting trends play an active part in encouraging and giving legitimacy to new styles of work. This is a role about which journal editors and conference organizers are usually quite aware, and lends a responsibility to them, and to their reviewers, that goes beyond simply filtering and selecting "the best" from the work that is submitted to them. For at the same time, they are helping to define, either narrowly or broadly, the field that they are representing. The circular process by which a field becomes what it is thought to be, in the minds of its members – and this can either be a highly conservative and static or a highly experimental and fluid intellectual process – is exemplified practically in these activities of peer review and selection (just as they are also exemplified in the courses and degree requirements of graduate programs that prepare students with the imprimatur of the field upon their degrees).

For philosophy of education in the post-analytic period, the contents of leading journals and conference publications became increasingly eclectic, interdisciplinary, and iconoclastic toward traditional conceptions of "the field." That this partly was an indication of a changing state of affairs, and partly a cause of it, was quite apparent to those involved in making such selections. Something else momentous was happening to philosophy of education during this period, I believe, represented by two related sets of changes. The first concerned the demographics of the field, especially during the 70s and into the 80s, as more and more women entered what had been virtually all-male organizations or, among those women who were already participants, as more shifted their interests away from analytic philosophy or other traditional topics toward women's status within education.

The second was the rise of feminism as a perspective on philosophical and professional issues within philosophy of education. Feminists pointed out that the questions of who was part of certain philosophical debates, and what philosophical language those debates privileged, were interdependent issues. They argued that the forms of philosophical argumentation, in which rigorous, aggressive debate was assumed to be the best way of testing new propositions, had the effect of narrowing the range of perspectives available for discussion and actively intimidating or silencing those who did not debate their points in that manner. They argued that the methods of analytic philosophy, such as the tendency to isolate conceptual issues from actual contexts, gave artificiality to philosophical discussions, notably in cases of ethics where, they believed, situated, interpersonal factors needed to be topics of philosophical consideration from the very start.

In these and other ways they argued the interdependence of issues of *content* and issues of *representation*. Which philosophical issues were being discussed, how they were discussed, and which issues were never discussed directly influenced and were influenced by the fact of who was part of those conversations, and who was not. Initially, this concern spoke directly to the underrepresentation of women in the professional organizations and journals of the field; eventually, such concerns began to be extended to other underrepresented groups as well – including, once again, the question of the relevance of philosophy of education to the concerns, needs, and interests of teachers (most of whom, of course, are female). One concrete manifestation of this shift has been a resurgence of interest in moral education, literature, and more relational views of personhood.

These changes – the increased eclecticism of philosophical sources seen as relevant to philosophy of education, and the increased awareness of the interdependence of issues of content and of representation – are fundamentally transforming the field today. Chambliss summarizes the contemporary scene in this way: "In the last decade of the twentieth century, philosophy of education scarcely resembles a discipline with a distinct purpose and a clearly established agenda. It is more accurately characterized as a field of study defined by the variety of its research and interpretive projects".

What is most interesting about this characterization is the implication that philosophy of education ever was a "discipline with a distinct purpose and a clearly established agenda." As noted, the very idea of "philosophy of education" as a distinct discipline is an artifact of a particular set of philosophical and institutional conditions, ones more typical of certain English-speaking contexts. Beyond this, the idea that this discipline ever had a unified purpose and agenda fits only certain brief periods of its development (notably, during the period of Progressivism and the period of analytic dominance) – yet even these periods were characterized by a good deal of internal friction and resistance to such unifying trends, and were followed by periods of reaction that explicitly challenged the boundaries established to define what truly counted as philosophy of education and what did not.

THE FUTURES OF PHILOSOPHY OF EDUCATION

Today, this reflexive awareness of how such philosophical boundaries also have institutional effects, and how these boundaries of inclusion and exclusion, in turn, feed back on which philosophical issues and perspectives are or are not represented within what officially counts as "philosophy of education," has ushered in a new period for the field. What Chambliss characterizes as a diffuse focus, or lack of focus, can be characterized just as accurately as a period of experimentation and expansion in philosophy of education. Consider, for example, Phillips' alternative characterization: "The situation in the 1990s is complex, and relatively healthy – philosophers are working with a variety of approaches, in a variety of fields, and the discipline is marked by an eclecticism perhaps unrivaled in previous periods" (1994, 4456).

There are paired centripetal and centrifugal forces at work in the field today, matching philosophers of education who prefer to draw the boundaries of the field more narrowly, around a strict disciplinary view of philosophical method (and within this view of philosophy a primary focus on matters of logic, epistemology, philosophy of science, and philosophy of mind), and those drawing the boundaries more broadly, blurring distinctions of philosophy and theory, and emphasizing the interdisciplinary cross-fertilization of philosophy with literary interpretation, political theory, women's studies, and other fields. These debates, it should be emphasized, arise as much from different views about who is a philosopher of education, who belongs at professional meetings, or who should be published in sponsored journals, as they do from the relative merits of disciplinary and interdisciplinary perspectives on the field. Yet, as Chambliss' assessment also reveals, if there is no disciplinary core whatsoever, is there anything that *does* characterize and unify philosophy of education as a field today? I will return to this question in a moment.

A related issue about such boundary-drawing is the effect of the professionalization of philosophy of education upon the involvement of philosophically minded practitioners and their concerns. As noted, from the very beginnings of the Philosophy of Education Society, for example, structures were put in place that would limit the involvement and influence of those without academic credentials in philosophy. While one can say that philosophers of education should continue to focus on issues of educational practice, this position stands in tension with actual policies that discourage the participation of those who hold these concerns closest to heart.

In the case of PES, for example, this tension is expressed in the uncomfortable, and occasionally alienated, relation between the national organization, which is the most philosophically sophisticated and professionally oriented, and which has the strongest representation in the major sponsored publications of the field, and the ten or so "regional" branches of the Society, many of which have a much higher rate of participation by colleagues in other fields of educational scholarship and practice – many of whom rarely attend, or would even consider attending, the national meeting. Similar interactions undoubtedly arise in other national contexts as well.

As a result of these dynamics, philosophy of education is once again in a period of self-examination about its scope and mission. The lead article in a recent collection of essays chosen to survey the field, written by Maxine Greene, is entitled "What counts as philosophy of education?" The responses by Feinberg and Phillips show how far from a consensual answer the field remains today.

Yet the title of that collection, *Critical Conversations in Philosophy of Education,* and its design as a series of constructive engagements around a set of educational concerns, gives a different and, I think, more hopeful characterization of the field. For if disciplinary boundary-drawing is regarded with more suspicion today, and if any prospective philosophical criteria for what counts as "philosophy of education" have come to be scrutinized partly in terms of which voices and perspectives they privilege and which they disadvantage or exclude, then the only alternative demarcations of the field must be more procedural and "boot-strapped." In this sense, philosophy of education today represents those engaged in ongoing conversations, in person or in print, about certain issues, in full awareness of their diversity and eclecticism of method, while retaining a degree of openness about who else might need to be drawn into those conversations. What counts as philosophy of education is simply what these collective processes of deliberation, paper reviewing, and public discourse acknowledge and accept as pertinent to a set of shared concerns.

At the same time, these processes tacitly invite or exclude different participants, and even set the standards of what it means to *be* involved. Hence adopting or changing these processes is a decision with immediate consequences for who is to be involved; and the converse is also the case. The identification of those concerns, the boundaries of the discipline, and the representation of participants in professional societies, graduate programs, and publications, are shifting, interdependent strands of what is the field, each changing in response to the others. Such a perspective itself raises a new challenge to the field, however, which is how this dynamic of self-examination and redefinition can maintain a sense of continuity; how a discipline that is continually remaking itself can respect the cumulative gains of sustained lines of inquiry, without discarding substantial bodies of scholarship as simply the outmoded musings of philosophical paradigms that have been transcended or surpassed.

Will contemporary philosophers of education read earlier academic work with respect and interest, for example? Or will each new generation of philosophers of education become amnesiac about their predecessors? Will the suspicion toward "canonical texts" mean that reading lists and syllabi are continually discarded with each passing fashion? Or will traditions of inquiry in such areas as ethics, democratic theory, what counts as "knowledge," and so forth, continue as sustained conversations among diverse texts and perspectives, to which each is regarded as making a distinct contribution? Finally, within this decentered characterization of philosophy of education, what trends stand out for the future? Without stipulating what the changing boundaries of the field will look like (a process I have obviously, painstakingly resisted throughout this essay), are there good guesses that can be offered about the future of philosophy of education?

One avenue, I have suggested, is to recognize how current topics of interest such as identity, difference, power, a suspicion toward "metanarratives," and so on, have become not only issues for philosophical investigation, but leverage points for reflection and critique within the field of philosophy of education itself. How difficult and sensitive this process has become can be seen in the dynamics surrounding the reception of Harvey Siegel's Presidential Address to a joint meeting of the Philosophy of Education Society and the Philosophy of Education Society of Australasia in 1995 – an interchange that perfectly crystallized some of the key issues at debate today, and an event that might come to be regarded, with hindsight, as a kind of watershed for the field. At heart an appeal to and argument for "inclusion," Siegel's account was sharply criticized for assuming as criteria for whom should be included, factors that are in fact exclusionary (some of these comments came from the responses of Bailin 1995 and Morgan 1995; others came from the floor).

Yet, of course, all criteria are exclusionary – or else they would not be criteria. For certain philosophers, such as Siegel, the question of standards of philosophical merit, and the matter of their social effects, are entirely separate issues – and a perspective excluded as being nonphilosophical, if it "is" nonphilosophical, need not be of concern to an organization devoted to establishing and maintaining standards of integrity and excellence within the discipline.

If prospective participants lack these criteria, the goal should be to find ways to help people acquire them, not to question the criteria. In criticism of this view, it was argued that the persistent effects of such standards, in terms of the exclusion of people, groups, and their perspectives, *must* be taken into account if a field is not to become increasingly hermetic and self-rationalizing – to say nothing of the possible effects of personal or professional harm upon those persons and groups by excluding them. Where there are important cultural or historical reasons why prospective participants have not acquired the characteristics defined by particular institutions as criteria of participation, one must consider the nature of those criteria as one potential factor.

Hence, as the boundaries of philosophy of education are being stretched and blurred, considerations of their role in including and excluding participation are becoming a topic of explicit, reflexive concern. If all criteria exclude someone, then the question of which exclusions will be found livable, and which ones not, is an element in weighing their relevance and merit. In my view, this is not a matter of abandoning all philosophical criteria, or of focusing solely on the question of inclusion and exclusion, but of becoming more sensitive to the complex interaction between them, and judging each in terms of the other.

To the extent that professional organizations, graduate programs, and journals and other publications are the institutional embodiment of the field, their decisions along these lines have profound implications for the intellectual and moral qualities of what the field turns out to be. This is particularly true in assessing the consequences of particular philosophical methods and content for attracting the interest and participation of educators from the arenas of policy, research, or practice.

The time has passed when the demographics of a field

can be regarded as irrelevant to its diversity and vitality. Just as women, once and for all, made the question of who was, and who was not, part of disciplinary conversations a matter of professional *and* philosophical concern, the field of philosophy of education must stand today in awareness of its roots in a particular conception of "philosophy of education" that emerged from predominantly English-speaking countries; and recognize that in certain contexts its participants are still predominantly male, and, where more equally male and female, almost entirely White.

The increased globalization of academic work, brought about by relative ease and speed of travel; the growth of international organizations and conferences (such as INPE, the International Network of Philosophers of Education, formed in 1990); the increase in contact among a multicultural group of colleagues; and the widespread use of the Internet as a means of global communication and electronic publication of scholarship, all portend a time when diversity and difference will move centrally onto the agenda of issues of concern to educational philosophers – including, naturally, the question of who is being respected as such.

As new partners enter the conversation, further questions of how, where, and under what terms that conversation is occurring will inevitably become objects of philosophical reflection. This shift is already taking place, and provides, I suggest, the best indicator of where the field called "philosophy of education" is headed. What this label will be taken to delimit, and by what criteria, will be the determination of *that* shifting population, as it has been for many previous generations of participants in the field. The one lasting change may be that the question, "What is philosophy of education?" will never again be asked in the expectation that a single, unified definition is either possible or desirable.

PHILOSOPHY AND EDUCATION

Philosophy of education is a field of applied philosophy, drawing from the traditional fields of philosophy (ontology, ethics, epistemology, etc.) and its approaches (speculative, prescriptive, and/or analytic) to address questions regarding education policy, human development, and curriculum theory, to name a few.

Put another way, philosophy of education is the philosophical study of the purpose, process, nature and ideals of education. For example, it might study what constitutes upbringing and education, the values and norms revealed through upbringing and educational practices, the limits and legitimization of education as an academic discipline, and the relation between educational theory and practice. Philosophy of education can be considered a branch of both philosophy and education.

The multiple ways of conceiving education coupled with the multiple fields and approaches of philosophy make philosophy of education not only a very diverse field but also one that is not easily defined. Although there is overlap, philosophy of education should not be conflated with educational theory, which is not defined specifically by the application of philosophy to questions in education. Although philosophers around the world have asked questions regarding education for millenia, as an academic discipline with its own place in the university it is relatively new. Nonetheless, it is an internationally well-established field, with departments and programs around the world. A chronological summary of the work of some of the most important and influential educational philosophers in Western culture follows.

BRANCHES OF PHILOSOPHY

The following branches are the main areas of study:

- Metaphysics investigates the nature of being and the world. Traditional branches are cosmology and ontology.
- Epistemology is concerned with the nature and scope of knowledge, and whether knowledge is possible. Among its central concerns has been the challenge posed by skepticism and the relationships between truth, belief, and justification.

- Ethics, or 'moral philosophy', is concerned with questions of how persons ought to act or if such questions are answerable. The main branches of ethics are meta-ethics, normative ethics, and applied ethics. Meta-ethics concerns the nature of ethical thought, comparison of various ethical systems, whether there are absolute ethical truths, and how such truths could be known. Ethics is also associated with the idea of morality. Plato's early dialogues include a search for definitions of virtue.
- Political philosophy is the study of government and the relationship of individuals and communities to the state. It includes questions about justice, the good, law, property, and the rights and obligations of the citizen.
- Aesthetics deals with beauty, art, enjoyment, sensory-emotional values, perception, and matters of taste and sentiment.
- Logic deals with patterns of thinking that lead from true premises to true conclusions, originally developed in Ancient Greece. Beginning in the late 19th century, mathematicians such as Frege focused on a mathematical treatment of logic, and today the subject of logic has two broad divisions: mathematical logic (formal symbolic logic) and what is now called philosophical logic.
- Philosophy of mind deals with the nature of the mind and its relationship to the body, and is typified by disputes between dualism and materialism. In recent years there has been increasing similarity between this branch of philosophy and cognitive science.
- Philosophy of language is the reasoned inquiry into the nature, origins, and usage of language.

Most academic subjects have a philosophy, for example the philosophy of science, the philosophy of mathematics, the philosophy of logic, the philosophy of law and the philosophy of history. In addition, a range of academic subjects has emerged to deal with areas which would have historically been the subject of philosophy. These include psychology, anthropology and science.

SIGNIFICANCE OF PHILOSOPHY OF EDUCATION

Teachers daily face the challenge daily of providing sincere and positive support to their students no matter what race they are. Teachers are human. Teachers up hold the most positive attitude when they are struggling with their own biases and insecurities in the world and within themselves. This requires an excellent teacher to put their personal problems behind. It demands that the educator follow his/her heart in acting genuinely in the student's best interest. The teacher carefully works through negative aspects and has the courage to face opposition. It takes guts to present to colleagues with a contrasting view or make suggestions to administrators on how to make the community better. Teachers must have the student's best interest always in mind! Being a teacher and having courage involves developing strong relationships among students despite the hard work this entails to break through their wall.

Time, respect, dedication, and hard work are all ingredients of developing productive relationships. These behaviors and attributes de- tail how teachers must contribute to professional leadership communities. Professional learning communities are built by strong, powerful minds who endeavor to develop sincere relationships and who demonstrate professional courage. Educators must contribute time and patience. The school always has to develop a rapport among all their educators and administrators so they are on the same path; "the idea of school as a learning community suggests a kind of connectedness among members that resembles what is found in a family, neighbour- hood, or some other closely knit group" PLCs must all have a shared purpose for all students, collective focus on student learning, collaboration, and shared norms.

Education is the key to success in America and the State of Connecticut. Education shapes our youngsters into weil-rounded individuals who succeed in the world. School turns students into adults who are respectful and have dignity for themselves. Students in America receive a free education to the twelfth grade. It gives the young generations the opportunity to have a stable routine in their lives and shows them that there is a world outside their realm. According to Eaton (2007), "kids in Hartford, as teachers and administrators had said, were not only poor but experientially impoverished, immersed in poverty, so surrounded by poverty that it shut out the rest of American life." in all reality, some students are unfortunate and do not have a steady home life or role model. Education therefore offers the best of teachers to give students the credential skills of life. Teachers are excellent role models for students to mirror.

If we didn't have education in America, our world would not be prosperous and we would not survive the trials of individual communities and the hardships of the world. Education relates to all children from the poverty-stricken communities, to the middle class, to the upper class. Every group has certain demands and special needs. When children come to a public school they are exposed to the realities of life. There should be no segregation among races; they should all be in same classroom. According to Eaton "The Sheff complaint alleged that Connecticut compelled Hartford kids – forced them-to attend racially separate, inherently unequal schools". Everybody needs a stable ground to enter and know that here at school everybody, regardless of ethnicity, religion and problems are equal. Education is important for every citizen in the United States.

Our country is changing everyday and new strategies among teaching are important for the success of every student.

- Teachers are required to obtain mental strength.?
- Parent, Pupil, and Teacher Harmony.?
- Different teaching strategies.?
- How to make lessons stick.?

The world is quickly changing there are many different types of families today. Sometimes the teacher has to go out of their way for the students' success school to learn that it shouldn't matter what their background is. When we have a school in a low-income neighborhood, it is hard for students not to be aware of the poverty around them. They come to school with a sense of hatred. Education relates to the need of every student. In the State of Connecticut, most inner city schools offer free breakfast and lunch for families who qualify for state aid. Education teaches everyone that they could be all that they can be in world if they want to.

School gives most students hope and skill on how to better their personal lives. Schools must develop a rapport among families and students. Families must understand that the teacher and the school administrators have the right to discipline the students if they feel the need to for wrong behaviour. The families must agree with the school and back certain decisions. Families must also discipline their children at home, to make them understand that they are in school for a reason. The student needs to be instilled with the ideas of having respect for school authority and have the ability to listen to school administrators. Families must encourage their children to do their assignments. They also should provide their child with clean clothes, proper supplies, and the most important manners. Families need to have their children to school on time and prepared. Education is to form students into well-rounded citizens.

When educators have high potential for their students, students succeed. When teachers don't have a high outlook for their students, the students do not have to worry about accomplishing goals. Therefore the teacher does not ever have to be frustrated when a lesson fails or the class bombs a test. If students realize that the teacher does not care about the class's success, the students become disheartened on what school is all about. When students are put to a challenge they are able to find themselves academically and realize they can exceed expectations. High expectations act as an excellent classroom motivator.

In the book Failure Is NOT an Option, Blankstein (2004) states the following: "Central to the success of high- achieving schools is a collaborative culture focused on teaching and learning." In order to develop an excellent school, all educators, administrators, faculty, and parents must develop a strong rapport. Once this link is developed, a strong goal must be developed. This goal must be powerful and valuable.

Teachers often have a bad frame of mind when it comes to data-based decision making. I think schools dedicate too much of their time, energy, and effort in reviewing for the state standardized test, for example the CMTs. I do believe it is a good way to determine what level they are at. I believe that the data collected in test scores must also reflect schools absentee rates, dropout rates, and report card grades, etc. Scores are simply not supposed to be used to pinpoint which school districts are succeeding and which ones are performing badly. Scores can help teachers see what areas the students are weak in. The problem once again with using the data to determine what the students progress is, many of the students in the inner city are immigrants and are many different levels. I believe that everybody needs to work and act like a huge family. Everybody of the family (administrators, teachers, parents/guardians, and students) must be fully engaged in order for the student to have a superb educational experience.

Teachers must be willing to take risks and have the courage to challenge not only the student but also themselves. The teachers must push the students to the max when it comes to their education career. Teachers must use many different methods and materials to teach lessons. Individual families of the students must show support in their student's education. Parents/guardians must also push their child to achieve healthy goals. Parents are very influential to their child. Administrators must provide the teachers with support to challenge the kids and to provide a healthy learning environment. When you are dedicated teacher, you are filled with dedication, compassion, and patience as a teacher. Every day you are presented with new trials of daily school life. First as a teacher you need to develop a respect and bond with each student. At first this may seem as a challenge because not all students want to develop a relationship with their teacher.

As a teacher you must go out of your way and make contact with students especially problem students. Part of your job when being an excellent educator you must go out of your way to let the parents know that he or she is not doing well in school. According to Eaton "Miss Luddy drove around after school, calling on parents who wouldn't answer the phone. She caught up with one father on the roof of a nearby bodega, hammering nails. "I have some concerns about your son." As an educator you must develop a rapport with the parents. Find out what their favourite sports team, singer or TV show, etc. Being a teacher you must realize that all students' backgrounds are different from ethnicity, to family's income level, to tragic events that have taken place. Having a smile on your face can simply make a difference in someone's life. When teaching a lesson you must be prepared for every student's special needs.

In lesson plans you must have activities for the special education students. Teachers must be interacting with students by using visual aids, etc. As teacher you must be resourceful with knowledge, and tools. Depending on where your teaching suburban or urban children are always going to come to school unprepared, with either no pens/pencils or paper, etc. As a teacher you are also seen as a role model for the students to look up to. Not every student at home receives TLC, so when you see an individual is doing something superb or making a huge improvement congratulate them. Even though the teacher is not able to go home with the student and continue making a difference they are still able to improve children's outlooks on life for the short time they spend with them each day.

For instance teachers must remind and let each student know that every individual can succeed as long as they get a superb education and put their all into it. The role of the teacher is greatly influenced on the local community because if a school is located in a suburb. Children have less likely to come to school in shambles, meaning the parents are financially more stable. Unlike the urban communities students are less fortunate. Urban communities are usually filled with hardships, abandoned buildings, smog, litter, poverty, etc, and some students have never even left their realms or know what the country is. The history of the school also could affect the children's mind frame for instance if the school is considered failing, the student may not be as positive to come to school and be goal oriented to do well. The teacher must act as a mediator at all times and balance children's mishaps.

Acting Within the Framework of Existing School Cultures

Teachers are very influential to students. Students spend an ample amount of time with teachers. The students spend about 180 days in their personal classroom. For a lot of students these days, the best role model they have to look up to is their teacher. This puts a lot of responsibility on teachers, having to be always conscious of their personality, their voice tone, and mannerisms. Every teacher has that day when they really don't want to teach their students today. That is when the teacher's passion should kick in and realize that the students need you! Being a teacher can be a very difficult job. A teacher has multiple tasks they must perform throughout the day and entire school year. The teacher must create lesson plans according to their schools framework. Every lesson plan that is produced must be creative and stimulating. The lesson must be able to hold every students attention span.

Since the No Child Left Behind law came instilled the teacher also has to make modified lesson plans to be able to fit every students learning needs in the class. Being a teacher I believe you learn to become very flexible, if you see a certain lesson plan is not working for a particular class, you must be able to intercept and make changes while you are standing in front of the class with 18-28 students in front of you. As a teacher you learn by student's expressions and reactions that they are having a difficult time grasping what is being taught in front of them. While this is happening you as a teacher must never show frustration. The environment in the classroom says it all to stranger or principal, if they shall ever unexpectedly walk in.

The structure of the classroom must be developed the first

day of school. You as the teacher must lay down the law with procedures, rules, and discipline. I believe if this is not developed right away students will take full advantage of you and your classroom. For example assigned seats, no talking when the teacher is speaking, or independent work must be done silently, etc. As a teacher the whole no talking issue is almost completely impossible to a certain extent. Everyone loves to talk, students get very excited and need to express. I remember being a student and loving to talk but knowing the right times when I was able to. "Happy children love to talk. They would rather talk to each other than do almost anything else."

Some classes you are able to create lesson plans that permit students to communicate with one another. But the students must realize that there is a time and place to socialize. I believe as a teacher, that if your students are staying on task throughout the period, you can reward them and give them a few minutes at the end of class to mingle. For block periods, at the half way point, give the students a few minutes to get up and stretch and chit chat, then continue on with their work. Spicing up your lesson plans also allows your students to learn in different ways, for example I have a passion for English, creating to different lesson plan that allows the students to work with hands on such as drawing/coloring out a story, or using the computer, it changes up the same boring routine.

Students adapt more to a nurturing environment. It is very important for teachers not to start to dislike certain students and directly point out a particular student; I know at times this seems almost impossible. Providing a classroom that is vibrant and nurturing to students, it allows them to become more adaptive to the class and its importance. Having a classroom that is inviting to students and the teacher is friendly but stern, allows the students to develop. Every classroom must be culturally friendly. Finally, every teacher must set a certain tone to the classroom so the teacher throughout the year is not taken advantage of. When a teacher teaches a lesson and students are following along, they are absorbing the information that they are being taught. "We have to think about things (reflect) and examine the images in our memory (observation). We stand back from our experience, look it over, and think about it. And what we look for is an image that fits all of our experience. We look for unity."

The Art of Changing the Brain

When a teacher is teaching students depending on grade level and development, we need to remember that everyone has different ways on how they remember information. Students and teachers use many different mnemonics, to help make the student understand, and remember information the best way, that is clear and precise. In the book Made to Stick written by C. Heath & D. Heath (2007), the book offers many suggestions on how to make memorization, fun and easy. Many people suffer on how to get their ideas across the most proficient way possible.

The Heath's express their thoughts very well; they make note that in order for the students make new lessons stick they have to tap into past experiences. The significance of remembering is powerful. The Heath's uses the example of JFK, to show that three random letters have a big impact on individuals. We all know that JFK stands for John F. Kennedy. By looking at the letters we are able to "think of all the associations with JFK –politics, relationships, his assassination, and his famous family". We as adults are able to make connections, so in all having our students remember information by bits and pieces, the overall meaning is great, and it is stored in our life time memory.

Unit II

Philosophies of Life and Education

CONCEPT AND IMPLICATIONS OF INDIVIDUALISM

Individualism and collectivism are conflicting views of the nature of humans, society and the relationship between them. Individualism holds that the individual is the primary unit of reality and the ultimate standard of value. This view does not deny that societies exist or that people benefit from living in them, but it sees society as a collection of individuals, not something over and above them. Collectivism holds that the group—the nation, the community, the proletariat, the race, etc.—is the primary unit of reality and the ultimate standard of value. This view does not deny the reality of the individual. But ultimately, collectivism holds that one's identity is determined by the groups one interacts with, that one's identity is constituted essentially of relationships with others.

Individualists see people dealing primarily with *reality*; other people are just one aspect of reality. Collectivists see people dealing primarily with other people; reality is dealt with through the mediator of the group; the group, not the individual, is what directly confronts reality. Individualism holds that every person is an end in himself and that no person should be sacrificed for the sake of another. Collectivism holds that the needs and goals of the individual are subordinate to those of the larger group and should be sacrificed when the collective good so requires. Individualism holds that the individual is the unit of achievement. While not denying that one person can build on the achievements of others, individualism points out that achievement goes beyond what has already been done; it is something *new* that is *created* by the individual.

Collectivism, on the other hand, holds that achievement is a product of society. In this view, an individual is a temporary spokesman for the underlying, collective process of progress. To further clarify the difference between individualism and collectivism, I'd like to discuss two widespread misconceptions about individualism.

ISOLATION

The first misconception is that individualism means isolation—being alone, being outside society. This misconception is reflected in the popular images of "individualism," images that stress being isolated, such as those of the lone cowboy, the fearless gumshoe, and the isolated prairie family. Such images can be exciting and heroic, but isolation is not the essence of individualism. In fact, the concept of individualism does not make sense in the absence of other human beings. Individualism and collectivism are contrasting views of the relationship between the individual and the group. Individualism is called "individualism" not because it exhorts the individual to seek a life apart from others, but because it asserts that the individual, and not the group, is the primary constituent of society.

The belief that individualism means being alone leads people to say that individualism is incompatible with cooperation. If one is too much of an "individualist," people say, one cannot "get along with groups," one is not a good "team player." Actually, a person who doesn't listen to others, the person who would rather do things an inefficient way as long as it's "my way," is not being an "individualist"—he's being closed minded. A true individualist wants the best for himself, so he seeks out the best, no mater who is the source. To the individualist, the truth is more important than any authority, including himself.

Living in society, cooperating with other people—these are tremendous benefits. Individualism does not deny this. But not all arrangements of living and working with other men are beneficial to the individual; the arrangement faced by American slaves is one example. Individualism is a theory of the conditions under which living and working with others is, in fact, beneficial.

BALANCE

Another widespread misconception about individualism is that it can somehow be mixed with or tempered by collectivism. In this view, neither "extreme" individualism nor "extreme" collectivism are correct. Rather, wisdom and truth lie somewhere in the middle. Individualism and collectivism are contradictory positions—there is no middle ground between them. Collectivism maintains that the group is an entity in its own right, a thing that can act upon people. Individualism denies this. Collectivism sees us being influenced by the group; individualism sees us being influenced by other individuals. Collectivism sees us cooperating with the team; individualism, with other people. Collectivism sees us building on the ideas and achievements of society; individualism, on the ideas and achievements of individuals. These are contradictory positions; it's either-or.

To accept the "balance" point of view is to accept collectivism. No collectivist has ever said that every single need of every individual must be frustrated for the sake of the society—if so, there wouldn't be any society left to serve. Collectivism *is* the balance point of view; it is a matter of fine-tuning here and there, constraining individuals when their interests get out of line with the "good of society." Indeed, the main debate between the "left" and the "right" today is not a debate over collectivism and individualism—its a debate over two forms of collectivism. The "left" holds that the needs of society lie in the materialistic realm, so they are into regulating that aspect of individual affairs. The "right" holds that the needs of society lie in the spiritual realm, so they are into regulating the spiritual aspect of individual affairs. Collectivism is, by its nature, an act of balancing the need of the individual against the need of "society." Individualism denies that society has any needs, so the issue of balance is not relevant to it.

Philosophic Implications of Individualism and Collectivism

Both collectivism and individualism rest on certain values and certain assumptions about the nature of man, which is what I want to explore next.

Responsibility vs. the Safety-net

The first issue I want to explore is responsibility versus the social safety-net. A primary element of individualism is individual responsibility. Being responsible is being *pro-active,* making one's choices consciously and carefully, and accepting accountability for everything one does—or fails to do. An integral part of responsibility is productivity. The individualist recognizes that nothing nature gives men is entirely suited to their survival; rather, humans must work to transform their environment to meet their needs. This is the essence of production. The individualist takes responsibility for his own production; he seeks to "earn his own way," to "pull his own weight."

Collectivism doesn't disparage responsibility; but ultimately, collectivism does not hold individuals accountable for the choices they make. Failing to save for retirement, having children one can't afford, making bad investments, becoming addicted to drugs or smoking—these actions are called "social problems" that "society" has to deal with. Thus, collectivists seek to build a social "safety-net" to protect individuals from the choices they make. To collectivism, responsibility is only to be expected of the productive, and consists of doing one's part in keeping the social "safety-net" in tact. Regarding production, collectivism sees society, not individuals, as the agent of production. As a result, wealth belongs to "society," so collectivists have no trouble dreaming up schemes to redistribute wealth according to their visions of "social justice."

Egoism vs. Altruism

The second issue I want to explore is egoism versus

altruism. Altruism holds "each man as his brother's keeper;" in other words, we are each responsible for the health and well-being of others. Clearly, this is a simple statement of the "safety-net" theory from above. This is incompatible with individualism, yet many people who are basically individualists uphold altruism as the standard of morality. What's going on?

The problem is wide-spread confusion over the meanings of "altruism" and "egoism." The first confusion is to confound altruism with kindness, generosity, and helping other people. Altruism demands more than kindness: it demands *sacrifice.* The billionaire who contributes $50,000 to a scholarship fund is not acting altruistically; altruism goes beyond simple charity. Altruism is the grocery bagger who contributes $50,000 to the fund, foregoing his own college education so that others may go. Parents who spend a fortune to save their dying child are helping another person, but true altruism would demand that the parents spend their money to save ten other children, sacrificing their own child so that others may live.

The second confusion is to confound selfishness with brutality. The common image of selfishness is the person who runs slip-shod over people in order to achieve arbitrary desires. We are taught that "selfishness" consists of dishonesty, theft, even bloodshed, usually for the sake of the whim of the moment. These two confusions together obscure the possibility of an ethics of non-sacrifice. In this ethics, each man takes responsibility for his own life and happiness, and lets other people do the same. No one sacrifices himself to others, nor sacrifices others to himself. The key word in this approach is *earn*: each person must earn a living, must earn the love and respect of his peers, must earn the self-esteem and the happiness that make life worth living.

It's this ethics of non-sacrifice that forms a lasting moral foundation for individualism. It's an egoistic ethics in that each person acts to achieve his own happiness. Yet, it's not the brutality usually ascribed to egoism. Indeed, by rejecting sacrifice as such, it represents a revolution in thinking on ethics. Two asides on the topic of egoism. First, just as individualism doesn't mean being alone, neither does non-sacrificial egoism. Admiration, friendship, love, good-will, charity, generosity: these are wonderful values that a selfishness person would want as part of his life. But these values do not require true *sacrifice,* and thus are not altruistic in the deepest sense of the word. Second, I question if brutality, the form of selfishness usually ascribed to egoism, is actually in one's self-interest in practice. Whim worship, dishonesty, theft, exploitation: I would argue that the truly selfish man rejects these, for he knows that happiness and self-esteem can't be stolen at the cost of others: they must be *earned* through hard work.

Reason

The third issue I want to explore is reason. The philosophic defence of individualism rests on the nature of reason and the role it plays in human life. Reason is the faculty of conceptual awareness; reason integrates the evidence of the senses into a higher-level of awareness. But beyond simple cognition, reason plays a key role in imagination, emotions, and creativity. Every thing we think, feel, imagine and do is based on our awareness and our thoughts. Our character, personal identity, and history of achievement are defined by our thoughts. Our very survival depends on reason. Our food, clothes, shelter, and medicine—all are products of thought. Reason is at the core of being human.

Reason is individualistic. No person can think for another; thought is an attribute of the individual. One can start with the ideas of another, but each new discovery, each creative step beyond the already known, is a product of the individual. And when an individual does build on the work and ideas of others, he is building on the work of other *individuals,* not on the ideas of "society." Individualism, then, is based on the fact that humans are rational beings, and that reason is an attribute of the individual. Humans can get together and share the products of reason, which is beneficial, but they cannot share the capacity to think.

Collectivist philosophers go out of their way to attack reason. One broad method of attack is skepticism, the denial that reason even works. This attack is illustrated in bromides like "you can't be sure of anything." A more sophisticated attack on reason aims at turning reason into a product of the group. Each nation, race, economic class, creed, or gender has its own concept, logic, and truth. But in the end, *all* attacks on reason have a common result: they deny or confuse the role reason plays as the foundation of individualism.

Political Implications of Individualism and Collectivism

These implications should be fairly clear. Under collectivism, the individual, in whole or in part, is a means to satisfying the needs of "society." The state is the instrument for organizing people to meet those needs. So it is the state, not the individual, that is sovereign. Under individualism, the individual is sovereign. The individual is an end in himself, whose cooperation is to be obtain only through voluntary agreement. All people are expected to act as traders, either *voluntarily* agreeing to interact or going separate ways; it's either "win-win, or no deal." The government is limited strictly to ensuring that coercion is banished from human relations, that "voluntary" is really voluntary, that *both* sides choose freely to deal and both sides live up to their agreements.

Radicals for Capitalism

Since I am representing the group Radicals for *Capitalism*, I do want to tie capitalism into the discussion so far. Radicals for Capitalism advocate the philosophy of individualism, and supports capitalism as the only political system compatible with individualism. Unfortunately, the word "capitalism" is misunderstood today; everybody seems to mean something different by the word. Many opponents of capitalism blame the market for the result of State interventions in the economy. Many so-called "capitalists" mix socialist and interventionist schemes in with free market rhetoric—and call the result Capitalism. Today, "capitalism" is much maligned and misunderstood, buried under false allegations.

We want to liberate the term from such baggage. By capitalism we mean: a "social system based on the recognition of individual rights, including property rights, in which all property is privately owned." "A system where any and all forms of government intervention in production and trade is abolished, and State and Economics are separated in the same way and for the same reasons as the separation of Church and State". As mentioned earlier, it's a system based on the notion that humans are traders—either voluntarily agreeing to interact or going separate ways—a system in which government is limited strictly to ensuring that coercion is banished from human relations, that "voluntary" is really voluntary, that *both* sides choose freely to deal.

Under capitalism, the government protects rights, including the right to property. Without the right to use and dispose what one has produced, one has no liberty. If individuals can't work and produce towards goals they can't pursue happiness. If one can't consume the product of one's effort, one cannot live. To the degree a government does not protect property rights, an individual is a slave at the mercy of someone or some group. Capitalism is *not* a system under which unproductive individuals can leach off the productive ones, whether the "unproductive" are the unambitious or politically-connected businessmen. Nor is capitalism a system in which the government acts not as a protector, but as a coercer of productive individuals. There are examples galore of unjust acts committed under the banner of law and justice, for example, when the government takes from one person to feed another, or when government takes taxpayer money to bail out foolhardy bankers.

Unfortunately, our vision of capitalism is not the current state of affairs and has only been approximated in the history of the man kind. No system in the world today is capitalistic to the extent we advocate. All could be, but not without changes; in particular, the wide-spread acceptance of individualism. I began this talk by mentioning the upcoming election. You might be wondering what the relevance of my words are to that election. In terms of effecting change, the fundamental issues we've touched on today have a time horizon much longer than the electoral process—we're talking decades and even generations. And yet, these fundamental issues are more important than the implementation details we hear about, in the sense that whether people accept individualism, moderate collectivism, or extreme collectivism has a tremendous impact on the range of implementation details considered at election time.

Our goal today, and the goal of RadCap's in general, is to help raise the level of abstraction of political discourse to a higher level, to the level of fundamental issues like individualism versus collectivism. Of course, RadCaps advocates a specific point of view—individualism—and we would like to convince people that it's the correct one. But just as important, we feel, is the more general goal of the level of discourse. So I hope that next time you hear a political advertisement or a debate between candidates, you'll try to see the collectivist and individualist angles in addition to the concrete policies advocated.

SOCIALISM

Socialism is undoubtedly in the throes of a crisis greater than at any time since 1917. The last half of 1989 saw the dramatic collapse of most of the communist party governments of Eastern Europe. Their downfall was brought about through massive upsurges which had the support not only of the majority of the working class but also a large slice of the membership of the ruling parties themselves. These were popular revolts against unpopular regimes; if socialists are unable to come to terms with this reality, the future of socialism is indeed bleak. The mounting chronicle of crimes and distortions in the history of existing socialism, its economic failures and the divide which developed between socialism and democracy, have raised doubts in the minds of many former supporters of the socialist cause as to whether socialism can work at all. Indeed, we must expect that, for a time, many in the affected countries will be easy targets for those aiming to achieve a reversion to capitalism, including an embrace of its external policies.

Shock-waves of very necessary self-examination have also

been triggered off among communists both inside and outside the socialist world. For our part, we firmly believe in the future of socialism; and we do not dismiss its whole past as an unmitigated failure. Socialism certainly produced a Stalin and a Ceaucescu, but it also produced a Lenin and a Gorbachev. Despite the distortions at the top, the nobility of socialism's basic objectives inspired millions upon millions to devote themselves selflessly to building it on the ground. And, no one can doubt that if humanity is today poised to enter an unprecedented era of peace and civilised international relations, it is in the first place due to the efforts of the socialist world. But it is more vital than ever to subject the past of existing socialism to an unsparing critique in order to draw the necessary lessons.

To do so openly is an assertion of justified confidence in the future of socialism and its inherent moral superiority. And we should not allow ourselves to be inhibited merely because an exposure of failures will inevitably provide ammunition to the traditional enemies of socialism: our silence will, in any case, present them with even more powerful ammunition. It is, for example, sad to record that among the early foreign policy initiatives of the new government in Hungary was to play host to South Africa's foreign minister. By doing this it has, without even the diplomatic niceties of consulting with the representatives of the repressed and dominated majority, moved away from one of the most humanitarian aspects of the policies of the socialist world, i.e. to be in the vanguard of those who shun apartheid.

Among other things, statistics recently published in The Economist (UK) show that in the Soviet Union - after only 70 years of socialist endeavour in what was one of the most backward countries in the capitalist world - there are more graduate engineers than in the US, more graduate research scientists than in Japan and more medical doctors per head than in Western Europe. It also produces more steel, fuel and energy than any other country (The World in the 1990s; Economist publication). How many capitalist countries can match the achievements of most of the socialist world in the provision of social security, child care, the ending of cultural backwardness, and so on? There is certainly no country in the world which can beat Cuba's record in the sphere of health care.

IDEOLOGICAL RESPONSES

The ideological responses to the crisis of existing socialism by constituents of what was previously known as the International Communist and Workers' movement (and among our own members) is still so varied and tentative that it is early days to attempt a neat categorisation. But at the risk of over-simplification, we identify a number of broad tendencies against which we must guard:

- Finding excuses for Stalinism
- Attributing the crisis to the pace of perestroika
- Acting as if we have declared a moratorium on socialist criticism of capitalism and imperialism and, worst of all,
- Concluding that socialist theory made the distortions inevitable.

STICKING TO STALINISM

The term 'Stalinism' is used to denote the bureaucratic-authoritarian style of leadership (of parties both in and out of power) which denuded the party and the practice of socialism of most of its democratic content and concentrated power in the hands of a tiny, self-perpetuating elite.

While the mould for Stalinism was cast under Stalin's leadership it is not suggested that he bears sole responsibility for its negative practices. The essential content of Stalinism - socialism without democracy - was retained even after Stalin in the Soviet Union (until Gorbachev's intervention), albeit without some of the terror, brutality and judicial distortions associated with Stalin himself.

Among a diminishing minority there is still a reluctance to look squarely in the mirror of history and to concede that the socialism it reflects has, on balance, been so distorted that an appeal to its positive achievements (and of course there have been many) sounds hollow and very much like special pleading.

It is surely now obvious that if the socialist world stands in tatters at this historic moment it is due to the Stalinist distortions. We should have little patience with the plea in mitigation that, in the circumstances, the Stalinist excesses (such as forced collectivisation) brought about some positive economic achievements. Statistics showing high growth rates during Stalin's time prove only that methods of primitive accumulation can stimulate purely quantitative growth in the early stages of capitalism or socialism - but at what human cost? In any case, more and more evidence is emerging daily that, in the long run, the excesses inhibited the economic potential of socialism.

Another familiar plea in mitigation is that the mobilising effect of the Stalin cult helped save socialism from military defeat. It is, however, now becoming clear that the virtual destruction of the command personnel of the Red Army, the lack of effective preparation against Hitler's onslaught and Stalin's dictatorial and damaging interventions in the conduct of the war could have cost the Soviet Union its victory. Vigilance is clearly needed against the pre-perestroika styles of work and thinking which infected virtually every party (including ours) and moulded its members for so many decades.

It is not enough merely to engage in the self-pitying cry: 'we were misled'; we should rather ask why so many communists allowed themselves to become so blinded for so long. And, more importantly, why they behaved like Stalinists towards those of their comrades who raised even the slightest doubt about the 'purity' of Stalin's brand of socialism. In the socialist world there are still outposts which unashamedly mourn the retreat from Stalinism and use its dogmas to 'justify' undemocratic and tyrannical practices. It is clearly a matter of time before popular revulsion leads to a transformation. In general, those who still defend the Stalinist model - even in a qualified way - are a dying breed; at the ideological level they will undoubtedly be left behind and they need not detain us here.

BLAMING GORBACHEV

Most communists, of course, concede that a great deal 'went wrong' and needs to be corrected. Some, however, fear that the corrective methods are so hasty and extreme that, in the end, they may do more harm than good. The enemies of socialism, so it is argued, are being given new powerful weapons with which to destroy socialism and to return to capitalism. The pace of Gorbachev's perestroika and glasnost are, either directly or indirectly, blamed for the 'collapse' of communist political hegemony in countries like Poland, Hungary, GDR and Czechoslovakia. In the countries mentioned, despite the advantage of over 40 years of a monopoly of education, the media, etc., the parties in power could not find a significant section of the class they claimed to represent (or, for that matter, even a majority of their own membership) to defend them or their version of socialism.

To blame perestroika and glasnost for the ailments of socialism is like blaming the diagnosis and the prescription for the illness. Indeed, the only way to ensure the future of socialism is to grasp the nettle with the political courage of a Gorbachev. When things go badly wrong (whether it be in a movement or a country) it is inevitable that some who have ulterior motives jump on to the bandwagon. When a gap develops between the leadership and the led, it always provides openings for real enemies. But to deal with the gap in terms only of enemy conspiracies is an ancient and discredited device. Equally, to fail to tackle mistakes or crimes merely because their exposure will give comfort to our adversaries is both short-sighted and counter-productive.

In any case, a number of additional questions still go begging:

Firstly, have we the right to conclude that the enemies of a discredited party leadership are the same as the enemies of socialism? If the type of socialism which the people have experienced has been rubbished in their eyes and they begin to question it, are they necessarily questioning socialism or are they rejecting its perversion? Secondly, what doctrine of pre-Stalinism and pre-Mao Marxism gives a communist party (or any other party for that matter) the moral or political right to impose its hegemony or to maintain it in the face of popular rejection? Thirdly, who has appointed us to impose and defend at all costs our version of socialism even if the overwhelming majority has become disillusioned with it?

In general, it is our view that the fact that the processes of perestroika and glasnost came too slowly, too little and too late in Eastern Europe did more than anything else to endanger the socialist perspective there. It is through these processes - and they must be implemented with all possible speed - that socialism has any hope of showing its essentially human face. When socialism as a world system comes into its own again - as it undoubtedly will - the 'Gorbachev revolution' will have played a seminal role.

ABANDONING THE IDEOLOGICAL CONTEST

We are impressed with the contribution which crusading pro-perestroika journals (such as *Moscow News* and *New Times*) are making to the renovation of socialism. At the same time, we must not overlook the alarming tendency among many media partisans of perestroika to focus so exclusively on the blemishes of the socialist experience that the socialist critique of capitalism and imperialism finds little, if any, place. In keeping with this excessive defensiveness, there is a tendency to underplay some of the most graphic pointers to the superior moral potential of socialist civilisation. For instance, it is a sad commentary on earlier socialist history that the Soviet people are now moved to erect monuments to the victims of the Stalin period. But the capitalist world is planning no monuments to those of its citizens ravaged by its cruelties nor to millions of victims of its colonial terror.

The transformations which have occurred in Poland, Hungary, the German Democratic Republic, Czechoslovakia and Bulgaria are revolutionary in scope. With the exception of Romania, is there another example in human history in which those in power have responded to the inevitable with such a civilised and pacific resignation? We should remember De Gaulle's military response in 1968 when ten million workers and students filled the streets of Paris. It is not difficult to forecast how Bush or Thatcher would deal with millions in their streets supported by general strikes demanding the overthrow of their system of rule.

Some Soviet journals have become so exclusively focused on self-criticism that the social inequalities within capitalism and the continuing plunder by international capital of the resources of the developing world through neo-colonial manipulation, unequal trade and the debt burden, receive little emphasis. Middle class elements, including many journalists within socialist societies, seem mesmerised by pure technocracy; the glitter of Western consumerism, and the quality of up-market goods, appear to overshadow the quality of life for society as a whole.

There is less visible than at any time a critique of imperialism's continuing human rights violations and its gross interference in the internal affairs of sovereign states through surrogates and direct aggression, and its continuing support for banditry and racist and military dictatorships.

The gloss which is put in some of these journals on social and political conditions inside the capitalist West itself has been described by Jonathan Steele in the British Guardian as little less than 'grotesque'. In some contributions capitalism is prettified in the same generalised and unscholarly way as it used to be condemned, i.e. without researched statistics and with dogma taking the place of information. The borderline between socialism and what is called welfare capitalism is increasingly blurred. In contrast to all this, whatever else may be happening in international relations, the ideological offensive by the representatives of capitalism against socialism is certainly at full blast.

The Western media gloat repeatedly with headlines such as 'Communism - R.I.P.'. Professor Robert Heilbroner, a luminary of the New York New School, has already raised his champagne glass with a victory toast for capitalism. Asserting that the Soviet Union, China and Eastern Europe have proved that capitalism organises the material affairs of humankind more satisfactorily than socialism, he goes on to proclaim:

'Less than 75 years after it officially began, the contest between capitalism and socialism is over; capitalism has won... the great question now seems how rapid will be the transformation of socialism into capitalism, and not the other way around.'

Just in case more is needed to fulfil this prediction, some of capitalism's most powerful representatives are there to give history a helping hand. Reagan's final boast for his eight years in office was that he saw to it that not one more inch of territory in the world 'went communist'. Bush takes up the baton with: 'We can now move from containment to bring the socialist countries into the community of free nations'. The Guardian reports a multi-million pound initiative, endorsed by British ministers, to encourage change in Eastern Europe. And so on.

In the face of all this, it is no exaggeration to claim that, for the moment, the socialist critique of capitalism and the drive to win the hearts and minds of humanity for socialism have been virtually abandoned. The unprecedented offensive by capitalist ideologues against socialism has indeed been met by a unilateral ideological disarmament. To the extent that this has come about through the need to concentrate on putting our own house in order it is, at least, understandable. But, in many cases, there is an inability to distinguish between socialism in general and the incorrect methods which were used to translate it on the ground. This has led to an unjustified flirtation with certain economic and political values of capitalism.

The perversion of democracy in the socialist experience is falsely contrasted to its practice in the capitalist West as if the latter gives adequate scope for the fulfilment of democratic ideals. The economic ravages caused by excessive centralisation and commandism under socialism seem also to have pushed into the background the basic socialist critique of capitalism that a society cannot be democratic which is ruled by profit and social inequality and in which power over the most vital areas of life is outside public control.

LOSING FAITH IN THE SOCIALIST OBJECTIVE

Some communists have been completely overwhelmed by

the soiled image of socialism which they see in the mirror of history. They conclude that it reflects not only what was (and in the case of some countries, what still is), but, in addition, what inevitably had to be in the attempts to build a socialist society as understood by the founding fathers of socialist doctrine. If, indeed, what happened in the socialist world had to happen because of some or all of our theoretical starting points, if the Stalin-type perversion is unavoidable, then there is no more to be said; we must clearly either seek an alternative to socialism or throw overboard, or at least qualify, some of its postulates.

We believe, however, that the theory of Marxism, in all its essential respects, remains valid and provides an indispensable theoretical guide to achieve a society free of all forms of exploitation of person by person. The major weaknesses which have emerged in the practice of socialism are the results of distortions and misapplications. They do not flow naturally from the basic concepts of Marxism whose core is essentially humane and democratic and which project a social order with an economic potential vastly superior to that of capitalism.

Marx used the term 'primitive accumulation' to describe the original process of capitalist accumulation which, he maintained, was not the result of abstinence but rather of acts (including brigandage) such as the expropriation of the peasantry as happened during the British Enclosures. Preobrazhensky in The New Economics (1926) talked about 'primitive socialist accumulation' involving the expropriation of resources from the better-off classes to generate capital for socialist industrial development. Here, the term is used to describe the arbitrary measures taken against the Soviet peasantry to forcibly 'enclose' them into collectives.

Socialism, as a transition phase to communism, is not based on full egalitarianism. But clearly the socialist maxim 'to each according to his contribution' is not applied absolutely in a socialist society which devotes a large slice of its resources to social services, subsidising basic necessities, and implementing the human right of guaranteed employment.

The middle strata in socialist society are inevitably worse off than their counterparts in the West. Access to the flesh-pots of consumer goods (which the West produces for the upper crust in almost mind-bending variations) is more restricted when society tries to use its surplus to achieve a more just distribution of wealth.

In the recent period a number of European and African political parties have 'officially' abandoned Marxism-Leninism as a theoretical guide. In the case of FRELIMO, the decision appears to be the result of second thoughts on what may, in the circumstances, have been a premature transformation of the movement into a communist vanguard. But in the case of some Western parties the decision seems to be a response (with undoubted electoral implications) to the distortions of the socialist experience rather than a reasoned conclusion that Marxism is not a viable tool in the socialist endeavour. A leading Soviet academic has predicted that South Africa has no chance of becoming socialist for a century.

MARXIST THEORY UNDER FIRE

Let us touch on some of the concepts which have come under fire in the post-perestroika polemics:

- Marxism maintains that the class struggle is the motor of human history. Some commentators in the socialist media are showing a temptation to jettison this theory merely because Stalin and the bureaucracy around him distorted it to rationalise tyrannical practices. But it remains valid both as an explanation of past social transformations and as a guide to the strategy and tactics of the struggle to win a socialist order; a struggle in which the working class plays the dominant role.
- The economic stagnation of socialism and its poor technological performance as compared to the capitalist world sector cannot be attributed to the ineffectiveness of socialist relations of production but rather to their distortion. Socialist relations of production provide the most effective framework for

maximising humanity's productive capacity and using its products in the interests of the whole society.

- Marxist ethical doctrine sees no conflict between the contention that all morality is class-related and the assertion that working class values are concerned, above all, with the supremacy of human values. The separation of these inter-dependent concepts (in later theory and practice) provided the context in which crimes against the people were rationalised in the name of the class. We continue to assert that it is only in a non-exploitative, communist, classless society that human values will find their ultimate expression and be freed of all class-related morality. In the meanwhile the socialist transition has the potential of progressively asserting the values of the whole people over those of classes.
- The great divide which developed between socialism and political democracy should not be treated as flowing naturally from key aspects of socialist doctrine. This approach is fuelled by the sullied human rights record and the barrack-room collectivism of some of the experiences of existing socialism. We believe that Marxism clearly projects a system anchored in deep-seated political democracy and the rights of the individual which can only be truly attained when society as a whole assumes control and direction of all its riches and resources.
- The crucial connection between socialism and internationalism and the importance of world working-class solidarity should not be underplayed as a result of the distortions which were experienced. These included excessive centralisation in the era of the Comintern, subordination of legitimate national aspirations to a distorted concept of 'internationalism', national rivalries between and within socialist states (including examples of armed confrontation). Working class internationalism

remains one of the most liberating concepts in Marxism and needs to find effective expression in the new world conditions.

In summary, we believe that Marxism is a social science whose fundamental postulates and basic insights into the historical processes remain a powerful (because accurate) theoretical weapon. But this is not to say that every word of Marx, Engels and Lenin must be taken as gospel; they were not infallible and they were not always correct in their projections. Lenin, for example, believed that capitalism was about to collapse worldwide in the post-October period.

It was a belief based on the incorrect premise that, as a system, capitalism was in an irreversible crisis and those capitalist relations of production constituted an obstacle to the further all-round development of the forces of production. This was combined with a belief in the imminence of global socialist transformation, which undoubtedly infected much of the earlier thinking about the perspectives of socialist construction in the Soviet Union.

Also, it could well be argued that the classical description of bourgeois democracy was an over-simplification and tended to underestimate the historic achievements of working class struggle in imposing and defending aspects of a real democratic culture on the capitalist state; a culture which should not disappear but rather needs to be expanded under true socialism. But we emphasise again that the fundamental distortions which emerged in the practice of existing socialism cannot be traced to the essential tenets of Marxist revolutionary science. If we are looking for culprits, we must look at ourselves and not at the founders of Marxism.

In some cases, the deformations experienced by existing socialist states were the results of bureaucratic distortions which were rationalised at the ideological level by a mechanical and out-of-context invocation of Marxist dogma. In other cases they were the results of a genuinely-motivated but tragic misapplication of socialist theory in new realities which were not foreseen by the founders of Marxism. The fact that socialist power was first won in the most backward outpost of European capitalism, without a democratic political tradition, played no small part in the way it was shaped. To this must be added the years of isolation, economic siege and armed intervention which, in the immediate post-October period, led to the virtual decimation of the Soviet Union's relatively small working class. In the course of time the party leadership was transformed into a command post with an overbearing centralism and very little democracy, even in relation to its own membership.

Most of the other socialist countries emerged 30 years later in the shadow of the cold war. Some of them owed a great deal to Soviet power for their very creation and survival, and the majority, for a great part of their history, followed the Stalinist economic and political model. Communists outside the socialist world and revolutionaries engaged in anti-colonial movements were the beneficiaries of generous aid and consistent acts of internationalist solidarity. They correctly saw in Soviet power a bulwark against their enemies and either did not believe, or did not want to believe, the way in which aspects of socialism were being debased.

All this helps to explain, but in no way to justify, the awful grip which Stalinism came to exercise in every sector of the socialist world and over the whole international communist movement. It was a grip which, if loosened by either parties (e.g. Yugoslavia) or individuals within parties, usually led to isolation and excommunication. We make no attempt here to answer the complex question of why so many millions of genuine socialists and revolutionaries became such blind worshippers in the temple of the cult of the personality. Suffice it to say that the strength of this conformism lay, partly, in an ideological conviction that those whom history had appointed as the custodians of humankind's communist future seemed to be building on foundations prepared by the founding fathers of Marxism. And there was not enough in classical Marxist theory about the nature of the transition period to provide a detailed guide to the future.

This under-developed state of classical Marxist theory in relation to the form and structure of future socialist society lent itself easily to the elaboration of dogma which could claim general 'legitimacy' from a selection of quotes from the masters. But the founders of Marxism 'never invented specific forms and mechanisms for the development of the new society. They elaborated its socialist ideal... they provided the historically transient character of capitalism and the historical need for transition to a new stage of social development. As for the structure of the future society to replace capitalism, they discussed it in the most general terms and mostly from the point of view of fundamental principles'.

In particular, let us consider two issues:

- Socialism and democracy, and the related question
- Social and economic alienation under socialism.

This must be understood as providing the immediate explanation of the way major social change manifests itself in a situation in which the relations of production have become obstacles to the development of productive forces. This type of formulation is preferred to the one occasionally used by Gorbachev that there are certain universal human values which take priority over class values.

This latter formulation tends to detract from the interdependence of working class and human morality. It also perhaps goes too far in separating morality from its class connection, even though it is clear that the assertion of certain values can be in the mutual interests of otherwise contending classes.

SOCIALISM AND DEMOCRACY

Marxist ideology saw the future state as 'a direct democracy in which the task of governing would not be the preserve of a state bureaucracy' and as 'an association in which the free development of each is a condition for the free development of all'. How did it happen that, in the name of this most humane and liberating ideology, the bureaucracy became so all-powerful and the individual was so suffocated?

To find, at least, the beginnings of an answer we need to look at four related areas:

- The thesis of the 'Dictatorship of the Proletariat'

which was used as the theoretical rationalisation for unbridled authoritarianism.

- The steady erosion of people's power both at the level of government and mass social organisations.
- The perversion of the concept of the party as a • vanguard of the working class, and
- Whether, at the end of the day, socialist democracy can find real expression in a single-party state.

Dictatorship of the Proletariat

The concept of the 'Dictatorship of the Proletariat' was dealt with rather thinly by Marx as 'a transition to a classless society' without much further definition. For his part Engels, drawing on Marx's analysis of the Paris Commune, claimed that it indeed 'was the Dictatorship of the Proletariat'. The Paris Commune of 1871 was an exceptional social experience which brought into being a kind of workers' city-state (by no means socialist-led) in which, for a brief moment, most functions of the state (both legislative and executive) were directly exercised by a popular democratic assembly. The concept of the 'Dictatorship of the Proletariat' was elaborated by Lenin in State and Revolution in the very heat of the revolutionary transformation in 1917.

Lenin quoted Engels approvingly when he said that 'the proletariat needs the state, not in the interests of freedom but in order to hold down its adversaries, and as soon as it becomes possible to speak of freedom the state as such ceases to exist'. In the meanwhile, in contrast to capitalist democracy which is 'curtailed, wretched, false... for the rich, for the minority... the dictatorship of the proletariat, the period of transition to communism, will, for the first time, create democracy... for the majority... along with the necessary suppression of the exploiters, of the minority.'

Lenin envisaged that working-class power would be based on the kind of democracy of the Commune, but he did not address, in any detail, the nature of established socialist civil society, including fundamental questions such as the relationship between the party, state, people's elected representatives, social organisations, etc. Understandably, the dominant preoccupation at the time was with the seizure of power, its protection in the face of the expected counter-revolutionary assault, the creation of 'democracy for the majority' and the 'suppression of the minority of exploiters'.

Rosa Luxemburg said, in a polemic with Lenin:

'Freedom only for the supporters of the government, only for the members of one party - however numerous they may be - is not freedom at all. Freedom is always and exclusively freedom for the one who thinks differently... its effectiveness vanishes when "freedom" becomes a special privilege.'

These words may not have been appropriate as policy (which is what Luxemburg argued for) in the special conditions of the phase immediately after the seizure of power in October 1917. Without a limitation on democracy there was no way the revolution could have defended itself in the civil war and the direct intervention by the whole of the capitalist world. But Luxemburg's concept of freedom is surely incontrovertible once a society has achieved stability. Lenin clearly assumed that whatever repression may be necessary in the immediate aftermath of the revolution would be relatively mild and short-lived.

The state and its traditional instruments of force would begin to 'wither away' almost as soon as socialist power had been won and the process of widening and deepening democracy would begin. Lenin was referring to the transitional socialist state (and not to the future communist society) when he emphasised that there would be an extension of 'democracy to such an overwhelming majority of the population that the need for a special machine of suppression will begin to disappear... it is no longer a state in the proper sense of the word (because) the suppression of the minority of exploiters... is easy, simple', entailing relatively little bloodshed, and hardly needing a machine or a special apparatus other than 'the simple organisation of the armed people (such as the Soviets)...'

We know that all this is a far cry from what happened in the decades which followed. The whole process was put in reverse. The complete 'suppression of the exploiters' was followed by the strengthening of the instruments of state suppression and the narrowing of democracy for the majority of the population, including the working class. The anti-Leninist theory advanced (in the name of Lenin) to 'justify' this process was that the class struggle becomes more rather than less intense with the entrenchment of socialism. In some respects this became a self-fulfilling prophecy; a retreat from democratic norms intensified social contradictions which, in turn, became the excuse for an intensification of the 'class struggle'.

One of the key rationalisations for this thesis was the undoubted threat, even after the end of the civil war, posed by imperialism and fascism to the very survival of the Soviet Union and the continuing Western conspiracies to prevent the spread of socialist power after 1945. But events have demonstrated that if the survival of the Soviet Union was at risk from the fascist onslaught it was, among other reasons, also the result of damage wrought to the whole Soviet social fabric (including its army) by the authoritarian bureaucracy. And if Western 'conspiracies' have succeeded in threatening the very survival of socialism in places like Eastern Europe, it is the narrowing rather than the extension of democracy which has played into their hands.

The term 'Dictatorship of the Proletariat' reflected the historical truth that in class-divided social formations state power is ultimately exercised by, and in the interests of, the class which owns and controls the means of production. It is in this sense that capitalist formations were described as a 'dictatorship of the bourgeoisie' whose rule would be replaced by a 'dictatorship of the proletariat' during the socialist transition period. In the latter case power would, however, be exercised in the interests of the overwhelming majority of the people and should lead to an ever-expanding genuine democracy - both political and economic.

On reflection, the choice of the word 'dictatorship' to describe this type of society certainly opens the way to ambiguities and distortions. The abandonment of the term by most communist parties, including ours, does not, in all cases, imply a rejection of the historical validity of its essential content. But, the way the term came to be abused bore little resemblance to Lenin's original concept. It was progressively denuded of its intrinsic democratic content and came to signify, in practice, a dictatorship of a party bureaucracy. For Lenin the repressive aspect of the concept had impending relevance in relation to the need for the revolution to defend itself against counter-revolutionary terror in the immediate post-revolution period. He was defending, against the utopianism of the anarchists, the limited retention of repressive apparatus.

But, unfortunately, practices justified by the exigencies of the earlier phases became a permanent feature of the new society. As time went on the gap between socialism and democracy widened; the nature and role of the social institutions (such as the Soviets, the party and mass organisations) which had previously given substance to popular power and socialist democracy, were steadily eroded.

ELECTED BODIES AND MASS ORGANISATIONS

The steady erosion of the powers and representative character of elected institutions led to the alienation of a considerable portion of society from political life. The electorate had no effective right to choose its representatives. Gone were the days when the party had to engage in a political contest to win a majority in the Soviets. The legislative organs did not, in any case, have genuine control over legislation; by their nature they could only act as rubber stamps for decisions which had already been taken by party structures. The executive and judicial organs were, for all practical purposes, under the direct control of the party bureaucracy. In practice the majority of the people had very few levers with which to determine the course of economic or social life. Democracy in the mass organisations was also more formal than real.

The enormous membership figures told us very little about the extent to which the individual trade unionist, youth or woman was able to participate in the control or direction of their respective organisations. At the end of the day these organisations were turned into transmission belts for decisions taken elsewhere and the individual members were little more than cogs of the vast bureaucratic machine. The trade union movement became an adjunct of the state and party. Workers had no meaningful role in determining the composition of the top leadership which was, in substance, answerable to the party apparatus. For all practical purposes the right to strike did not exist. The extremely thin dividing line between management and the trade union collective on the factory floor detracted from the real autonomy of trade unions.

Apart from certain welfare functions, they tended, more and more, to act like Western-style production councils, but without the advantage of having to answer for their role to an independent trade union under the democratic control of its membership. Much of the above applied to the women's and youth organisations. Instead of being guided by the aspirations and interests of their constituencies, they were turned into support bases for the ongoing dictates of the state and party apparatus. In the immediate aftermath of the October revolution, the Bolshevik party shared power with other political and social tendencies, including Mensheviks and a section of the left Social Revolutionaries. In the elections for the constituent assembly in 1918, the Bolsheviks received less than a third of the popular vote.

There may be moments in the life of a revolution which justify a postponement of full democratic processes. And we do not address the question of whether the Bolsheviks were justified in taking a monopoly of state power during the extraordinary period of both internal and external assault on the gains of the revolution. Suffice it to say that the single-party state and the guiding and leading role of the party subsequently became permanent features of socialist rule and were entrenched in the constitutions of most socialist states. Henceforth the parties were 'vanguards' by law and not necessarily by virtue of social endorsement. This was accompanied by negative transformations within the party itself. Under the guise of 'democratic centralism' inner-party democracy was almost completely suffocated by centralism.

All effective power was concentrated in the hands of a

Political Bureau or, in some cases, a single, all-powerful personality. The control of this 'leadership' by the party as a whole was purely formal. In most cases the composition of the highest organ - the congress which finalised policy and elected the leadership - was manipulated from the top. The Central Committee (elected by variations of a 'list' system emanating from the top) had only the most tenuous jurisdiction over the Political Bureau. Within this latter body a change of leaders resembled a palace coup rather than a democratic process; invariably the changes were later unanimously endorsed.

The invigorating impact of the contest of ideas in Marxist culture was stifled. In practice, the basic party unit was there to explain, defend, exhort and support policies in whose formulation they rarely participated. The concept of consensus effectively stifled dissent and promoted the completely unnatural appearance of unanimity on everything. Fundamental differences were either suppressed or silenced by the self-imposed discipline of so-called democratic centralism. In these conditions the democratic development of party policy became a virtual impossibility.

The Single-Party State

Hegel coined the profound aphorism that truth is usually born as a heresy and dies as a superstition. With no real right to dissent by citizens or even by the mass of the party membership, truth became more and more inhibited by deadening dogma; a sort of catechism took the place of creative thought. And, within the confines of a single-party state, the alternative to active conformism was either silence or the risk of punishment as 'an enemy of the people'. Is this suppression of the right to dissent inherent in the single-party state? Gorbachev recently made the point that:

'Developing the independent activities of the masses and prompting democratisation of all spheres of life under a one-party system is a noble but very difficult mission for the party. And a great deal will depend on how we deal with it'.

Gorbachev's thought has special relevance to many parts

of our own continent where the one-party system abounds. It straddles both capitalist and socialist-oriented countries and in most of them it is used to prevent, among other things, the democratic organisation of the working people either politically or in trade unions.

This is not to say that all one-party states in our continent have in fact turned out to be authoritarian; indeed some of them are headed by the most humane leaders ho passionately believe in democratic processes. Nor can we discuss the role they have played in preventing tribal, ethnic and regional fragmentation, combatting externally inspired banditry, and correcting some of the grave distortions we inherited from the colonial period. In relation to the socialist perspective, it is sometimes forgotten that the concept of the single-party state is nowhere to be found in classical Marxist theory.

And we have had sufficient experience of one-party rule in various parts of the world to perhaps conclude that the 'mission' to promote real democracy under a one-party system is not just difficult but, in the long run, impossible. But, in any case, where a single-party state is in place and there is not even democracy and accountability within the party, it becomes a short-cut to a political tyranny over the whole of society. And at different points in time this is what happened in most socialist states. The resulting sense of political alienation of the great majority of the people was not the only negative feature of existing socialism. Of equal importance was the failure to overcome the sense of economic alienation inherited from the capitalist past.

TOTALITARIANISM

Uniquely a twentieth-century phenomenon, students will encounter the concept of totalitarianism in many courses on the period. Care should be taken to distinguish the concept from autocracy, dictatorship and single-party rule. A simple definition of totalitarianism can be taken to be 'a system of rule, driven by an ideology, that seeks direction of all aspects of public activity, political, economic and social, and uses to that end, at least to a degree, propaganda and terror'. This definition, through brevity, is incomplete. To move toward a more complete understanding, a look at the history of its use can be helpful. This will indicate that initially it was not used as a critical judgement on a government. The word was probably first used by the Italian philosopher, Giovanni Gentile, in 1925, during the earlier years of Italian Fascist rule, to describe a comprehensive socio-political system. Mussolini happily used the word, and while in general it usefully describes Nazism and Stalinism, Hitler avoided its use and Stalin saw it as applicable to Fascist Italy and Nazi Germany but not to Russia.

The concept gained wider currency and became prominent in schoolbooks during the post-1945 Cold War period. It was at that time that it was defined more fully, notably by US historians Carl Friedrich and Zbigniew Brzezinski in *Totalitarian Dictatorship and Autocracy* (1956). Friedrich and Brzezinski's theoretical model, derived from the history of the twentieth century, had six key features.

- An official ideology to which general adherence was demanded, the ideology intended to achieve a 'perfect final stage of mankind'.
- A single mass party, hierarchically organised, closely interwoven with the state bureaucracy and typically led by one man.
- Monopolistic control of the armed forces.
- A similar monopoly of the means of effective mass communication.
- A system of terroristic police control.
- Central control and direction of the entire economy.

During the Cold War time of ideological combat the concept was used by liberal democracies to condemn the political systems of communist states. While some will wish to amend parts of Friedrich and Brzezinski's depiction of totalitarianism, nevertheless their classification provides a six-part instrument with which to compare and assess the workings of states in the last century. If this conceptual model is applied to individual states, differences in the *form* of totalitarianism and *variations in degree* can be identified. Here are one or two examples but readers can make more extensive and detailed assessments of the totalitarianism of the states considered.

ITALY AND MUSSOLINI

Mussolini never created an exclusive ideology: Fascism existed alongside the Roman Catholic Church, illustrated by the Lateran Treaty of 1929, and the monarchy, that dismissed him in 1943. Italian Fascism has been likened to a *style* of government and compared to Germany and the USSR, Italian terrorist police activity was limited: Mussolini's singular economic policy, corporatism, was loosely executed. What Mussolini, with his grounding in journalism, did achieve was a skilful projection of Fascist ideas through propaganda. Hitler acknowledged that he learned from these successes.

THE USSR AND STALIN

Stalin vigorously followed a policy of strengthening Communist party power and, from the late 1920s, social and economic transformation but how far this can be seen as ideologically Marxist-Leninist policy continues to be debated among historians, as discussed by Jane Redfern in this issue.

THE THIRD REICH AND HITLER

When Hitler gained power he had already promoted a strongly nationalist/ racist ideology for some time, not least in his prison book, *Mein Kampf* (1923), and he, with Dr Joseph Goebbels were outstanding practitioners of the use of mass communication, but Hitler's control of the armed forces, with their embedded Prussian officer corps mentality, took some time to achieve. Effective control of the entire economy required a struggle and was successful only midway through the Second World War. Edgar Feuchtwanger has described the policy of Nazification, in his concise '*Gleichshaltung*' concept article and, in the next issue, David Welch charts the party/ state administrative muddle in the Third Reich.

DEMOCRACY AND TOTALITARIANISM

This writer has proposed elsewhere that liberal democracy

can develop only where certain circumstances exist. These include a degree of industrialisation, an active media and expressions and discussions of opinion. Also needed are attitudes, held in common within society, of tolerance, respect for minority and individual rights and the absence of fixed goals. Alert readers will note that a totalitarian system uses the same circumstances needed for liberal democracy and, harnessed to a fixed goal, acts to negate or reverse the attitudes that underpin democracy. Twentieth-century technology has provided the possibilities for the use of media (newspapers, radio, film and television) to 'brainwash'citizens, and modern communications to identify dissidents and co-ordinate action against them.

It is inconceivable that a person in their right mind would wish to loose two of democracy's greatest gifts, pluralism (a plurality of power centres) and the rule of law. It is noteworthy, therefore, that the roots of totalitarianism have been traced to the 1890s, thought by many to be the high point of liberalism. Liberalism, with its emphasis on individual liberty, contained a contradiction. Unrestrained pursuit of individual liberty was a threat to others, that is to the society, without which individual liberty was worthless.

With their stress on the social rather than the individual, the three main totalitarian systems mentioned and other lesser systems, in their own crudely inhuman ways redressed this contradiction. If this latter view unsettles readers, then this last will do so more. It has been suggested by some thinkers that liberal democracies have totalitarian characteristics in the sense that the assumptions of capitalism, and the appropriate way of life, are remorselessly inferred in all that is public and creates a homogenised mind set among the population.

DEMOCRACY

The crucial assumption behind the anti-globalizers' skepticism is that the increasing transactions across the border of nation-states are eroding the efficiency of national governing structures, especially democratic ones. This The hypothesis that economic globalization erodes the ability of democratic governments to manage economic and social affairs in interests of the people, has been challenged in a number of studies but remains exceptionally influential: "The tradeoffs can be represented in the form of a trilemma: the nation-state system, democratic politics, and full economic integration are mutually incompatible. Of the three, at most two can be had together".

This "trilemma" becomes especially sensitive in the context of the increasing democratic aspirations around the world, the phenomenon, which Samuel Huntington has called the "Third Wave of Democratization". As David Held has mentioned: "There is... a striking paradox to note about the contemporary era: from Africa to Eastern Europe, Asia to Latin America, more and more nations and groups are championing the idea of "the rule by the people"; but they are doing so at just that moment when the very efficacy of democracy as a national form of political organization appears open to question". Are globalization and the "Third Wave of Democratization" two inherently controversial trends?

There are various models of democracy, whose diversity is imbedded in different normative approaches toward the democratic idea. The limited frame of the present paper does not allow us to elaborate in detail discussing these controversies; but one can hardly disagree with the argument that the modern democratic state is primarily a nation-state. The ideas of democracy and national sovereignty are deeply interrelated. The philosophers of the Enlightenment developed both these concepts with a logical interdependence between them. People, while they are joining into a society, erect the state and, as a consequence, constitute the nation; therefore, the sovereignty should remain with the people; and thus, the only proper government is a democratic one.

Two main arguments supporting the thesis that economic globalization threatens democracy are present in the literature:

- Globalization erodes the ability of nation-states to exercise the effective control over the political agenda;
- Globalization eliminates the social correctives to the market economy. This loosening of the social safety net together with the on-going restructuring of the

economic system (frequently labeled as "New Economy") increase social inequality: the rich richer and the poor poorer. A result of these developments is the threat to the very social foundations of contemporary democracies.

Thus, modern democracy seems to be in the squeeze between the external pressure and unfavorable internal shifts in the domestic social structures.

EXTERNAL PRESSURE

The impact of globalization on modern democracies is usually debated under the name "crisis of the state": "Globalization increases the potential mobility of financial capital, real investments, goods and services, and to a more limited extent, highly skilled labour. Consequently, mobile economic actors are better able to avoid undesirable state regulations, or to profit from ones that are more advantageous. To the extent that countries depend on these actors, or on the resources they control, they are forced into a competition for locational advantage that has all the characteristics of a Prisoner's Dilemma game, and that reduces the capacity of the territorial state to shape the conditions under which capitalist economies must operate".

The widespread vision is that globalization has directly challenged the ability of states to govern autonomously, even in the domain of domestic policy. States are losing their control over:

- *Financial flows and transnational organization of production,* due to the huge world-wide electronic money transfers, growing significance of off-shore zones, increasing ability of transnational corporations decide upon organization of production across national borders;
- *Information flows,* because the rise of satellite communications, computer data transmissions, international mass-media, which cover ever larger parts of the world.

The lack of the ability to control information flows has

increasing importance in the ostensible information age. In the 20th century, the means of mass communication (cheap newspapers, radio translators, TV-sets, computers) became more and more ubiquitous. Control over the centers transmitting this information became an effective tool of manipulating the public opinion. Growth of international mass-media and consequent decline in governmental ability to control information being delivered to almost every house is therefore apparently challenging for authoritarian regimes, but it also creates some risks for a democracy since the latter can hardly guarantee access of different social groups to leading mass-media.

Paradoxically, these two trends may have different effects on democratic and authoritarian political regimes. Increased information flows challenge autocracies and, perhaps, were a cause of the major democratization wave in the late twentieth century. At the same time, financial flows and transnational organization of production may jeopardize democratic governance at the national level. Because the financial autonomy and ability to modify systems of taxation according to recognized social needs has been considered as a fundamental property of a modern sovereign state, the relative release of financial flows from direct national regulation is expected to undermine the authority of nation-states. In the case of contemporary democratic regimes, these developments are likely to weaken one of their basic pillars, namely, the social safety net. Thus, globalization is expected to challenge the basic principle of democratic governance, the authority of representative institutions to establish the rules of wealth re-distribution in a country.

The constraints on the financial capacities of nation-states are most frequently pointed to as the threat to national sovereignty and democratic decision-making in the "globalized world". However, their existence is debatable. As F. Scharpf argues: "Empirical studies on tax policies also produce ambivalent findings, especially if they fail to distinguish between mobile and immobile tax bases. There is, for instance, no theoretical reason to assume that the liberalization of capital markets should be associated with a reduction of social security charges."

Thus, Scharpf attacks a central proposition of the globalization theory, which maintains that higher taxes inevitably push the capital out of a country and negatively effect economic growth. He hypothesizes that this is not the overall level of taxation but its composition that affects economic growth. In order to test these contradictory hypotheses – those by the pundits of the globalization theory and by Scharpf, – I have analyzed statistical associations between economic growth (average annual change in 1990-98, in per cent) and direct investment inflows (in per cent of GDP, in 1997), on the one hand; and government tax receipts (total and from different classes of taxation, in per cent of GDP, in 1996), on the other hand.

The analysis focuses on the advanced industrial nations of the OECD because of the following reasons. First, these countries are democratic and engaged in the global economic and, thus, provide us with evidence directly related to the topic under study. Second, these nations are similar in many respects (including political stability, the level of development, etc.) and, therefore, innumerable controls may be relaxed. There is marginally significant correlation between the overall taxation burden, conventionally operationalized as the ratio of total tax receipts to GDP and economic growth in the 1990s. The respective Pearson coefficient is - 0.328 and significant at 0.1 probability level. This means that increasing the overall level of taxation *may* have a negative effect economic growth.

Do all types of taxation have a negative effect? The decomposition of the explanatory variable offers interesting results. First, the explanatory power of the model greatly increases: from 10.7% of the explained variance in the initial model to 57.8% after the decomposition. The F-statistic is equal to 2.89, which is significant at 0.05 probability level, a high standard for an estimation based on merely 29 cases. The model is reported below. The estimations indicate that the effect of so-called "social security contributions", which in fact are a heavy tax on labour, especially unskilled labour, has a strong detrimental effect on growth. At the same time, the impact of taxes on goods and sales and, surprisingly for pundits of the globalization theory, the impact of corporate profit taxation appears to be either neutral or marginally positive.

Is the redistributive effect of the social security system or its currently widespread mode of finance through the special taxation on labour detrimental for economic growth? In order to address this question, the model for the average annual growth in the 1990s with the ratio of social security budget to GDP as explanatory variable was estimated; and, then, the ratio of social security contributions to GDP was included in the model. The budget of the social security system (as the ratio to GDP) has a seemingly negative association with economic growth in the 1990s. The respective Pearson coefficient is 0.398 and significant at 0.1 probability level. However, this association vanishes as soon as the ratio of "social security contributions" to GDP is controlled.

The model for the average annual growth in the 1990s with the ratios of social security budget and social security contributions to GDP as explanatory variables explains 33.2% of variance; the respective F-statistic equals 4.72 and is significant at 0.05 probability level.

In the model, only the second explanatory factor appears significant. The respective t-statistic is -2.22 and significant at 0.05 probability level. This observation is supportive for the hypothesis that not the volume of the social security of network but the usage of *de-facto* labour taxation in order to finance it is the source of troubles. The same four models have been run in order to explain the international variance in investment rates.

The association with the ratio of investment to GDP appeared to be marginally *positive*; the finding should be surprising to the pundits of globalization theory. The Pearson correlation is 0.339 and significant at the 0.1 probability level. The probable explanation is that investors are ready to pay higher taxes for the investment environment better in other respects, perhaps, including the socio-political stability, which a developed social security system may bring about. The result of the multivariate model, where the taxation factors has been decomposed, may be puzzling indeed. The model is efficient. It explains 36.8% of variance and is significant at the 3% probability level.

The most surprising finding is that the ratio of the fiscal incomes from corporate profit taxation has strong *positive* partial correlation with the investment rate. This finding is challenging for further investigations. The linear models for investment rates with the ratios of social security budget and social security contributions to GDP as explanatory variables did not show any significant correlations.

The results of the above analysis can be explained in terms of effective governmental policy:

There is... not one best way through which advanced welfare states could maintain their economic viability in an environment of internationalized capitalism without abandoning their employment, social security and egalitarian aspirations. But as countries like Denmark, Switzerland, Australia, or the Netherlands demonstrate, there is no reason to think that economic viability should be incompatible with the successful pursuit of these aspirations.

Our findings indicate the need to reform the systems of taxation and, especially, social security funding. In the latter case, either public funding out of indirect taxation or quasi-private finding with fixed contributions, or their mixture may be preferable to the currently most widespread system based on the heavy taxation of labour. Apparently, labour will be a crucial input of the "new economy" in whichever form the latter may develop. Thus, the fiscal suppression of the key developmental factor is detrimental.

However, the need for reform does not imply the necessity to abandon. Nation-states have much space for maneuvering. Neither their ability to tax, nor their capacity to maintain social security networks seems to be endangered from the viewpoint of international economics. However, both, the fisc and the social security provision, are under siege. The reasons may be ideological rather than economic in nature.

INTERNAL SHIFTS

As the above analysis indicates, neoliberal theory is questionable, but even if it had accurately predicted that the effects of governmental policy and economic openness and liberalization are prerequisites for growth, there is no actual threat for democratic decision-making. Political decisions were always supposed to be made in the frame of rational choice. Democratic governance never meant that the public should be inconsiderate of economic realities.

On the contrary, the development of representative democracy is a system of checks and balances aimed at binding the popular vote by reasons of economic rationality and the preservation of human rights. The goal of unlimited democratic sovereignty was never pursued in modern democracies after the Jacobin period of the French revolution. Even if the neoliberal theory were true, this would not mean that democracy should be replaced by a "technocratic government" of economic experts.

The issue presently confronting democracy is not the narrowing of the democratically controlled political agenda, but the new urgency of the old contradictions between economic rationality and other democratic values: equality and solidarity. These contradictions encompass the whole history of democratic development in capitalist society, and contemporary urgency over the problem is not caused by the (envisaged) reduction of opportunities for the democratic regulation of economic affairs, but rather by the complication of the political agenda; while the latter is a result of globalization processes.

This complication of the contemporary political agenda requires new solutions on the part of policy-makers. The problem of suitable instruments for a national democratic government has at least two dimensions: democratic governments need new instruments of social regulation and they need to change themselves in order to be able to employ these instruments. The prospects of an adequate response to these challenges are rather obscure: "The modern welfare state is based on democracy. Low voting rates, minor respect for politics and politicians, perspectives of the coming non-transparent and simultaneously very complex information society – these anti-participating phenomena are simultaneous significant threats for efforts to conduct the reforms of social policy". One can say that the problems brought about by globalization seem to be political rather than economic in nature.

The "competition state" and representative democracy. The main points of neoliberalism as the leading ideology of "globalization" are: *(1)* the rule of the market; *(2)* cutting public expenditure for social services; *(3)* deregulation; *(4)* privatization; *(5)* eliminating the concept of "the public good" or "community". Application of these ideas leads, in particular, to the complication or, better said, "technologicalization" of the political agenda. Good examples are problems of deregulation, issues of the international division of labour, creation and regulation of quasi-markets for public goods (like educational vouchers or competing pension funds).

The complication of the political agenda and the vision of only one "correct" economic policy are employed in order to legitimize the shift of power within national governments. G. Baecker has demonstrated this tendency, using as an example the current developments in Switzerland:

The perception of [new] internal and external affairs Â... in connection with the increased number of social issues regulated in international regimes leads to a shift of political power from the Parliament to the Executive. Many problems that have been treated through national legislation before can now be negotiated by the Federal Council within international treaties. Democratic legitimization for these issues is weakened by the fact that Parliament can no longer perform its deliberating function.

This is only an illustration. Similar tendencies are observed in many other parliamentary as well as presidential democracies, and the reader can, perhaps, recall many other examples. The complication of the political agenda requires increasing specialization of the political class. At the first sight, it creates additional opportunities for representative democracy (parliamentary procedures and organized groups of interests). Political deliberations should be more open to representative organizations; while in practice: "Associations are dismissed [by governments] as hide-bound purveyors of the lowest common denominator sectoral view".

At the moment, the structural weakness of traditional political parties, civic associations and the former "drivers" of the political system is a characteristic feature of many democratic political systems. The institutions of representative democracy (political parties, trade unions, other public organizations, and, to some extend, parliaments) appear not to be ready to bear the increasing load. Because of the change of their internal structure and pattern of conduct in "the golden time" of deliberative democracy (late 1960s - early 1980s), they have ceased to be the tools of fast reaction. In a short paper on "Political crisis as the crisis of communication", P. Glotz describes problems of the modern German political parties as follows: "Parties are today one-sidedly constituted, rather closed and rather old, hierarchically organized circles of communication, in which miscellaneous needs of the differentiated civil society make the way for themselves hard and slow".

This situation creates an environment that favors the priority of institutional interests over the interests of represented social groups. The question of whether the set of traditional representative groups continues to reflect real cleavages within a modern society becomes relevant. Investigating the new patterns of social regulation formed during globalization, G. Wewer noticed the crisis of other representative institutions, and, first of all, those of them who are being overloaded to the largest extent. If P. Glotz sounds the alarm because of the increasing alienation of the organized political elite, G. Wewer draws an even more unpleasant picture of the crisis of representative democracy today:

Not only parties, but also churches, trade unions and public organizations lose their supporters. Even the industrial and trade chambers should struggle with "rebels", who do no longer want to pay contributions, and question their purpose.

If, however, there are no longer public conditions, under which legitimacy was founded in the past, then it seems disputable, whether the problem can be solved by other ways. It results in the question, what will actually consolidate a society in the future.

To what extent can these structural changes in society and political communication be attributed to the globalization processes? As far as increasing external (international) similarities require internal (within a nation-state) differentiation, and as far as the theoretical prediction of a new emerging cleavage between "globalized" social groups and "the rest of population" is true, we would suggest the positive answer. However, the question remains open and points out a new dimension of the discussion on the political effects of globalization.

Globalization and Plebiscite Democracy

The matter of the above-mentioned claims is the crisis of the deliberative model of democracy, the ideal type of democratic government outlined by J. Habermas. Several kinds of mechanisms for compensating unsatisfactory work of the institutions of representative democracy emerge within modern political systems.

P. Glotz describes the reaction *within* representative organizations, to inadequate adaptation to new circumstances:

As the political elite naturally feel this deficiency, it tries to find a solution. If the elite are already moved by democratic routines ("democracy within the party") from the increasingly distant voter, it has to invent a device, which reproduces some kind of telepathic relation to this unknown being, the voter. This is the top candidate, the hero, the embodying. Thus, in order to correct an erratic development, another erratic development emerges: one could label it - by a paradoxical concept - the democratic Caesarism. For the correction of the sluggish interior communications of the time-rich, a populist on the top was invented.

Simultaneously, there are growing demands from public groups that do not consider their interests as adequately represented by traditional political institutions, because the parties are too inert: public organizations are either corrupted or do not respond to the changed structure of the society. The unsatisfactorily represented social groups insist on expansion of plebiscite elements in the democratic political systems. This demand corresponds also with the tendencies inside the representative organizations. As a result, the growth of the plebiscite elements is often combined with the increase of political populism.

Certainly, economic globalization highlights or even exaggerates structural weaknesses of contemporary democratic regimes. However, none of these developments indicate that globalization has an inevitably debilitating effect on the foundations of democratic governance at the national level. Politicians are not obliged to focus exclusively on mentoring of the public in neoliberal ideas. Representative institutions may accommodate newly developed social interests and articulate the cleavages that globalization deepens. Thus, opportunities for political populism can be reduced. At the same time, there is no fully convincing evidence that developments in democratic society *have to* follow such an optimistic scenario and the effect of globalization on democratic political systems *will be* ultimately positive. My argument is that globalization, as a catalyst of change, *may* have a positive effect in terms of democratic representation and governance.

The linkage between economic globalization and erosion of the democratic nation-state is more political than economic in nature. The main problem is not the negative effects of the increasing influence of financial market players, but the structural crisis of deliberative democracy caused by:

- Inadequacy of the traditional representative institutions in managing the complication of policy tasks brought about by globalization;
- Erosion of the linkage between representative institutions and represented social groups due to the shifts in social structure as well as structural weakness of the institutions themselves;

- Neoliberal ideological reaction to globalization, whose assumptions are often used by the political elite for legitimization of its functional failure.

Recent developments within contemporary democracies suggest two possible scenarios of reinvesting the democratic government. According to the optimist view, the tasks of current economic and social regulation will be transferred to the independent public institutions and market players through privatization, mechanisms of "new public management", etc.; while the government will gain a new glance of democratic legitimization by the plebiscite mechanisms and maintain the role of the main innovator and moderator. A more skeptical vision draws the picture of uncontrolled segmentation of policy regulation and populist political leadership challenging popular demands.

It implies also a new cultural cleavage within society: the development from rather homogeneous (at least, in cultural aspects) national society to a society with two coexisting types of culture: "traditional" national culture of the industrial society and "globalized" culture of economic and political elite, focused on the values of the post-industrial society. This discrepancy can be demonstrated both on national level, between the new elite and "less globalized" social groups, as well as on an international level, where the gap between the countries, which are spearheading globalization, and "the rest of the world" rapidly increases. Again, as in the case of external challenges of economic globalization, we should say that the risks are serious and reforms are necessary. However, all the above problems are domestic problems of national political systems, and they, respectively, have domestic solutions. It remains implausible that the development of supranational political structures – a "world government", for example – may be an efficient means to ameliorate the problems associated with the on-going reconstruction of political systems within nation-states.

IDEALISM

Idealism is the philosophical theory that maintains that

the ultimate nature of reality is based on mind or ideas. It holds that the so-called external or "real world" is inseparable from mind, consciousness, or perception. In the philosophy of perception, idealism is contrasted with realism in which the external world is said to have a so-called absolute existence prior to, and independent of, knowledge and consciousness. Epistemological idealists (such as Kant), it is claimed, might insist that the only things which can be directly *known for certain* are just ideas (abstraction).

In the philosophy of mind, idealism is contrasted with materialism, in which the ultimate nature of reality is based on physical substances. Idealism and materialism are both theories of monism as opposed to dualism and pluralism. Idealism also refers to a tradition in Western thought that represents things in an ideal form, or as they ought to be rather than as they really are, in the fields of ethics, morality, aesthetics, and value. In the ancient philosopy of the Vedas, idealism refers to the dynamic consciousness of living beings that emanates from the divine cosmic source.

Idealism is a philosophical movement in Western thought, and names a number of philosophical positions with sometimes quite different tendencies and implications in politics and ethics, for instance; although in general, at least in popular culture, philosophical idealism is associated with Plato and the school of platonism.

IDEALISM AND ANCIENT PHILOSOPHY

Antiphon

In his chief work *Truth*, Antiphon wrote: "Time is a thought or a measure, not a substance". This presents time as an ideational, internal, mental operation, rather than a real, external object. Plato is called an idealist because of his theory of Forms or doctrine of Ideas, which are "ideal" in the dictionary sense. Most interpreters, ancient and modern, hold that Plato does not describe the Forms as being in any mind. Instead, he describes them as having their own independent existence—for which the textual evidence is adduced from various translations of the dialogues. Indeed, some anti-idealist commentators say that in the dialogues Socrates often denies the reality of the material world.

However, it is clear that the Platonic Socrates merely denies the ideal reality of the non-ideal realm, namely the world of appearances, which he sometimes compares to shadows. An exact interpretation of the dialogues, which are notoriously misrepresented, involves knowledge of linguistics, hermeneutics, philology, semantics, and the philosophy of language, as well as good grounding in classical studies. Athenian Greek philosophical terms, like most English abstract nouns, have more than one meaning. It seems clear that Plato is not, at any rate, a subjective idealist, like Berkeley.

Plato's Allegory of the Cave is sometimes interpreted by anti-platonists as drawing attention to the modern European philosophical problem of knowing external objects—the question that is often attributed to Descartes, Locke, Berkeley, and other early modern philosophers. According to certain materialistic interpretations of Plato, which construe matter as an entirely external reality, the Forms that the Cave-dwellers are ignorant of are not external to them in the way that so-called material objects are for modern thinkers. Again, some anti-idealistic readers hold that for Plato the Forms are true realities, but they are not outside of us in a spatial sense like material objects, which some natural scientists call physical bodies. For these interpreters, one might say, the issue that Plato's allegory addresses is the problem of how one can know what is truly real and good—a theme which apparently is opposed to the so-called modern question of our knowledge of the external world.

However, speaking in the realm of pure abstract theory, even if Plato doesn't share the specific concerns of modern philosophy, and of George Berkeley, in particular, Plato could still be a *non-subjective* idealist. Plato could believe that matter has no so-called independent existence, that ultimate reality (distinct from mere appearance) is known only in the world of ideas—should we care to speculate in purely hypothetical terms. Bernard Williams and Myles Burnyeat have surmised that Greek philosophers never conceived of so-called idealism as an option, because they lacked Descartes's conception of an independently existing mind.

Perhaps Williams and Burnyeat did not consider the apparent possibility that Plato could have held an idealism like Kant's, which appears to argue from the nature of knowledge to the nature of the objects of knowledge; or he might have subscribed to a form of Absolute Idealism, like that of G.W.F. Hegel which, say commentators, denies that matter is ultimately real—without perhaps (in either case) reducing so-called material objects to ideas in a mind or minds. Moreover, we conjecture, Plato's theory of the separation of soul and body could be seen as an earlier, primitive form of Cartesian dualism. The German neo-kantian scholar, Paul Natorp, argued in his *Plato's Theory of Ideas. An Introduction to Idealism* that Plato was a non-subjective, "transcendental" idealist, somewhat like Kant. Natorp's thesis has received some support from commentators and neo-kantian scholars.

Plotinus

Nathaniel Alfred Boll wrote of this Neoplatonist philosopher: "With Plotinus there even appears, probably for the first time in Western philosophy, *idealism* that had long been current in the East even at that time, for it taught that the soul has made the world by stepping from eternity into time, with the explanation: 'For there is for this universe no other place than the soul or mind' (neque est alter hujus universi locus quam anima), indeed the ideality of time is expressed in the words: 'We should not accept time outside the soul or mind' (oportet autem nequaquam extra animam tempus accipere)."

Similarly, professor Ludwig Noiré wrote: "For the first time in Western philosophy we find idealism proper in Plotinus, where he says, "The only space or place of the world is the soul," and "Time must not be assumed to exist outside the soul." It is worth noting, however, that like Plato but unlike Schopenhauer and other modern philosophers, Plotinus does not worry about whether or how we can get beyond our ideas in order to know external objects.

MODERN PHILOSOPHY

Malebranche

Malebranche, a student of the Cartesian School of Rationalism, disagreed that if the only things that we know for certain are the ideas within our mind, then the existence of the external world would be dubious and known only indirectly. He declared instead that the real external world is actually God. All activity only appears to occur in the external world. In actuality, it is the activity of God. For Malebranche, we directly know internally the ideas in our mind. Externally, we directly know God's operations. This kind of idealism led to the pantheism of Spinoza.

LEIBNIZ

Leibniz expressed a form of Idealism known as Panpsychism in his theory of monads, as exposited in his Monadologie. He held Monads are the true atoms of the universe, and are also entities having perception. The monads are "substantial forms of being" They are indecomposable, individual, subject to their own laws, un-interacting, and each reflecting the entire universe. Monads are centers of force; substance is force, while space, matter, and motion are phenomenal.

For Leibniz, there is an exact pre-established harmony or parallel between the world in the minds of the alert monads and the external world of objects. God, who is the central monad, established this harmony and the resulting world is an idea of the monads' perception. In this way, the external world is ideal in that it is a spiritual phenomenon whose motion is the result of a dynamic force. Space and time are ideal or phenomenal and their form and existence is dependent on the simple and immaterial monads. Leibniz's cosmology, with its central monad, embraced a traditional Christian Theism and was more of a Personalism than the naturalistic Pantheism of Spinoza.

GEORGE BERKELEY

Bishop Berkeley, in seeking to find out what we could know with certainty, decided that our knowledge must be based on our perceptions. This led him to conclude that there was indeed no "real" knowable object behind one's perception, that what was "real" was the perception itself. This is characterised by Berkeley's slogan: "Esse est aut percipi aut percipere" or "To be is to be perceived or to perceive", meaning that something only exists, in the particular way that it is seen to exist, when it is being perceived (seen, felt, etc.) by an observing subject. This subjective idealism or dogmatic idealism led to his placing the full weight of justification on our perceptions. This left Berkeley with the problem of explaining how it is that each of us apparently has much the same sort of perceptions of an object. He solved this problem by having God intercede, as the immediate cause of all of our perceptions.

Schopenhauer wrote: "Berkeley was, therefore, the first to treat the subjective starting-point really seriously and to demonstrate irrefutably its absolute necessity. He is the father of idealism...." (*Parerga and Paralipomena,* Vol. I, "Fragments for the History of Philosophy") Schopenhauer could have said, instead, that Berkeley was the "father" of the modern variety of idealism that is motivated, primarily, by epistemological considerations—as distinct from the more purely metaphysical idealism of (for example) Plotinus or Hegel. Bishop Berkeley therefore is considered the first modern philosopher known as an idealist. His *immaterialism* held that objects exist by the good quality of our perception of them. In other words, they are ideas residing in our awareness - as well as in the consciousness of the Divine Being.

ARTHUR COLLIER

Arthur Collier published the same assertions that were made by Berkeley. However, there seemed to have been no influence between the two contemporary writers. Collier claimed that the represented image of an external object is the only knowable reality. Matter, as a cause of the representative image, is unthinkable and therefore nothing to us. An external world, as absolute matter, unrelated to an observer, does not exist for human perceivers. As an appearance in a mind, the universe cannot exist as it appears if there is no perceiving mind. Collier was influenced by John Norris's (1701) *An Essay Towards the Theory of the Ideal or Intelligible World.* The idealist statements by Collier were generally dismissed by readers who were not able to reflect on the distinction between a mental idea or image and the object that it represents.

IMMANUEL KANT

Immanuel Kant held that the mind shapes the world as we perceive it to take the form of space-and-time. It is said that Kant focused on the idea drawn from British empiricism (and its philosophers such as Locke, Berkeley, and Hume) that all we can know is the mental impressions, or *phenomena,* that an outside world, which may or may not exist independently, creates in our minds; our minds can never perceive that outside world directly. Kant made the distinction between things as they appear to an observer and things in themselves, "... that is, things considered without regard to whether and how they may be given to us...."

... if I remove the thinking subject, the whole material world must at once vanish because it is nothing but a phenomenal appearance in the sensibility of ourselves as a subject, and a manner or species of representation. – *Critique of Pure Reason A383*

Kant's postscript to this added that the mind is not a blank slate, tabula rasa, (contra John Locke), but rather comes equipped with categories for organising our sense impressions. Perhaps this Kantian sort of idealism opens up a world of abstractions (i.e., the universal categories minds use to understand phenomena) to be explored by reason, but perhaps, in sharp contrast to Plato's, confirms uncertainties about a (un)knowable world outside our own minds. We cannot approach the *noumenon,* the "Thing in Itself" (German: *Ding an Sich*) outside our own mental world. (Kant's idealism is called *transcendental idealism.*)

Apparently Kant distinguished his transcendental or critical idealism from previous varieties:

The dictum of all genuine idealists, from the Eleatic school to Bishop Berkeley, is contained in this formula: "All knowledge through the senses and experience is nothing but sheer illusion, and only in the ideas of the pure understanding and reason is there truth." The principle that throughout dominates and determines my idealism is, on the contrary: "All knowledge of things merely from pure understanding or pure reason is nothing but sheer illusion, and only in experience is there truth." – *Prolegomena, 374*

FICHTE

Johann Fichte denied Kant's noumenon, and held that consciousness constitutes its own foundation, that the mental life of the Ego, of pure selfhood, relies upon nothing wholly external to itself, and that the hypothesis of an outer world of any kind is the same thing as admitting a Kantian realm. We may say that Fichte was the first German philosopher to make an attempt at a presuppositionless theory of knowledge, wherein nothing outside of thought is assumed to exist apart from the primordial analysis of the Ego. So that his philosophy could be solely grounded in itself, he assumed nothing without his Fichtean deductions from first principles, and elaborated what he called a Wissenschaftslehre. (Apparently Fichte's theory is very similar to Giovanni Gentile's Actual Idealism, except that Gentile's theory appears to go even further by denying any grounds, derived from pure thought, for the Ego or personality.)

SCHELLING

Friedrich Wilhelm Joseph Schelling (1775 - 1854) claimed that the Fichte's "I" needs the Not-I, because there is no subject without object, and vice versa. So there is no difference between the subjective and the objective, that is, the ideal and the real. This is the Schelling's "absolute identity": the ideas or mental images in the mind are identical to the extended objects which are external to the mind.

HEGEL

Hegel, another German philosopher whose dialectical system has been called *idealistic.* In his *Science of Logic* (1812-1814) Hegel argued that finite qualities are not fully "real," because they depend on other finite qualities to determine them. Qualitative *infinity,* on the other hand, would be more self-determining, and hence would have a better claim to be called fully real. Similarly, finite natural things are less "real"—because they're less self-determining—than spiritual things like morally responsible people, ethical communities, and God.

So any doctrine, such as materialism, that asserts that finite qualities or merely natural objects are fully real, is mistaken. Hegel called his philosophy *absolute idealism,* in contrast to the "subjective idealism" of Berkeley and the "transcendental idealism" of Kant and Fichte, philosophies which were not based (like Hegel's idealism) on a critique of the finite, and a dialectical philosophy of history. Some commentators have maintained that Hegel's dialectical system most closely resembles that of Plato and Plotinus, however, there is an exact historical difference between ancient and modern thought, at least in the history of philosophy. One might say that none of these three thinkers associate their idealism with the so-called epistemological thesis that what we know are ideas in our minds.

It is perhaps a noteworthy fact that some commentators of Hegel fail to distinguish Hegelian idealism from either the philosophy of Berkeley or Kant. Hegel certainly intends to preserve what he takes to be true of German idealism, in particular Kant's insistence that ethical reason can and does go beyond finite inclinations. However, some commentators hold that Hegel does not endorse Kant's conception of the thing-in-itself, or the type of epistemological perplexities that led Kant to that view. Still less does Hegel endorse Berkeley's doctrine that to be is to perceive or to be perceived—in the purely Berkeleyian sense.

The guiding ideal behind Hegel's absolute idealism is the scientific thought, which he shares with Plato and other great idealist thinkers, that the exercise of reason and intellect enables the philosopher to know ultimate historical reality, which in the Hegelian system is the phenomenological constitution of self-determination,—the dialectical development of self-awareness and personality in the realm of History. By giving this Ideal a central role in his philosophy, Hegel made a lasting contribution to that part of the Western mindset, beginning in earnest with Plato and his Pre-Socratic predecessors, which makes Idealism the basis of civilization and progress in the world.

SCHOPENHAUER

In the first volume of his *Parerga and Paralipomena,* Schopenhauer wrote his "Sketch of a History of the Doctrine of the Ideal and the Real". He defined the ideal as being mental pictures that constitute subjective knowledge. The ideal, for him, is what can be attributed to our own minds. The images in our head are what comprise the ideal. Schopenhauer emphasized that we are restricted to our own consciousness. The world that appears is only a representation or mental picture of objects. We directly and immediately know only representations. All objects that are external to the mind are known indirectly through the mediation of our mind.

Schopenhauer's history is an account of the concept of the "ideal" in its meaning as "ideas in a subject's mind." In this sense, "ideal" means "ideational" or "existing in the mind as an image." He does not refer to the other meaning of "ideal" as being qualities of the highest perfection and excellence. In his *On the Freedom of the Will,* Schopenhauer noted the ambiguity of the word "idealism" by calling it a "term with multiple meanings." [T]rue philosophy must at all costs be *idealistic*; indeed, it must be so merely to be honest.

For nothing is more certain than that no one ever came out of himself in order to identify himself immediately with things different from him; but everything of which he has certain, sure, and therefore immediate knowledge, lies within his consciousness. Beyond this consciousness, therefore, there can be no *immediate* certainty.... There can never be an existence that is objective absolutely and in itself; such an existence, indeed, is positively inconceivable. For the objective, as such, always and essentially has its existence in the consciousness of a subject; it is therefore the subject's representation, and consequently is conditioned by the subject, and moreover by the subject's forms of representation, which belong to the subject and not to the object. – *The World as Will and Representation, Vol. II, Ch. 1*

It is evident that Schopenhauer's "idealism" is based primarily on considerations having to do with the relation between our ideas and external reality, rather than being based (like Plato's, Plotinus's, or Hegel's "idealism") on considerations having to do with the nature of reality as such.

BRITISH IDEALISM

British idealism enjoyed ascendancy in English-speaking philosophy in the later part of the 19th century. F. H. Bradley of Merton College, Oxford, saw reality as a monistic whole, which is apprehended through "feeling", a state in which there is no distinction between the perception and the thing perceived.

Like Berkeley, Bradley thought that nothing can be known to exist unless it is known by a mind. We perceive, on reflection, that to be real, or even barely to exist, must be to fall within sentience.... Find any piece of existence, take up anything that any one could possibly call a fact, or could in any sense assert to have being, and then judge if it does not consist in sentient experience.

Try to discover any sense in which you can still continue to speak of it, when all perception and feeling have been removed; or point out any fragment of its matter, any aspect of its being, which is not derived from and is not still relative to this source. When the experiment is made strictly, I can myself conceive of nothing else than the experienced. – *F.H. Bradley, 'Appearance and Reality', Chapter 14*

Bradley was the apparent target of G. E. Moore's radical rejection of idealism. Moore claimed that Bradley did not understand the statement that something is real. We know for certain, through common sense and prephilosophical beliefs that some things are real, whether they are objects of thought or not, according to Moore. In this way, he disagreed with Bradley's assertion that we cannot think of anything that really exists unless we have a thought of it in our mind. J. M. E. McTaggart of Cambridge University, argued that minds alone exist, and that they only relate to each other through love. Space, time and material objects are for McTaggart unreal. He argued, for instance, in *The Unreality of Time* that it was not possible to produce a coherent account of a sequence of events in time, and that therefore time is an illusion.

His book *The Nature of Experience* (1927) contained his arguments that space, time, and matter cannot possibly be real. In his *Studies in Hegelian Cosmology*, Cambridge, 1901, p. 196, he declared that metaphysics are not relevant to social and political action. McTaggart "... thought that Hegel was wrong in supposing that metaphysics could show that the state is more than a means to the good of the individuals who compose it." For McTaggart, "...philosophy can give us very little, if any guidance in action.... Why should a Hegelian citizen be surprised that his belief as to the organic nature of the Absolute does not help him in deciding how to vote? Would a Hegelian engineer be reasonable in expecting that his belief that all matter is spirit should help him in planning a bridge?

American philosopher Josiah Royce described himself as an objective idealist. Thomas Hill Green and Bernard Bosanquet are also prominent members of the British idealism movement.

KARL PEARSON

In *The Grammar of Science*, Preface to the 2nd Edition, 1900, Karl Pearson wrote, "There are many signs that a sound idealism is surely replacing, as a basis for natural philosophy, the crude materialism of the older physicists." This book influenced Einstein's regard for the importance of the observer in scientific measurements. In § 5 of that book, Pearson asserted that "...science is in reality a classification and analysis of the contents of the mind...." Also, "...the field of science is much more consciousness than an external world."

CRITICISM OF IDEALISM

Immanuel Kant

In the 1st edition (1781) of his Critique of Pure Reason, Kant described Idealism as such. We are perfectly justified in maintaining that only what is within ourselves can be immediately and directly perceived, and that only my own existence can be the object of a mere perception. Thus the existence of a real object outside me can never be given immediately and directly in perception, but can only be added in thought to the perception, which is a modification of the internal sense, and thus inferred as its external cause.... In the true sense of the word, therefore, I can never perceive external things, but I can only infer their existence from my own internal perception, regarding the perception as an effect of something external that must be the proximate cause.... It must not be supposed, therefore, that an idealist is someone who denies the existence of external objects of the senses; all he does is to deny that they are known by immediate and direct perception.... – *Critique of Pure Reason, A367 f.*

In the 2nd edition (1787) of his Critique of Pure Reason, he wrote a section called Refutation of Idealism to distinguish his transcendental idealism from Descartes's Sceptical Idealism and Berkeley's Dogmatic Idealism. In addition to this refutation in both the 1781 & 1787 editions the section "Paralogisms of Pure Reason" is an implicit critique of Descartes' Problematic Idealism, namely the Cogito. He says that just from "the spontaneity of thought" (cf. Descartes' Cogito) it is not possible to infer the 'I' as an object. In his Notes and Fragments Kant defines idealism in the following manner:

"The assertion that we can never be certain whether all of our putative outer experience is not mere imagining is idealism."

Søren Kierkegaard

Kierkegaard's primary criticism against Hegel is based

around Hegel's claim to have developed a fully comprehensive system that could explain the whole of reality. The quote commonly used to express this idea, whether fair to Hegel or not, is, "What is rational is actual; and what is actual is rational," in the *Elements of the Philosophy of Right* (1821). Kierkegaard asserts that reality can be a system for God, but it cannot be so for any human individual, because both reality and humans are incomplete, and all philosophical systems imply completeness. Kierkegaard attacked Hegel's idealist philosophy in several of his works, but most succinctly in *Concluding Unscientific Postscript* (1846).

In the *Postscript*, Kierkegaard, as the pseudonymous philosopher Johannes Climacus, argues that a logical system is possible but an existential system is impossible. Hegel argues that once one has reached an ultimate understanding of the logical structure of the world, one has also reached an understanding of the logical structure of God's mind. Climacus claims Hegel's absolute idealism mistakenly blurs the distinction between existence and thought. Climacus also argues that our mortal nature places limits on our understanding of reality. As Climacus argues:

So-called systems have often been characterized and challenged in the assertion that they abrogate the distinction between good and evil, and destroy freedom. Perhaps one would express oneself quite as definitely, if one said that every such system fantastically dissipates the concept existence.... Being an individual man is a thing that has been abolished, and every speculative philosopher confuses himself with humanity at large; whereby he becomes something infinitely great, and at the same time nothing at all.

A major concern of Hegel's *Phenomenology of Spirit* (1807) and of the philosophy of Spirit that he lays out in his *Encyclopedia of the Philosophical Sciences* (1817-1830) is the interrelation between individual humans, which he conceives in terms of "mutual recognition." However, what Climacus means by the aforementioned statement, is that Hegel, in the *Philosophy of Right*, believed the best solution was to surrender one's individuality to the customs of the State, identifying right and wrong in view of the prevailing bourgeois morality. Individual human will ought, at the State's highest level of development, to properly coincide with the will of the State. Climacus rejects Hegel's suppression of individuality by pointing out it is impossible to create a valid set of rules or system in any society which can adequately describe existence for any one individual. Submitting one's will to the State denies personal freedom, choice, and responsibility.

In addition, Hegel does believe we can know the structure of God's mind, or ultimate reality. Hegel agrees with Kierkegaard that both reality and humans are incomplete, inasmuch as we are in time, and reality develops through time. But the relation between time and eternity is outside time and this is the "logical structure" that Hegel thinks we can know. Kierkegaard disputes this assertion, because it eliminates the clear distinction between ontology and epistemology. Existence and thought are not identical and one cannot possibly think existence.

Thought is always a form of abstraction, and thus not only is pure existence impossible to think, but all forms in existence are unthinkable; thought depends on language, which merely abstracts from experience, thus separating us from lived experience and the living essence of all beings. In addition, because we are finite beings, we cannot possibly know or understand anything that is universal or infinite such as God, so we cannot know God exists, since that which transcends time simultaneously transcends human understanding.

Friedrich Nietzsche

Friedrich Nietzsche was the first to mount a logically serious criticism of Idealism that has been popularised by David Stove. He pre-empts Stove's GEM by arguing that Kant's argument for his transcendental idealism rests on a confusion between a tautology and/or petitio principii; therefore is an invalid argument. In his book *Beyond Good and Evil,* Part 1 On the Prejudice of Philosophers Section 11, he ridicules Kant for admiring himself because he had undertaken and (thought he) succeeded in tackling "the most difficult thing that could ever be undertaken on behalf of metaphysics."

Quoting Nietzsche's prose:

"But let us reflect; it is high time to do so. 'How are synthetic judgements a priori possible?' Kant asked himself-and what really is his answer? 'By virtue of a faculty' - but unfortunately not in five words,...The honeymoon of German philosophy arrived.

All the young theologians of the Tübingen seminary went into the bushes all looking for 'faculties.'...'By virtue of a faculty' - he had said, or at least meant. But is that an answer? An explanation? Or is it not rather merely a repetition of the question? How does opium induce sleep? 'By virtue of a faculty,' namely the virtus dormitiva, replies the doctor in Moliére."

Thus Nietzsche contstructs Kant's Critique of Pure Reason as such. 'How are synthetic judgments a priori possible?' and Kant's answer to that question is 'By virtue of a faculty'.

Stock examples of answers that beg the question:

"Why am I the boss? It's because I call the shots around here." "Of course I had a reason, or I wouldn't have done it."

This argument Nietzsche advances can also be contructed to read that Kant was making a tautological argument (aka Necessarily True). An argument that has a necessarily true premise cannot make any synthetic a priori statments. Because the synthetic cannot be necessarily true.

In addition to the Idealism of Kant, Nietzsche in the same book attacks the idealism of Schopenhauer and Descartes via a similar argument to Kant's original critique of Descartes. Quoting Nietzsche:

There are still harmless self-observers who believe that there are "immediate certainties"; for example, "I think," or as the superstition of Schopenhauer put it, "I will"; as though knowledge here got hold of its objects purely and nakedly as "the thing in itself," without any falsification on the part of either the subject or the object. But that "immediate certainty," as well as "absolute knowledge" and the "thing in itself," involved a *contradictio in adjecto,* (contradiction between the noun and the adjective) I shall repeat a hundred times; we really ought to free ourselves from the seduction of words!

G. E. Moore

The first criticism of Idealism that falls within the analytic philosophical framework is by one of its co-founders G. E. Moore. This 1903 seminal article, *The Refutation of Idealism*. This one of the first demonstrations of Moore's commitment to analysis as the proper philosophical method. Moore proceeds by examining the Berkeleian aphorism *esse est percipi*: "to be is to be perceived". He examines in detail each of the three terms in the aphorism, finding that it must mean that the object and the subject are *necessarily* connected. So, he argues, for the idealist, "yellow" and "the sensation of yellow" are necessarily identical - to be yellow is necessarily to be experienced as yellow. But, in a move similar to the open question argument, it also seems clear that there is a difference between "yellow" and "the sensation of yellow". For Moore, the idealist is in error because "that *esse* is held to be *percipi*, solely because what is experienced is held to be identical with the experience of it".

Though far from a complete refutation, this was the first strong statement by analytic philosophy against its idealist predecessors—or at any rate against the type of idealism represented by Berkeley—this argument did not show that the GEM is logically invalid. Arguments advanced by Nietzsche (prior to Moore), Russell (just after Moore) & 80 years later Stove put a nail in the coffin for the "master" argument supporting (Berkeleyan) idealism.

BERTRAND RUSSELL

Despite Bertrand Russell's hugely popular book *The Problems of Philosophy* (this book was in its 17th printing by 1943) which was written for a general audience rather than academia, few ever mention his critique even though he completely anticipates David Stove's GEM both in form and content.

Quoting Russell's prose (1912:42-43):

"If we say that the things known must be in the mind, we

are either un-duly limiting the mind's power of knowing, or we are uttering a mere tautology. We are uttering a mere tautology if we mean by 'in the mind' the same as by 'before the mind', i.e. if we mean merely being apprehended by the mind. But if we mean this, we shall have to admit that what, in this sense, is in the mind, may nevertheless be not mental. Thus when we realize the nature of knowledge, Berkeley's argument is seen to be wrong in substance as well as in form, and his grounds for supposing that 'idea'-i.e. the objects apprehended-must be mental, are found to have no validity whatever. Hence his grounds in favour of the idealism may be dismissed."

A.C. Ewing

Published in 1933, A. C. Ewing, according to David Stove, mounted the first full length book critique of Idealism, entitled *Idealism; a critical survey*. Stove does not mention that Ewing anticipated his GEM.

David Stove

The Australian philosopher David Stove argued in typical acerbic style that idealism rested on what he called "the worst argument in the world". From a logical point of view his critique is no different from Russell or Nietzsche's — but Stove has been more widely cited and most clearly highlighted the mistake of proponents (like Berkeley) of subjective idealism. He named the form of this argument - invented by Berkeley — "the GEM". Berkeley claimed that "[the mind] is deluded to think it can and does conceive of bodies existing unthought of, or without the mind, though at the same time they are apprehended by, or exist in, itself". Stove argued that this claim proceeds from the tautology that nothing can be thought of without its being thought of, to the conclusion that nothing can exist without its being thought of. Alan Musgrave recently extended this argument to attack Conceptual Idealism.

John Searle

In *The Construction of Social Reality*, John Searle offers an attack on some versions of idealism. Searle conveniently summarises two important arguments for (subjective) idealism. The first is based on our perception of reality:

- All we have access to in perception are the contents of our own experiences
- The only epistemic basis we can have for claims about the external world are our perceptual experiences therefore,
- The only reality we can meaningfully speak of is the reality of perceptual experiences (The Construction of Social Reality p. 172)

Whilst agreeing with (2), Searle argues that (1) is false, and points out that (3) does not follow from (1) and (2).

The second argument for (subjective) idealism runs as follows:

- *Premise: Any cognitive state occurs as part of a set of cognitive states and within a cognitive system*
- *Conclusion 1: It is impossible to get outside of all cognitive states and systems to survey the relationships between them and the reality they are used to cognize*
- *Conclusion 2: No cognition is ever of a reality that exists independently of cognition* (The Construction of Social Reality *p. 174)*

Searle goes on to point out that conclusion 2 simply does not follow from its precedents.

Alan Musgrave

Alan Musgrave in an article titled *Realism and Antirealism* in R. Klee (ed), *Scientific Inquiry: Readings in the Philosophy of Science,* Oxford, 1998, 344-352 - later re-titled to *Conceptual Idealism and Stove's GEM* in A. Musgrave, Essays on Realism and Rationalism, Rodopi, 1999 also in M.L. Dalla Chiara et al. (eds), *Language, Quantum, Music,* Kluwer, 1999, 25-35 - Alan Musgrave argues in addition to Stove's GEM, Conceptual Idealists compound their mistakes with use/mention confusions and proliferation of unnecessary hyphenated entities.

Hyphenated entities are "warning signs" for conceptual

idealism according to Musgrave because they over emphasise the epistemic (ways in which people come to learn about the world) activities and will more likely commit errors in use/mention. These entities do not exist (strictly speaking and are ersatz entities) but highlight the numerous ways in which people come to know the world.

In Sir Arthur Eddington's case use/mention confusions compounded his problem when he thought he was sitting at two different tables in his study. In fact Eddington was sitting at one table but had two different perspectives or ways of knowing about that one table. Richard Rorty and Postmodernist Philosophy in general have been attacked by Musgrave for committing use/mention confusions. Musgrave argues that these confusions help proliferate GEM's in our thinking and serious thought should avoid GEM's.

Philip J. Neujahr

"Although it would be hard to legislate about such matters, it would perhaps be well to restrict the idealist label to theories which hold that the world, or its material aspects, are dependent upon the specifically cognitive activities of the mind or Mind in perceiving or thinking about (or 'experiencing') the object of its awareness."

Idealism in Religious Thought

A broad enough definition of idealism could include most religious viewpoints. The belief that personal beings (e.g., God/s, angels & spirits) preceded the existence of insentient matter seems to suggest that an experiencing subject is a necessary reality. Also, the existence of an omniscient God suggests, regardless of the actual nature of matter, that all of nature is the object of at least one consciousness.

Materialism sees no incoherence in a scenario of there being a cosmos where no sentient subject ever develops; a wholly unknown universe where neither any subject, nor any object of a subject's experience ever exists. Historically, *Mechanistic Materialism* has been the favourite viewpoint of Atheist philosophers. Still, idealistic viewpoints that have not included God, supernatural beings, or a post-mortem existence have sometimes been advanced.

While many religious philosophies are indeed specifically idealist, for example, some Hindu denominations view regarding the nature of Brahman, souls, and the world are idealistic, some have favored a form of substance dualism. Early Buddhism was not subjective idealistic. Some have misinterpreted the Yogâcâra school of Mahayana Buddhism that developed the consciousness-only approach as a form of metaphysical idealism, but this is incorrect. Yogâcâra thinkers did not focus on consciousness to assert it as ultimately real (Yogâcâra claims consciousness is only conventionally real since it arises from moment to moment due to fluctuating causes and conditions), but rather because it is the cause of the karmic problem they are seeking to eliminate.

Some Christian theologians have held idealist views, substance dualism has been the more common view of Christian authors, especially with the strong influence of the philosophy of Aristotle among the Scholastics. Several modern religious movements, for example the organizations within the New Thought Movement and the Unity Church, may be said to have a particularly idealist orientation. The theology of Christian Science includes a form of subjective idealism: it teaches that all that exists is God and God's ideas; that the world as it appears to the senses is a distortion of the underlying spiritual reality, a distortion that may be corrected by a reorientation (spiritualization) of thought. Such a reorientation, Christian Science teaches, results in healing, as the world of appearance adjusts to approximate more nearly to the underlying divine reality.

Christian Science is consequently a form of monistic (theistic) idealism, since it teaches that there is in reality no matter: all is Spirit (God) and its manifestation. In Christian Science teaching, there is no ultimate division or dualism between Spirit and its expression (the spiritual universe including the true identity of each one of us) any more than there is between the sun and the light which shines forth from it. *A Course in Miracles,* a spiritual self-study course published in 1976, represents an explicitly idealist, pure nondualistic thought system. In the Course, only God and His Creation, which is Spirit and has nothing to do with the world, are real. The physical universe is an illusion and does not exist.

The Course compares the world of perception with a dream. It arises from the projection of the dreamer, i.e. the mind ("projection makes perception," T-21.in.1:5), according to its wishes. The purpose of the perceptual world is to ensure our separate, individual existence apart from God but avoid the responsibility and project the guilt onto others. As we learn to give the world *another purpose* and recognize our perceptual errors, we also learn to look past them or "forgive," as a way to awaken gradually from the dream and finally remember our true Identity in God. The Course's nondualistic metaphysics is similar to Advaita Vedanta. However, *A Course in Miracles* differs in that it adds a "motivation" for the illusory existence of the perceptual world.

Other Uses

In general parlance, "idealism" or "idealist" is also used to describe a person having high ideals, sometimes with the connotation that those ideals are unrealisable or at odds with "practical" life. The word "ideal" is commonly used as an adjective to designate qualities of perfection, desirability, and excellence. This is foreign to the epistemological use of the word "idealism" which pertains to internal mental representations. These internal ideas represent objects that are assumed to exist outside of the mind.

REALISM

For many years, there have been attempts to rationalize physics. But, since the first part of this century the Berkeley-Copenhagen interpretation of modern physics has taught that there is no reality in physics. It claims that what we perceive as real does not have its own independent existence. It exists only in our imagination. Descriptions in modern physics cannot be compatible with reality since some fundamental definitions are not compatible with realism. The concept of realism was accepted and used in all fields of physics from the beginning of history until the beginning of this century. However, since the development of modern physics, the interpretation of quantum mechanics has rejected realism.

Before discussing the concept of realism, let us examine with great care what it means. Realism has been defined in various ways. One of the definitions of realism is: "The quality of the universe existing independently of ourselves." However, the Berkeley-Copenhagen interpretation denies the existence of realism. According to modern physics, matter starts to exist only at the moment the observer learns about its existence. This bizarre belief is illustrated by one of the great masters of the Berkeley-Copenhagen interpretation. Heisenberg states:

"But then one sees that not even the quality of being (if that may be called a "quality") belongs to what is described. It is a possibility for being or a tendency for being." (Parentheses and quotation marks are from Heisenberg's book.)

Let us recall that Cramer makes the same claim in different words:

"It is the change in the observer's knowledge that precipitates the state vector collapse"

Heisenberg also insists on this lack of reality in the Berkeley-Copenhagen interpretation. He writes:

"In the Copenhagen interpretation of quantum mechanics, the objective reality has evaporated, and quantum mechanics does not represent particles, but rather, our knowledge, our observations, or our consciousness of particles."

If nature does not even have the *quality of being,* and if it is the observer's knowledge that *precipitates* that *being,* the universe did not exist before life began on earth, as suggested by Davies. The universe will therefore cease to exist at the moment all life disappears on earth. If matter cannot have its own existence, independent of human mind, as dictated by the Berkeley-Copenhagen interpretation, cosmologists cannot study the birth of galaxies or the origin of the universe.

There was no observer before humans started to observe. If the creation of the universe is the result of the *observer's knowledge,* then the universe could not exist before we did.

Then the observer had to be there at the very first instant of creation in order to *precipitate* the creation. In other words, the universe is a creation of our mind and will disappear with it. How can such an absurd theory be considered as the best interpretation of modern physics of the 20th century?

CONFUSION ON THE MEANING OF REALISM

A logical understanding of realism is central to a rational science. Definitions of realism are not given here for the pleasure of giving a good definition. They are absolutely essential to achieve coherence and logic in science. Not enough efforts have been made to describe with sufficient intelligibility what is meant by *realism* or *reality*. It is quite inadequate to say that reality is the *quality of being real* or that realism is a *faithful portrayal of reality*. A lot of confusion remains. One can find at least three different example, in which the expression *reality* is used with different meanings. Let us consider what sort of reality is involved when we speak of:

- The reality of existence of a mass;
- The reality of existence of thoughts; and
- The reality of existence of lengths, time, an electric charge, a mass distribution, etc.

The same expression *reality of existence* is used in all three cases, but each example has different implications. We know that a mass exists independently of our mind, while our thoughts evidently do not. However, both *thoughts* and *masses*are usually considered to have a real existence. It certainly does not mean the same kind of *real existence*. There is a clear and fundamental difference between these "realities". It is impossible to have a clear understanding of realism (reality of existence) in physics when the same word *reality*, is applied to both *thoughts* or*masses*. The difference between the reality of matter and the reality of thoughts is not usually taken into account. Finally, it must also be noted that reality of time and the reality of lengths are still other kinds of reality.

Let us go back to the three cases mentioned above. Let us give a specific name to each kind of realism. We consider:

- *Physical Realism,* when one deals with the reality of existence of masses.
- *Mental Realism,* when one deals with the reality of existence of thoughts, and
- *Distinctive Realism,* when one deals with the reality of existence of *specific qualities* like lengths, time, electric charges etc.

These are qualities that belong to masses and consequently are distinguishable from masses themselves. Geometrical properties also possess some kind of reality. Definitions given to realism are usually vague because they fail to show these fundamental differences. Among some interesting definitions of realism is this:

"The doctrine that material objects exist in themselves, apart from the mind's consciousness of them."

In more simple terms, one says that in realism, "Matter has its own existence independently of our mind." Such definitions require some more analysis. One notices that the words *matter* or *material objects* are essential in the above definition when we define physical realism. In fact, in the *reality of thoughts* one must realize that there is no physical reality because thoughts do not exist outside our mind.

One arrives at the realization that in physics, realism is limited only to its relation to matter, since it is the only case for which objects really exist independently of the observer. This shows the necessity to use the word *mass* in the definition of reality. Many scientists in search of an adequate description of realism have realized the subtle difficulty of excluding *mental realism*. Instead of excluding *soft* realism, like mental realism, they insist more strongly on the opposite materialistic aspect. They then used very original descriptions. Popper reports:

"I regard as excellent Landé's suggestion that we call physically real what is 'kickable' (and able to kick back if desired)."

Much more recently, Popper also gives much support to realism in describing physics during an interview by Horgan. Popper said:

"Subjectivism has no place in physics, quantum or otherwise.

Physics, he [Popper] exclaims, grabbing a book from a table and slamming it down, is that!"

Samuel Johnson was actually refuting Berkeley when he kicked the stone with mighty force. It is clear that you cannot grab a *thought* and slam it down on a table! You cannot *slam down* a velocity or a (mass) distribution. Only the mass can be slammed down. Those definitions by Landé Popper and Johnson are exactly equivalent to our definition of physical reality since what is *kickable* or *slammable* has to be a mass, existing independently of our mind.

VELOCITIES, LENGTHS AND TIME ARE NOT MATTER

Let us consider properties qualifying matter. We have parameters like velocities, lengths time, (mass) distribution etc. These are distinctive properties that do not exist without matter. The fact that a velocity is given to a mass or that an observer moves with respect to it does not change the physical reality or the fundamental nature of that mass. The *velocity with respect to the observer* is not a physical reality. It is a description of the relative motion of the observer with respect to the physical reality (the mass). The *velocity of the observer* does not exist without the observer.

Autonomous Existence

We must conclude that mass has the unique property of having an independent existence. The electric charge is only a property of masses since in physics, there exists no electric *charge* without mass. We have found that *only masses* have a completely *autonomous existence* independently of anything else. Lengths, time, charges and (mass) distributions do not have their autonomous existence without a mass to support them. Mass is the *support* of all other physical quantities. The existence of lengths, time and charges is bound to the existence of mass. Needless to say thoughts do not have an autonomous existence. So, one must conclude that in physics, physical reality necessarily implies *autonomous existence.* Autonomous existence is a key condition for realism.

The difficulty of deciding whether a physical description involves reality or not appears mostly when we consider a description that uses partly physical reality and partly some non-physical reality. Most of the time it is claimed that a description implies physical reality simply because a part of the phenomenon implies physical reality. It is not noticed that only one part of the description involves physical reality. That difference is sometimes very subtle and thus often remains unnoticed. This error exists at many cases in physics and *is responsible for most of the absurdities in modern physics.*

A simple example is the case of mass distribution. It is clear that a mass has an autonomous existence but the distribution of that mass does not have an autonomous existence, since there cannot be any distribution without mass. One can multiply these examples. The case of a description of sound waves in air is quite interesting. Sound waves propagate as a variation of air pressure in space and time. Waves exist independently of the relative motion of the observer. Independent observers can come to the same fundamental description compatible with reality. However, waves do not exist independently of the gas carrying them.

The description of waves is nothing but a description of the distribution of matter in space. Without matter, there could not be waves. Waves do not have an autonomous existence. Since waves have no autonomous existence, they have no absolute physical reality. Furthermore, when an observer moves with respect to air, he can observe a Doppler effect. That change of frequency is completely due to the observer's motion, or to the motion of the experimental apparatus. There is no physical reality in the Doppler effect itself, since the relative velocity has no autonomous existence. The frequency shifted Doppler effect is true but it has no physical reality.

Let us conclude with a practical description of physical reality. Physical reality exists only in the case of matter, since it is the only thing that has its own autonomous existence, independently of any observer's mind, location or time. Furthermore, the objective description of fundamental reality implies that there is no relative motion with respect to the mass observed, since relative motion (with respect to the observer) does not exist independently of the observer and can distort observations. We must finally point out that the family of words related to realism and reality includes the word realistic. However, we must avoid using the word *realistic*in this context, because it simply means that it is not absurd. Also, the word *real*is often confused with *true*.

Test of Physical Reality

In order to see if there is some physical reality in the phenomenon observed, it is useful to devise a test. We consider that physical reality exists if the description of one thing (a mass) given by one observer is compatible with another description of the same thing, given by another independent observer. To be completely sure of the independent existence, the observer must not be aware of the observations made by others. This is the way to show that observations are independent of the observer's mind. There must also be more than one observer, and the experiment must be done at various times, so that when the observational results are compiled, the observations lead to independent and compatible descriptions. Finally, the description of the object must be compatible with a complete autonomous existence.

Those conditions are essential to test physical reality that is a necessary condition for realism. Multiple independent observers are required because, if a thing does not have its own existence, independent of the observer, it is logically impossible that all independent observers who are not aware of each other can always give a compatible description by chance. Let us give an example. Let us suppose that many people, having independently seen the moon, give a compatible description of it. In that case, one should not have any reasonable doubt that the moon has an independent existence, even if during some short instants, nobody looks at it. The description of the moon does not become fundamentally different because it is observed at a different time and from a different direction. As seen above, time, direction and velocities do not change the nature of the moon. If one day, somebody discovers that the moon does not actually exist for an instant, then this last observation will be a new discovery that will require the total revision of the physical model.

NATURALISM

Secular humanism, at least the naturalistic variety, is predicated on the idea that reliable knowledge of the world is best attained via science - the empirical, experimental, and intersubjective investigation of phenomena. Allegiance to science is an expression of the basic human need to predict and control circumstances to bring about outcomes we desire. Responsiveness to the way the world is, as opposed to the way we might want it to be, is a cognitive trait that obviously serves complex organisms such as ourselves well in the quest for survival. Science is the culturally evolved refinement of such responsiveness, and it has turned native human curiosity into a powerful tool of prediction and control, while giving us a coherent, unified picture of the world.

The ultimate constituents of the universe, according to science, are those micro-level phenomena described by physical theory, and the rest of what exists is, in one way or another, composed of these constituents. The scientific mode of knowing thus leads to an overarching ontological naturalism, in that whatever science incorporates into its explanations is likewise incorporated into a single, natural world, not divided into two distinct realms, the natural and the supernatural. The latter division is the hallmark of non-empirical, non-experimental epistemologies, those driven by a commitment to revealed knowledge, authoritative texts, personal revelation, and traditional world views that often ascribe supernatural status to gods, spirits, souls, and other non-physical entities.

Because of their commitment to science as an epistemology, secular humanists tend toward a non-dualist, naturalist conception of ourselves as embedded in nature. There is nothing that fundamentally sets us apart, or above, the natural world. We are fully physical, caused creatures, even in our highest capacities, and the various characteristics of persons, whether idiosyncratic or universal, are a entirely a function of the environmental and genetic situation in which they develop. But at the start of the 21st century such a view is held by a small minority, at least in the United States. Human nature, it seems, prevents the optimally rational allegiance to science that secular humanists hold as the ideal epistemic commitment.

The overriding desire for survival implanted in us by evolution generates the opposite, anti-scientific tendency: the wishful thinking that denies the empirical evidence that we are simply material creatures doomed to die and disappear. Hence the widespread, often religiously expressed supposition that the causal physical story told by science can't be the whole story: there's something within us that transcends nature and survives death, namely the supernatural soul.

This soul, this mental essence or non-physical agent, escapes being fully included in the natural order. But not only does it survive death, it has contra-causal free will (what philosophers sometimes call libertarian free will), the capacity to cause without itself being fully the causal product of surrounding and prior conditions. Like God, it is causally *privileged* over the rest of nature. I will call this commitment to the soul and contra-causal free will the dualist stance, since it supposes that we are of fundamentally two natures, the natural and the supernatural.

NATURALISM, ATTITUDES, AND SOCIAL POLICY

Because they imply radically different things about ourselves as agents, these two fundamentally different world views, the non-dual, naturalist stance and the dualist, supernaturalist stance, help drive deeply divergent attitudes and social policies.

The naturalist stance, based in science, acknowledges that human beings and their successes and failures are completely a function of prior and surrounding conditions, both genetic and environmental. Human behaviour is the result of complex interactions between an individual's biology and their upbringing, education, peer group, community, and other factors, many of which are potentially affected by social policy. In seeking to explain and ameliorate sub-standard social conditions and criminal behaviour, and to create a more flourishing society, those inclined towards a naturalist view of human nature will be led to consider, in the light of scientific findings, all the factors which influence individual growth and community health. Likewise, when evaluating the impact of policies on persons, societies, and the planet, secular humanists will seek out the best available empirical evidence that bears on a policy's effects. Moreover, their acute and steadfast appreciation of causality leads, or should lead, to a compassionate understanding of those who, by virtue of their genetic and environmental circumstances, end up on the bottom rungs of the economic ladder, or who exhibit dysfunctional or anti-social behaviour.

After all, there but for the luck of the environmental and genetic draw go you or I, experiencing the same deprivation and dysfunction. By virtue of this causality-based empathy and compassion, the naturalist stance *motivates* humanists toward progressive social policies that work to maximize opportunity for the disadvantaged, while simultaneously showing the effective *means* of personal and social change based in a scientific understanding of human behaviour. The dualist stance, on the other hand, leads in much the opposite direction, both in terms of the perceived effectiveness of policy interventions and the motivation to implement them.

Dualists suppose that there is something – the freely willing, supernatural soul – that acts independently of heredity, environment, and any and all policy initiatives. True, as partially material creatures we are to some extent influenced by those factors cited by naturalists, but as partially *supernatural* creatures we can transcend any and all influences in making choices in life, should we choose to exercise our capacity for free choice. Despite the impact of various influences upon us, we essentially create ourselves and our character by virtue of having contra-causal free will. What we do, and the sorts of people we become, is therefore essentially and finally up to us.

So however much society invests in creating conditions under which people might become productive, flourishing individuals, it is the soul which has the final, determining say on behaviour. If such is the case, then social policies that seek to ameliorate conditions that give rise to crime and economic inequality can only have limited effects, in which case why invest much time and energy on such policies? Because individuals, not social conditions, are the ultimate determining factor behind success in life, then it really isn't within our capacity to help much, and so it's really not that much our concern or responsibility. Belief in free will, therefore, lets us off the hook with respect to others' welfare.

Not only can the dualist view undercut the perceived efficacy of social policies, and thus our motivation to pursue them, it suggests that the less fortunate simply deserve their lot in life. As freely willing agents, we alone merit ultimate credit and blame for success or failure in becoming morally upright, productive, gainfully employed citizens. Those who are poor are ultimately at fault for not having competed successfully in the marketplace of education, jobs, and careers, and those that end up in the criminal justice system are likewise the ultimate, buck-stopping source of their offenses and so deeply deserve punishment. The homeless, Ronald Reagan famously said, simply choose to be homeless, and addicts, because they simply refuse to stop using drugs and alcohol, deserve to die of needle-borne diseases, overdoses, or liver failure.

Those who succeed in life, on the other hand, are fully deserving of whatever rewards they can lay their hands on, including, for instance, the hugely inflated salaries of corporate CEOs and university presidents, and the vast unearned income from stock trade windfalls. The differential outcomes following from failure and success are just deserts for the differential exercise of free will, not disparities stemming from social conditions that should be remedied via social policy.

CRIMINAL JUSTICE

Some of the starkest differences in policy objectives driven by the naturalist and dualist conceptions of human nature are found in the arena of criminal justice. The last quarter of the 20th century in the United States saw an increasing emphasis on non-rehabilitative punishment as the preferred "get tough" response to crime. The American criminal justice system underwent a retrenchment in training programs and substance abuse treatment for offenders, reductions in inmate amenities, and sometimes even the denial of basic privileges such as exercise, books, and television. There was a corresponding increase in punitive control, such as maximum security units, solitary confinement and physical restraints.

Criminal sanctions on juveniles became more severe, even as juvenile crime declined, and many states passed "3 strike" laws, some of which permit sentences of up to life for simple theft. High rates of mental illness and addiction in prison suggest mental and behavioral disorders figure prominently in the cause of crime, but these remain notoriously unaddressed by the criminal justice system. Underlying such policies are more or less unquestioned retributive attitudes supporting harsh sanctions, attitudes stemming from a dualist conception of the criminal, who freely chose to become an offender.

If criminals, not the conditions that produced them, are seen as the ultimate source of their criminality, then they are deemed deserving of punishment on grounds that they could have overcome their environmental and biological circumstances, but simply and willfully refused to do so. This sense of strong, ultimate desert is used to justify both capital punishment and incarceration far more punitive than necessary for rehabilitation or deterrence. Such punishment simply models and perpetuates violent, retaliatory behaviour, leaving in its wake vast and unnecessary suffering. To the extent that criminality and harmful deviance are understood to arise from individuals' undetermined, freely willed choices, their actual biological, social and economic causes will necessarily go unexplored and unaddressed.

The myth of contra-causal free will essentially releases us from the obligation to thoroughly investigate and remedy the origins of maladaptive and anti-social behaviour, which lie in mental illness, poverty, child abuse, lack of education and economic opportunity. Free will is the bottom line excuse and justification for harsh and ineffective criminal justice policies which guarantee continuing high levels of dysfunction and alienation, and which perpetuate the cycle of crime and punitive response. The scientific view that people don't create themselves, but instead are fully included in the causal matrix of environmental and biological conditions, can help to defuse retributive blaming focused on the person alone. As the metaphysical assumption of free will is questioned, and replaced with a naturalist understanding of how offenders are shaped by their genetic and environmental circumstances, retributive attitudes should soften, which in turn will help reduce the demand for capital punishment and punitive prison conditions.

Simultaneously, more attention will be paid to the factors which generate criminality. Under pressure from naturalism, the aims of criminal justice will shift from the retributive imposition of just deserts to policies that support the prevention of crime and recidivism, rehabilitation of offenders, and victim restoration and reconciliation. These policies will do far more to increase public safety than the punitive orientation of our current criminal justice system. Such reforms have long been contemplated, of course, and some are underway, but the secular humanist commitment to the science of human nature adds a powerful rationale for their adoption.

As of this writing, there is evidence that under severe budgetary constraints brought about by the recession of the early 2000s, some states are reconsidering "tough on crime" criminal justice policies. It turns out that long prison sentences for non-violent offenses, such as drug possession, are simply too expensive to justify their punitive objectives, even for those who favor punishment over treatment or training. The financial incentive to be "smart on crime," therefore, is shifting attention away from the merely retributive aims of criminal justice to the practical, pragmatic aim of keeping the peace cheaply.

It turns out that *less* punitive criminal justice policies, involving alternatives to incarceration for non-violent offenders, and rehabilitation for those who must be incarcerated, might well be more economical and more effective. It is to be hoped that the budgetary inducement to rethink retributive justice will carry over into an increased appreciation of how more humane criminal justice polices, those that emphasize prevention, rehabilitation, and community restoration, are indeed smarter, more efficient policies. A naturalistic understanding of ourselves will help accelerate this process.

SOCIAL INEQUALITY

During the 1980's and 90's, voter support of get-tough criminal justice coincided with declining enthusiasm for public programs designed to address unequal opportunities in access to housing, education, job training, child care, and other necessities strongly associated with economic success in life. The 1960's vision of a "Great Society" in which government would play a central role in equalizing opportunity was, by the end of the century, largely usurped by a narrower, private sector philosophy in which individuals sink or swim in competitive market economies without much government assistance. Efforts to better the lot of those born into disadvantaged circumstances are now more likely to be dismissed as paternalistic infringements on a person's right (and obligation) to be a self-sufficient self-starter instead of praised as altruistic attempts to level the playing field.

Helping to motivate this retrenchment is the widespread assumption of libertarian, contra-causal freedom, the Western radical individualism which supposes that persons are at bottom self-made. This works to justify and excuse the increasing differences in material well-being and social advantages that have followed the dismantling of the Great Society. On this dualist understanding of ourselves, those that fail economically fail partially because of a willful refusal to apply themselves or follow the rules. Since it was their *choice* not to get ahead, they deserve their impoverishment. Likewise, those that succeed deserve their riches, however excessive or disproportionate, since they made themselves who they are.

The huge and growing inequalities between rich and poor, driven by conservative policies such as tax cuts for the wealthy, welfare reform, and disinvestments in public infrastructure and education, are tolerated partially because they are thought by many to reflect differences in metaphysical merit derived from the differential exercise of free will. Inequality, at bottom, is simply the reflection of what people deserve. To the extent that economic and social inequalities are believed to result from human choices unaffected by surrounding conditions (the definition of libertarian freedom), such inequality will be perceived as the natural outcome of self-originated individual differences, not anything that could or should be remedied by social policy.

Progressive social interventions, therefore, will be only thought capable of operating around the margins of what is essentially up to human free will. The free will assumption, therefore, disempowers and defeats interventions to reduce inequality *in advance* by implying they cannot be effective, or that they somehow infringe our right to ultimate self-determination. (Of course if we really had contra-causal free will, our self-determination couldn't be infringed upon.) In contradicting the myth of radical individualism, inclusive naturalism shows that a person's economic and social success is entirely a function of family status at birth, innate talents, access to education and other social resources, and numerous other environmental and biological factors, not free will.

As John Rawls put it in *A Theory of Justice* "It seems to be one of the fixed points of our considered judgments that no one deserves his place in the distribution of native endowments, any more than one deserves one's initial starting place in society. The assertion that a man deserves the superior character that enables him to make the effort to cultivate his abilities is equally problematic; for his character depends in large part upon fortunate family and social circumstances for which he can claim no credit. The notion of desert seems not to apply to these cases."

If we take science as our guide to truth, successful individuals can no longer claim that their riches are deserved in the deep, metaphysical sense of having created themselves and their success *ex nihilo*. There are no literally self-made men or women. Nor can those who end up on the bottom be blamed for their failure on the grounds they could have chosen otherwise, given the circumstances that obtained. Social and economic inequality will be understood as the luck of the draw, a matter of environmental and biological conditions, not a matter of self-created will and hence not a reflection of metaphysical merit. Accepting a naturalist view of ourselves will therefore weaken justifications for inequality based on the notions of deserved success and deserved failure.

Those of us living comfortable lives will see that but for circumstances we, not they, would have been denied such comforts, and this insight will increase our empathy for the less fortunate. It will undercut support for social policies that have generated huge discrepancies in wealth and opportunity, while increasing support for interventions that improve both opportunities and outcomes for the disadvantaged. Although incentives must still exist to encourage hard work, initiative, and risk-taking, they need not, and should not, result in a grossly skewed distribution of resources. Inclusive naturalism will shift the justification for having a reasonable standard of living from what's *deserved* to what's *needed* to live a fulfilled, satisfying life. It will also challenge the implicit assumption that nearly unlimited riches in the hands of a few are an acceptable outcome of a just economic system.

There are many other arenas in which naturalism suggests progressive policy reform, including our approaches to such behavioral issues as mental health, addiction, obesity, and learning disabilities. Whenever the individual's free will is assumed to play a role in causing behaviour, as it often is in these domains, the secular humanist response should be to challenge that assumption, and initiate a scientific investigation into the actual causes. Such inquiry will serve to reduce the stigma surrounding the behaviour in question, since it will no longer be considered to originate from the individual alone.

This helps to supply the empathetic motivational *basis* for pursuing non-punitive, rehabilitative interventions. And by illuminating the causal story of how interventions actually work (or don't, as is too often the case), naturalism will make them more *effective*. An increase in the awareness and acceptance of an inclusive, thorough-going naturalism, therefore, should result in the adoption of progressive social policies and humane behavioral interventions that work better than those premised on the existence of free will.

THE PROSPECTS FOR NATURALISM

If naturalism is both true and a basis for enlightened social action, the question arises of how secular humanists can promote naturalism within a culture that seems increasingly inimical to science and critical thinking. The challenge to free will, like earlier secular humanist challenges to god, the supernatural and the paranormal, will not receive a warm welcome, given the widespread assumption that contra-causal freedom is the basis for all we hold near and dear. In fact, the scientific threat to our cherished causal exceptionalism is already beginning to spark anxiety in some quarters. In a 1998 conference on *Neuroscience and the Human Spirit*, conference organizer Dr. Frederick K. Goodwin put it this way in his opening remarks:

"Do ...scientific advances challenge the first principles that the majority of our citizens believe provide the very foundation upon which our civilization rests – free will and the capacity to make moral choices?...Does this growing understanding of genetic and environmental influences on human behaviour leave any room for free will?...How can the ever-mounting discoveries of biological, genetic, and environmental factors shaping human behaviour be integrated into our culture without contributing to further erosion of individual responsibility?...To the extent that our choices are not truly free, it would seem that we have less moral responsibility for them."

Some philosophers, notably philosopher Saul Smilansky in his book *Free Will and Illusion*, claim that although inclusive naturalism is true, it is dangerous and counterproductive to make it widely known. He recommends that the truth about free will be kept an academic secret, so that what he considers to be the *fictional* but nevertheless irreplaceable basis for morality and values remains intact. Daniel Dennett, in *Freedom Evolves*, also warns about the "environmental impact" of spiking the myth of libertarian freedom. Demoralization might ensue, he worries, if people mistakenly conclude that they've lost something essential when they cease to believe that they're causally privileged.

Such concerns suggest what must be done to make the naturalist view of ourselves palatable: secular humanists must defuse the common "determinist anxieties," as they might be called, that arise when we discover we are entirely natural creatures. Just as they strive to show that we can be good without God, they must also show that we can be moral, effective, and fully individual agents without belief in free will. In addition, they must also demonstrate, as I have attempted above in discussing criminal justice and social inequality, the positive motivational and practical benefits of taking a consistently scientific, causal view of ourselves. Allaying anxieties and showing the positive consequences of naturalism will help to generate acceptance of a world view that, although empirically well-founded, now has barely a foothold in a public consciousness dominated by the myths of free will and radical individualism.

Although it is beyond the scope of this essay, anxieties about determinism having to do with responsibility, morality, individuality, personal efficacy, and rationality (to name some of the fears most frequently encountered) can be successfully addressed. This requires showing how, in each case, the assumption of a freely willing agent is unnecessary for a self-image that supports robust and socially adequate conceptions of moral agency, cognition, action, and personhood. As Daniel Dennett has put it, nothing *valuable* gets lost in this revised picture of ourselves – everything we need is afforded under naturalism, and the myth of contra-causal freedom ultimately does far more harm than good. Facing the naturalistic facts about ourselves, including the sometimes emotionally fraught denial of free will, involves a firm commitment to science as one's epistemology.

Secular humanists, nearly universally, find this commitment to be second nature, but many will find it sorely tested as they confront the initially discomfiting realization that we are not exceptions to causality. Nevertheless, as the positive personal and social implications of a fully consistent naturalism sink in, accepting this truth about ourselves will become easier. Secular humanists will be in the vanguard (as they always have been) in this next revolution in our understanding of our place in the universe. Their humane motives, reinforced by the empathy generated by taking the fully causal view, will ensure that the immense power of causal understanding will be used wisely and for the good as we seek to create a more flourishing, sustainable world.

For the majority not committed to science as the route to truth, naturalism stands as a clear threat to some dearly cherished notions of human nature and the proper social order. Their response to the view proposed here is likely to be increasingly heated denials that science does or should have the final say about who we are, and a more fervid embrace of dualistic faiths that proclaim human causal exceptionalism. The ideologically driven rejection of naturalism in the face of our increasing scientific understanding of ourselves may well emerge as the defining schism of the culture wars. In facing such opposition, secular humanists must apply the same causal thinking that informs their approach to all other phenomena.

Understanding the various factors that contribute to supernatural thinking, including needs for emotional security, lack of education, and growing up within religious traditions, will help humanists avoid the counterproductive demonization of their opponents.

Supernaturalists, just as naturalists, are fully caused to believe and act as they do, and do not willfully choose to remain unenlightened. An intelligent, empathetic appreciation of the causal story behind supernaturalism itself will allow secular humanists to be more skillful and more humanistic in their quest to make known the virtues, and truth, of naturalism.

PRAGMATISM

A great part of our communicative behaviour takes place between the explicitly expressed words: It happens implicitly. What we mean is hardly ever exhausted by what we explicitly say. Normally we don't have any difficulties in grasping what the speaker is trying to communicate implicitly. How can we explain this fact? Paul Grice gave the following answer: We grasp the implicit meaning by assuming cooperation on the part of the speaker (especially the observance of certain conversational maxims). And as speakers we rely on this assumption when we expect that our hearers will understand us. This starting point has already proven to be very fruitful for the philosophy of language and linguistic pragmatics. Nevertheless we still do not have a theory in an narrow sense. This situation should be changed by this project. Our first two main goals are:

- (G1) The development of a theory of conversational implicatures, which is embedded in the already developed General Theory of Communication and also in Intention-Based-Semantics
- (G2) The reconstruction and evaluation of the most important alternative theories of pragmatic implications

THE GRICEAN PROGRAMME

Foundation of the project is essentially the intentionalistic communication theory, which goes back to the ideas of Grice in (1957), (1968) and (1975). The so-called "Gricean Programme" has three parts:

- *General Communication Theory*

In the first step of the Programme a general concept of communicative behaviour is explicated, which does not presuppose notions of intersubjective meaning (especially not the notion of the linguistic meaning of an expression type).

- *Intentionalistic Semantics*

In the second step of the Programme the concepts of the conventional and linguistic meaning of an expression type get explicated with the help of the in part I already developed concepts of communicative behaviour.

- *Theory of Implicit Communication*

Step I and II form the basis of the Explanation of those cases of communicative behaviour in which the meaning of the expression doesn't cover the content of the communicated message.

All distinctions already developed in the General Theory of Communication and in Intention Based Semantics (cp. Meggle (1981), (1984)) are also relevant in the Theory of Pragmatic Implications. With respect to the results that have been reached in the General Theory of Communication we have to take into account the following distinctions:

- between implicatures in a wider and implicatures in a narrow sense. This distinction is parallel to the distinction between attempts at communication and successful attempts at communication
- between the understanding of the complete attempt at communication and the understanding of the implicature
- between the success of the complete attempt at communication and the success of the implicature.

THE CLASSIFICATION OF THE COMMUNICATIVE CONTENT OF AN UTTERANCE

In (1975) Grice divided "the total signification" of an utterance in two ways. Firstly, he distinguished between what is part of the meaning of the uttered sentence and what is not. Secondly, he distinguished between what is said and what is implicated. A speaker has said that p only if p must be the case in order for the sentence to be true. On the other hand, the truth of what is implicated is not required by the truth of the uttered sentence (or what is said). These two distinctions form a cross classification.

Firstly, there are communicative contents that cover partly the meaning of the uttered sentence but don't have to be the case in order for the sentence to be trues (the so-called conventional implicatures). Secondly, the meaning of the uttered sentence only helps to determine what is said by uttering the sentence, but it cannot be identified with what is said. According to Grice to determine what was said one has to disambiguate the sentence (i.e. to select one of its possible readings), and assign referents to all referential expressions. Grice claimed that this is everything one has to do.

Nowadays many authors assume that the gap between the meaning of the sentence and what is said is wider than Grice suggested. In many cases the underdetermination is not limited to reference-assignment and disambiguation. For example: What is said with "The bat is too big"? A bat is too big *for something*. If one does not know what that something is, one does not understand what is said with an utterance of this sentence. Hence many authors have tried to find new criteria to distinguish between what was said and what was implicated.

One aim of our project will be the discussion and evaluation of the different versions of the under determination argument and the developed new criteria for the distinction between what was said and what was implicated. With respect to this discussion we have to consider two important topics that normally are neglected. Firstly the concept of the literal meaning of a sentence. Secondly a systematic discussion of the different test for an implicat (nondetachability, cancelability etc.) given by Grice.

The Calculation of Conversational Implicatures

For Grice the most important feature of a conversational implicature is that the conversational implicatures of an utterance should be recoverable by a reasoning process. Essentially in this reasoning process is thereby the assumption, that the speaker fulfills the Cooperative Principle and the Conversational Maxims: "... to calculate a conversational implicature is to calculate what has to be supposed in order to preserve the supposition that the Cooperative Principle is being observed". But Grices own account of the derivation process is rather sketchy and little progress has been made in specifying this calculability requirement. We mention three important issues of the discussion.

It is even unclear what has to be calculated. Sometimes the calculability requirement is treated as an epistemological requirement. It is presupposed, that the speaker intends to communicate implicitly such-and-such and it has just to be explained how the speaker can expect that the hearer will understand what the speakers intends to communicate. Sometimes it is assumed that even the existence of the implicature depends on fulfillment of the cooperative principle and the maxims. (Even Grice did not distinguish between these two cases very sharply)

Furthermore: What is the exact nature of the inference process by which conversational implicatures are worked out? Levinson for example says that implicatures are like inductive inferences. Bach & Harnish claim that the inference "might be called an inference to a plausible explanation" On the other hand Sperber & Wilson believe that deductive inferences play a crucial role in the recovery of implicatures As far as the answer to the question is concernd which type of inference is being used by the recovery of implicatures, we expect a lot of help from project 4 (Explanatory Coherence).

Grice claims that background assumptions must play a role in the calculation of conversational implicatures. So: What is the epistemic status of context assumptions? Many authors suppose that context assumptions must be mutual knowledge. Against this claim Sperber & Wilson have argued that mutual knowledge is psychological impossible and superfluous in a theory of communication). Their argument has created a heavy discussion. Our project is intended to interfere into this discussion.

The Conversational Maxims

Finally the conversational maxims raise a lot of questions. Firstly, the content of the cooperative principle and of many maxims is unclear. What does it mean, that a contribution is as informative as required? When is a contribution relevant?

Secondly: What is the status of the maxims? Are they rules, conventions, or just empirical generalizations? What is the rationale behind the cooperative principle and the conversational maxims? And finally: Are there just the nine maxims Grice mentioned, or might others be needed? Or could the number of the maxims be reduced? Of course, in our project we want to answer these questions.

EXISTENTIALISM

Existentialism is a term that has been applied to the work of a number of nineteenth and twentieth century philosophers who, despite profound doctrinal differences, took the human subject — not merely the thinking subject, but the acting, feeling, living human individual and his or her conditions of existence — as a starting point for philosophical thought. Existential philosophy is the "explicit conceptual manifestation of an existential attitude" that begins with a sense of disorientation and confusion in the face of an apparently meaningless or absurd world. Many existentialists have also regarded traditional systematic or academic philosophy, in both style and content, as too abstract and remote from concrete human experience. One gives one's life meaning through action; life has no value unless one gives it value.

Existentialism emerged as a movement in twentieth-century literature and philosophy, foreshadowed most notably by nineteenth-century philosophers Søren Kierkegaard and Friedrich Nietzsche, though it had forerunners in earlier centuries. In the 20th century the German philosopher Martin Heidegger influenced other existentialist philosophers such as Sartre, Simone de Beauvoir and Albert Camus. Fyodor Dostoyevsky and Franz Kafka also described existential themes in their literary works. Although there are some common tendencies amongst "existentialist" thinkers, there are major differences and disagreements among them (most notably the divide between atheistic existentialists like Sartre and theistic existentialists like Tillich); not all of them accept the validity of the term as applied to their own work.

The term "existentialism" seems to have been coined by

the French philosopher Gabriel Marcel around 1943 and adopted by Jean-Paul Sartre who, on October 29, 1945, discussed his own existentialist position in a lecture to the *Club Maintenant* in Paris. The lecture was published as *L'existentialisme est un humanisme,* a short book which did much to popularize existentialist thought. The label has been applied retrospectively to other philosophers for whom existence and, in particular, human existence were key philosophical topics.

Martin Heidegger had made human existence (*Dasein*) the focus of his work since the 1920s, and Karl Jaspers had called his philosophy *"Existenzphilosophie"* in the 1930s. Both Heidegger and Jaspers had been influenced by the Danish philosopher, Søren Kierkegaard. For Kierkegaard the crisis of human existence had been a major theme. He came to be regarded as the first existentialist, and has been called the "father of existentialism". In fact he was the first to explicitly make existential questions a primary focus in his philosophy. In retrospect, other writers have also implicitly discussed existentialist themes throughout the history of philosophy.

Examples include:

- The Buddha's teachings,
- The Bible in the Books of Genesis, Ecclesiastes, and Job,
- Saint Augustine in his *Confessions,*
- Averroes' school of philosophy,
- Saint Thomas Aquinas' writings,
- Mulla Sadra's transcendent theosophy,
- William Shakespeare's *Hamlet.*

As early as 1835 in a letter to his friend Peter Wilhelm Lund, the Danish philosopher Søren Kierkegaard wrote one of his first existentially sensitive passages. In it, he describes a truth that is applicable for him:

What I really lack is to be clear in my mind what I am to do, not what I am to know, except in so far as a certain knowledge must precede every action. The thing is to understand myself, to see what God really wishes me to do: the thing is to find a truth which is true for me, to find the idea for which I can live and die.... I certainly do not deny that

I still recognize an imperative of knowledge and that through it one can work upon men, but it must be taken up into my life, and that is what I now recognize as the most important thing. —Søren Kierkegaard, Letter to Peter Wilhelm Lund dated August 31, 1835, emphasis added.

The early thoughts of Kierkegaard would be formalized in his prolific philosophical and theological writings, many of which would later form the modern foundation of 20th century existentialism.

KIERKEGAARD AND NIETZSCHE

Søren Kierkegaard and Friedrich Nietzsche were two of the first philosophers considered fundamental to the existentialist movement, though neither used the term "existentialism" and it is unclear whether they would have supported the existentialism of the 20th century. They focused on subjective human experience rather than the objective truths of mathematics and science, which they believed were too detached or observational to truly get at human experience. Like Pascal, they were interested in people's quiet struggle with the apparent meaninglessness of life and the use of diversion to escape from boredom.

Unlike Pascal, Kierkegaard and Nietzsche also considered the role of making free choices, particularly regarding fundamental values and beliefs, and how such choices change the nature and identity of the chooser. Kierkegaard's knight of faith and Nietzsche's Übermensch are exemplars who define the nature of their own existence. These idealized individuals invent their own values and create the very terms under which they excel. Kierkegaard and Nietzsche were also precursors to other intellectual movements, including postmodernism, nihilism, and various strands of psychology.

DOSTOYEVSKY AND KAFKA

Two of the first literary writers who were important to existentialism were the Czech author Franz Kafka and the Russian author Fyodor Dostoevsky. Dostoevsky's *Notes from Underground* details the story of a man who is unable to fit into society and unhappy with the identities he creates for himself. Many of Dostoevsky's novels, such as *Crime and Punishment*, covered issues pertinent to existential philosophy while offering story lines divergent from secular existentialism: for example in *Crime and Punishment* one sees the protagonist, Raskolnikov, experience existential crises and move toward a worldview similar to Christian Existentialism, which Dostoevsky had come to advocate.

Kafka created often surreal and alienated characters who struggle with hopelessness and absurdity, notably in his most famous novella, *The Metamorphosis*, or in his master novel, *The Trial*. In his philosophical essay *The Myth of Sisyphus*, the French existentialist Albert Camus describes Kafka's *oeuvre* as "absurd in principle", although he also finds present the same "tremendous cry of hope" as is to be found in religious existentialists such as Kierkegaard and Shestov, and which Camus himself rejects.

EARLY 20TH CENTURY

In the first decades of the 20th century, a number of philosophers – some working independently, but all influenced in varying degrees by Kierkegaard, Nietzsche and Dostoevsky – developed positions which were existentialist in all but name. The Spanish philosopher Miguel de Unamuno y Jugo, in his 1913 book *The Tragic Sense of Life in Men and Nations*, emphasized the life of "flesh and bone" as opposed to that of abstract rationalism. Unamuno rejected systematic philosophy in favor of the individual's quest for faith. He retained a sense of the tragic, even absurd nature of the quest, symbolized by his enduring interest in Cervantes' fictional character Don Quixote.

A novelist, poet and dramatist as well as philosophy professor at the University of Salamanca, Unamuno's short story about a priest's crisis of faith, "Saint Manuel the Good, Martyr" has been collected in anthologies of existentialist fiction. Another Spanish thinker, Ortega y Gasset, writing in 1914, held that the human existence must always be defined as the individual person combined with the concrete circumstances of his life: *"Yo soy yo y mi circunstancia"* ("I am myself and my circumstances"). Sartre likewise believed that human existence is not an abstract matter, but is always situated (*"en situation"*).

Although Martin Buber wrote his major philosophical works in German, and studied and taught at the Universities of Berlin and Frankfurt, he stands apart from the mainstream of German philosophy. Born into a Jewish family in Vienna in 1878, he was also a scholar of Jewish culture and involved at various times in Zionism and Hasidism. In 1938, he moved permanently to Jerusalem. His best-known philosophical work was the short book I and Thou, published in 1922. For Buber, the fundamental fact of human existence, too readily overlooked by scientific rationalism and abstract philosophical thought, is "man with man", a dialogue which takes place in the so-called "sphere of between" (*"das Zwischenmenschliche"*).

Two Russian thinkers, Lev Shestov and Nikolai Berdyaev became well-known as existentialist thinkers during their post-Revolutionary exiles in Paris. Shestov, born into a Russian-Jewish family in Kiev, had launched an attack on rationalism and systematization in philosophy as early as 1905 in his book of aphorisms *All Things Are Possible*. Berdyaev, also from Kiev but with a background in the Eastern Orthodox Church, drew a radical distinction between the world of spirit and the everyday world of objects. Human freedom, for Berdyaev, is rooted in the realm of spirit, a realm independent of scientific notions of causation. To the extent the individual human being lives in the objective world, he is estranged from authentic spiritual freedom. "Man" is not to be interpreted naturalistically, but as a being created in God's image, an originator of free, creative acts. He published a major work on these themes, *The Destiny of Man* in 1931.

Gabriel Marcel, long before coining the term "existentialism", introduced important existentialist themes to a French audience in his early essay "Existence and Objectivity" (1925) and in his *Metaphysical Journal* (1927). A dramatist as well as a philosopher, Marcel found his philosophical starting point in a condition of metaphysical alientation; the human individual searching for harmony in a transient life. Harmony, for Marcel, was to be sought through "secondary reflection", a "dialogical" rather than "dialectical" approach to the world, characterized by "wonder and astonishment" and open to the "presence" of other people and of God rather than merely to "information" about them.

For Marcel, such presence implied more than simply being there (as one thing might be in the presence of another thing); it connoted "extravagant" availability, and the willingness to put oneself at the disposal of the other. Marcel contrasted "secondary reflection" with abstract, scientific-technical "primary reflection" which he associated with the activity of the abstract Cartesian ego. For Marcel, philosophy was a concrete activity undertaken by a sensing, feeling human being incarnate — embodied — in a concrete world. Although Jean-Paul Sartre adopted the term "existentialism" for his own philosophy in the 1940s, Marcel's thought has been described as "almost diametrically opposed" to that of Sartre. Unlike Sartre, Marcel was a Christian, and became a Catholic convert in 1929.

In Germany, the psychologist and philosopher Karl Jaspers — who later described existentialism as a "phantom" created by the public, — called his own thought, heavily influenced by Kierkegaard and Nietzsche — *Existenzphilosophie*. For Jaspers, "*Existenz*-philosophy is the way of thought by means of which man seeks to become himself...This way of thought does not cognize objects, but elucidates and makes actual the being of the thinker." Jaspers, a professor at the University of Heidelberg, was acquainted with Martin Heidegger, who held a professorship at Marburg before acceding to Husserl's chair at Freiburg in 1928. They held many philosophical discussions, but later became estranged over Heidegger's support of National Socialism.

They shared an admiration for Kierkegaard, and in the 1930s Heidegger lectured extensively on Nietzsche. Nevertheless, the extent to which Heidegger should be considered an existentialist is debatable. In *Being and Time* he presented a method of rooting philosophical explanations in human existence (*Dasein*) to be analysed in terms of existential categories (*existentiale*); and this has led many commentators to treat him as an important figure in the existentialist movement. One of the most known novels of Hermann Hesse, *Steppenwolf*, is considered a clear example of an existential novel. It is the reflexion of a deep spiritual crisis of Hesse in the 1920s. The main character, Harry Haller, is a portrait of a man who faces a human condition dilemma: "who am I?". There are two living souls within his chest: a man and a wolf. The eternal struggle between virtues and instincts takes him to a journey through his inner desert, to some answers related to buddhist-like doctrines.

AFTER THE SECOND WORLD WAR

Following the Second World War, existentialism became a well-known and significant philosophical and cultural movement, mainly through the public prominence of two French writers, Jean-Paul Sartre and Albert Camus, who wrote best-selling novels, plays and widely-read journalism as well as theoretical texts. These years also saw the growing reputation outside Germany of Heidegger's book *Being and Time*. Sartre had dealt with existentialist themes in his 1938 novel *Nausea* and the short stories in his 1939 collection *The Wall*, and had published a major philosophical statement, *Being and Nothingness* in 1943, but it was in the two years following the liberation of Paris from the German occupying forces that he and his close associates — Camus, Simone de Beauvoir, Maurice Merleau-Ponty, and others — became internationally famous as the leading figures of a movement known as existentialism.

In a very short space of time, Camus and Sartre in particular, became the leading public intellectuals of post-war France, achieving by the end of 1945 "a fame that reached across all audiences." Camus was an editor of the most popular leftist (former French Resistance) newspaper *Combat*; Sartre launched his journal of leftist thought, *Les Temps Modernes*, and two weeks later gave the widely reported lecture on existentialism and humanism to a packed meeting of the Club

Maintenant. Beauvoir wrote that "not a week passed without the newspapers discussing us"; existentialism became "the first media craze of the postwar era." By the end of 1947, Camus's earlier fiction and plays had been reprinted, his new play *Caligula* had been performed and his novel *The Plague* published; the first two novels of Sartre's *The Roads to Freedom* trilogy had appeared, as had Beauvoir's novel *The Blood of Others*.

Works by Camus and Sartre were already appearing in foreign editions. The Paris-based existentialists had become famous. Sartre had travelled to Germany in 1930 to study the phenomenology of Edmund Husserl and Martin Heidegger, and he included critical comments on their work in his major treatise *Being and Nothingness*. Heidegger's thought had also become known in French philosophical circles through its use by Alexandre Kojève in explicating Hegel in a series of lectures given in Paris in the 1930s. The lectures were highly influential; members of the audience included not only Sartre and Merleau-Ponty, but Raymond Queneau, Georges Bataille, Louis Althusser, André Breton and Jacques Lacan. A selection from Heidegger's *Being and Time* was published in French in 1938, and his essays began to appear in French philosophy journals.

Heidegger read Sartre's work and was initially impressed, commenting: "Here for the first time I encountered an independent thinker who, from the foundations up, has experienced the area out of which I think, Your work shows such an immediate comprehension of my philosophy as I have never before encountered." Later, however, in response to a question posed by his French follower Jean Beaufret, Heidegger distanced himself from Sartre's position and existentialism in general in his *Letter on Humanism*. Heidegger's reputation continued to grow in France during the 1950s and 1960s. In the 1960s, Sartre attempted to reconcile existentialism and Marxism in his work *Critique of Dialectical Reason*. A major theme throughout his writings was freedom and responsibility.

Albert Camus was a friend of Sartre, until their falling-out, and wrote several works with existential themes including *The Rebel, The Stranger, The Myth of Sisyphus,* and *Summer in Algiers.* Camus, like many others, rejected the existentialist label, and considered his works to be concerned with people facing the absurd. In *The Myth of Sisyphus,* Camus uses the analogy of the Greek myth to demonstrate the futility of existence. In the myth, Sisyphus is condemned for eternity to roll a rock up a hill, but when he reaches the summit, the rock will roll to the bottom again. Camus believes that this existence is pointless but that Sisyphus ultimately finds meaning and purpose in his task, simply by continually applying himself to it.

Simone de Beauvoir, an important existentialist who spent much of her life as Sartre's partner, wrote about feminist and existential ethics in her works, including *The Second Sex* and *The Ethics of Ambiguity.* Although often overlooked due to her relationship with Sartre, de Beauvoir integrated existentialism with other forms of thinking such as feminism, unheard of at the time, resulting in alienation from fellow writers such as Camus. Frantz Fanon, a Martiniquan-born critic of colonialism, has been considered an important existentialist. Paul Tillich, an important existential theologian following Søren Kierkegaard and Karl Barth, applied existential concepts to Christian theology, and helped introduce existential theology to the general public.

His seminal work *The Courage to Be* follows Kierkegaard's analysis of anxiety and life's absurdity, but puts forward the thesis that modern man must, via God, achieve selfhood in spite of life's absurdity. Rudolf Bultmann used Kierkegaard's and Heidegger's philosophy of existence to demythologize Christianity by interpreting Christian mythical concepts into existential concepts. Maurice Merleau-Ponty, an existential phenomenologist, was for a time a companion of Sartre. His understanding of Husserl's phenomenology was far greater than that of Merleau-Ponty's fellow existentialists. It has been said that his work, Humanism and Terror, greatly influenced Sartre.

However, in later years they were to disagree irreparably,

dividing many existentialists such as de Beauvoir, who sided with Sartre. Michel Foucault would also be considered an existentialist through his use of history to reveal the constant alterations of created meaning, thus proving history's failure to produce a cohesive version of reality. Colin Wilson, an English writer, published his study The Outsider in 1956, initially to critical acclaim. In this book and others (e.g. *Introduction to the New Existentialism*), he attempted to reinvigorate what he perceived as a pessimistic philosophy and bring it to a wider audience. He was not, however, academically trained, and his work was attacked by professional philosophers for lack of rigor and critical standards.

CONCEPTS

Existentialist thinkers focus on the question of concrete human existence and the conditions of this existence rather than hypothesizing a human essence. However, even though the concrete individual existence must have priority in existentialism, certain conditions are commonly held to be "endemic" to human existence. What these conditions are is better understood in light of the meaning of the word "existence," which comes from the Latin "existere," meaning "to stand out." Man exists in a state of distance from the world that he nonetheless remains in the midst of. This distance is what enables man to project meaning into the disinterested world of in-itselfs. This projected meaning remains fragile, constantly facing breakdown for any reason — from a tragedy to a particularly insightful moment.

In such a breakdown, we are put face to face with the naked meaninglessness of the world, and the results can be devastating. It is in relation to the concept of the devastating awareness of meaningless that Albert Camus claimed that "there is only one truly serious philosophical problem, and that is suicide" in his *The Myth of Sisyphus*. Although "prescriptions" against the possibly deleterious consequences of these kinds of encounters vary, from Kierkegaard's religious "stage" to Camus' insistence on persevering in spite of absurdity, the concern with helping people avoid living their lives in ways that put them in the perpetual danger of having everything meaningful break down is common to most existentialist philosophers.

Existence Precedes Essence

A central proposition of existentialism is that existence precedes essence, which means that the actual life of the individual is what constitutes what could be called his "essence" instead of there being a predetermined essence that defines what it is to be a human. Although it was Sartre who explicitly coined the term, similar notions can be found in the thought of many existentialist philosophers, from Kierkegaard to Heidegger. It is often claimed in this context that man defines himself, which is often perceived as stating that man can "wish" to be something – anything, a bird, for instance – and then be it. According to most existentialist philosophers, however, this would rather be a kind of inauthentic existence. What is meant by the statement is that man is defined only insofar as he acts and that he is responsible for his actions.

To clarify, it can be said that a man who acts cruelly towards other people is, by that act, defined as a cruel man and in that same instance, he (as opposed to his genes, or "the cruel nature of man", for instance) is defined as being responsible for *being* this cruel man. As Sartre puts it in his Existentialism is a Humanism: "man first of all exists, encounters himself, surges up in the world – and defines himself afterwards." Of course, the more positive, therapeutic aspect of this is also implied: You can choose to act in a different way, and to be a good person instead of a cruel person. Here it is also clear that since man can choose to be either cruel or good, he is, in fact, neither of these things *essentially*.

ANGST

Angst, sometimes called dread, anxiety or even anguish is a term that is common to many existentialist thinkers. It is generally held to be the experience of our freedom and responsibility. The archetypal example is the experience one has when standing on a cliff where one not only fears falling off it, but also dreads the possibility of throwing oneself off. In this experience that "nothing is holding me back", one senses the lack of anything that predetermines you to either throw yourself off or to stand still, and one experiences one's own freedom. It can also be seen in relation to the previous point how angst is before *nothing,* and this is what sets it apart from fear which has an object. While in the case of fear, one can take definitive measures to remove the object of fear, in the case of angst, no such "constructive" measures are possible.

The use of the word "nothing" in this context relates both to the inherent insecurity about the consequences of one's actions, and to the fact that, in experiencing one's freedom as angst, one also realizes that one will be fully responsible for these consequences; there is no *thing* in you (your genes, for instance) that acts in your stead, and that you can "blame" if something goes wrong. Not every choice is perceived as having dreadful possible consequences (and, it can be claimed, our lives would be unbearable if every choice facilitated dread), but that doesn't change the fact that freedom remains a condition of every action.

One of the most extensive treatments of the existentialist notion of Angst is found in Søren Kierkegaard's monumental work *Begrebet Angest (The Concept of Dread).* Angst is often described as the drama an adolescent troubles with during their developmental years. In pop-culture 'angst' is used to describe a particular attitude, often towards family or governmental systems. In this light, the angst of popular teenage life could be used to describe the often-theorized 'existential crisis' that is adolescence.

FREEDOM

The existentialist concept of freedom is often misunderstood as a sort of liberum arbitrium where almost anything is possible and where values are inconsequential to choice and action. This interpretation of the concept is often related to the insistence on the absurdity of the world and that there are no relevant or absolutely good or bad values. However, that there are no values to be found in the world *in-itself* does not mean that there are no values: each of us usually already has his values before a consideration of their validity is carried through, and it is, after all, upon these values we act. In Kierkegaard's Judge Vilhelm's account in *Either/Or,* making choices without allowing one's values to confer differing values to the alternatives, is, in fact, choosing not to make a choice — to flip a coin, as it were, and to leave everything to chance.

This is considered to be a refusal to live in the consequence of one's freedom; an inauthentic existence. As such, existentialist freedom isn't situated in some kind of abstract space where everything is possible: since people are free, and since they already exist in the world, it is implied that their freedom is only in this world, and that it, too, is restricted by it. What *is not* implied in this account of existential freedom, however, is that one's values are immutable; a consideration of one's values may cause one to reconsider and change them.

A consequence of this fact is that one is not only responsible for one's actions, but also for the values one holds. This entails that a reference to common values doesn't excuse the individual's actions: Even though these are the values of the society the individual is part of, they are also his own in the sense that s/he could choose them to be different at any time. Thus, the focus on freedom in existentialism is related to the limits of the responsibility one bears as a result of one's freedom: the relationship between freedom and responsibility is one of interdependency, and a clarification of freedom also clarifies what one is responsible for.

FACTICITY

A concept closely related to freedom is that of facticity, a concept defined by Sartre in *Being and Nothingness* as that "in-itself" of which you are in the mode of not being. This can be more easily understood when considering it in relation to the temporal dimension of past: Your past is what you are in the sense that it co-constitutes you. However, to say that you are *only* your past would be to ignore a large part of reality (the present and the future) while saying that your past is only what you *were* in a way that would entirely detach it from you *now*. A denial of one's own concrete past constitutes an inauthentic lifestyle, and the same goes for all other kinds of facticity (having a body (e.g. one that doesn't allow you to run faster than the speed of sound), identity, values, etc.).

In relation to freedom, facticity is both a limitation and a condition of your freedom. It is a limitation in that a large part of your facticity consists of things you couldn't have chosen (birthplace, etc.), but a condition in the sense that your values most likely will depend on it. However, even though your facticity is "set in stone" (as being past, for instance), it cannot *determine* you: The value ascribed to your facticity is still ascribed to it freely *by you*. As an example, consider two men, one of which has no memory of his past and the other remembers everything. They have both committed many crimes, but the first man, knowing nothing about this, leads a rather normal life while the second man, feeling trapped by his own past, continues a life of crime, blaming his own past for "trapping" him in this life. There is nothing essential about his committing crimes, but he ascribes this meaning to his past.

However, to disregard your facticity when you, in the continual process of self-making, project yourself into the future, would be to put yourself in denial of yourself, and would thus be inauthentic. In other words, the origin of your projection will still have to be your facticity, although in the mode of not being it (essentially). Another aspect of facticity is that it entails angst, both in the sense that freedom "produces" angst when limited by facticity, and in the sense that the lack of the possibility of having facticity "step in" for you to take responsibility for something you have done also produces angst.

AUTHENTICITY AND INAUTHENTICITY

The theme of authentic existence is common to many existentialist thinkers. It is often taken to mean that one has to "find oneself" and then live in accordance with this self, but in one sense, if one considers the self to be substantial or "fixed," that the self truly is some thing you can find if you look hard enough, this is a misunderstanding. What is meant by authenticity is that in acting, one should act as oneself, not as *One, one's genes* or any other essence. The authentic act is one that is in accordance with one's freedom. Of course, as a condition of freedom is facticity, this includes one's facticity, but not to the degree that this facticity can in any way *determine* one's choices (in the sense that one could then blame one's background for making the choice one made).

The role of facticity in relation to authenticity involves letting one's actual values come into play when one makes a choice (instead of, like Kierkegaard's Aesthete, "choosing" randomly), so that one also takes responsibility for the act instead of choosing either-or without allowing the options to have different values. In contrast to this, the inauthentic is the denial to live in accordance with one's freedom. This can take many forms, from pretending choices are meaningless or random, through convincing oneself that some form of determinism is true, to a sort of "mimicry" where one acts as "*One* should." How "One" should act is often determined by an image one has of how one such as oneself (say, a bank manager) acts. This image usually corresponds to some sort of social norm, but this does not mean that all acting in accordance with social norms is inauthentic: The main point is the attitude one takes to one's own freedom and responsibility, and the extent to which one acts in accordance with this freedom.

DESPAIR

Commonly defined as a loss of hope, Despair in existentialism is more specifically related to the reaction to a breakdown in one or more of the "pillars" of one's self or identity. If one has invested a lot of oneself in being some*thing*, a waiter or an "upstanding citizen," and one finds oneself in a situation in which one has done something or had something happen to oneself that compromises this being-thing, one would normally find oneself in a state of Despair, a *hopeless* state.

An athlete who loses his legs in an accident may despair if he has nothing to "fall back on," for instance. What sets the existentialist notion of Despair apart from the dictionary definition is that Despair is a state one is in even when one isn't overtly in Despair: As long as one has based one's identity on such pillars so that one is vulnerable to *having one's world break down*, one is considered to be in perpetual Despair. As Kierkegaard defines it in his Either/or: "Any life-view with a condition outside it is despair." In other words, it is possible to be *in despair* without *despairing*.

The Other (when written with a capital "o") is a concept more properly belonging to phenomenology and its account of intersubjectivity. However, the concept has seen widespread use in existentialist writings, and the conclusions drawn from it differ slightly from the phenomenological accounts. The experience of the Other is the experience of another free subject who inhabits the same world as you do. In its most basic form, it is this experience of the Other that constitutes intersubjectivity and objectivity. To clarify, when one experiences someone else, and that this Other person experiences the world (the same world that you experience), only from "over there", the world itself is constituted as objective in that it is something that is "there" as identical for both of the subjects; you experience the other person as experiencing the same as you. This experience of the Other's look is what is termed the Look (sometimes The Gaze).

While this experience, in its basic phenomenological sense, constitutes the world as objective, and yourself as objectively existing subjectivity (you experience yourself as seen in the Other's Look in precisely the same way that you experience the Other as seen by you, as subjectivity), in existentialism, it also acts as a kind of limitation of your freedom. This is because the Look tends to objectify what it sees. As such, when one experiences oneself in the Look, one doesn't experience oneself as nothing (no thing), but as something. Sartre's own example of a man peeping at someone through a keyhole can help clarify this: At first, this man is entirely caught up in the situation he is in; he is in a pre-reflexive state where his entire consciousness is directed at what goes on in the room. Suddenly, he hears a creaking floorboard behind him, and he becomes aware of himself *as seen by the Other*.

He is thus filled with shame for he perceives himself as he would perceive someone else doing what he was doing, as a Peeping Tom. The Look is then co-constitutive of one's facticity. Another characteristic feature of the Look is that no Other *really* needs to have been there: It is quite possible that the creaking floorboard was nothing but the movement of an old house; the Look isn't some kind of mystical telepathic experience of the *actual* way the other sees you (there may also have been someone there, but he could have not noticed that you were there). It is only your *perception* of the way another might perceive you.

REASON

Emphasizing action, freedom, and decision as fundamental, existentialists oppose themselves to rationalism and positivism. That is, they argue against definitions of human beings as primarily rational. Rather, existentialists look at where people find meaning. Existentialism asserts that people actually make decisions based on the meaning to them rather than rationally. The rejection of reason as the source of meaning is a common theme of existentialist thought, as is the focus on the feelings of anxiety and dread that we feel in the face of our own radical freedom and our awareness of death. Kierkegaard saw strong rationality as a mechanism humans use to counter their existential anxiety, their fear of being in the world: "If I can believe that I am rational and everyone else is rational then I have nothing to fear and no reason to feel anxious about being free." However, Kierkegaard advocated rationality as means to interact with the objective world (e.g. in the natural sciences), but when it comes to existential problems, reason is insufficient: "Human reason has boundaries".

Like Kierkegaard, Sartre saw problems with rationality, calling it a form of "bad faith", an attempt by the self to impose structure on a world of phenomena — "the Other" — that is fundamentally irrational and random. According to Sartre, rationality and other forms of bad faith hinder us from finding meaning in freedom. To try to suppress our feelings of anxiety and dread, we confine ourselves within everyday experience, Sartre asserts, thereby relinquishing our freedom and acquiescing to being possessed in one form or another by "the look" of "the Other" (i.e. possessed by another person – or at least our idea of that other person). In a similar vein, Camus believed that society and religion falsely teach humans that "the Other" has order and structure. For Camus, when an individual's consciousness, longing for order, collides with the Other's lack of order, a third element is born: absurdity.

THE ABSURD

The notion of the Absurd contains the idea that there is no meaning to be found in the world beyond what meaning we give to it. This meaninglessness also encompasses the amorality or "unfairness" of the world. This contrasts with "karmic" ways of thinking in which "bad things don't happen to good people"; to the world, metaphorically speaking, there is no such thing as a good person or a bad thing; what happens happens, and it may just as well happen to a "good" person as to a "bad" person. This contrasts our daily experience where most things appear to us as meaningful, and where good people do indeed, on occasion, receive some sort of "reward" for their goodness.

Most existentialist thinkers, however, will maintain that this is not a necessary feature of the world, and that it definitely isn't a property of the world in-itself. Because of the world's absurdity, at any point in time, anything can happen to anyone, and a tragic event could plummet someone into direct confrontation with the Absurd. The notion of the absurd has been prominent in literature throughout history. Søren Kierkegaard, Franz Kafka, Fyodor Dostoevsky and many of the literary works of Jean-Paul Sartre and Albert Camus contain descriptions of people who encounter the absurdity of the world. Albert Camus studied the issue of "the absurd" in his essay *The Myth of Sisyphus*.

Though nihilism and existentialism are distinct philosophies, they are often confused with one another. A primary cause of confusion is that Friedrich Nietzsche is an important philosopher in both fields, but also the existentialist insistence on the absurd and the inherent meaninglessness of the world. Existentialist philosophers often stress the importance of Angst as signifying the absolute lack of any objective ground for action, a move that is often reduced to a moral or an existential nihilism.

A pervasive theme in the works of existentialist philosophy, however, is to persist *through* encounters with the absurd, as seen in Camus' The Myth of Sisyphus, and it is only very rarely that existentialist philosophers dismiss morality or one's self-created meaning: Kierkegaard regained a sort of morality in the religious (although he wouldn't himself agree that it was ethical; the religious suspends the ethical), and Sartre's final words in Being and Nothingness are "All these questions, which refer us to a pure and not an accessory (or impure) reflection, can find their reply only on the ethical plane. We shall devote to them a future work." Hence, existentialists believe that one can create value and meaning, whilst nihilists will deny this.

Herbert Marcuse criticised Existentialism, especially *Being and Nothingness* (1943), by Jean-Paul Sartre, for projecting anxiety and meaninglessness onto the nature of existence itself: "Insofar as Existentialism is a philosophical doctrine, it remains an idealistic doctrine: it hypostatizes specific historical conditions of human existence into ontological and metaphysical characteristics. Existentialism thus becomes part of the very ideology which it attacks, and its radicalism is illusory". In 1946, Sartre already had replied to Marxist criticism of Existentialism in the lecture *Existentialism is a humanism.* In *Jargon of Authenticity,* Theodor Adorno criticised Heidegger's philosophy, especially his use of language, as a mystifying ideology of advanced, industrial society, and its power structure.

In *Letter on Humanism,* Heidegger criticized Sartre's existentialism:

Existentialism says existence precedes essence. In this statement he is taking existentia *and* essentia *according to their metaphysical meaning, which, from Plato's time on, has said that* essentia *precedes* existentia. *Sartre reverses this statement. But the reversal of a metaphysical statement remains a metaphysical statement. With it, he stays with metaphysics, in oblivion of the truth of Being.*

In *From Descartes to Wittgenstein*, Roger Scruton says that Heidegger's concept of inauthenticity and Sartre's concept of bad faith were self-inconsistent; both deny any universal moral creed, yet speak of these concepts as if everyone were bound to abide them. "In what sense Sartre is able to 'recommend' the authenticity, which consists in the purely self-made morality, is unclear. He does recommend it, but, by his own argument, his recommendation can have no objective force." However, despite the seemingly moral tone present in each, both Heidegger and Sartre stress throughout their respective works that these are not to be taken as evaluative concepts, and if we take their word for this (as Scruton does not), there is no inconsistency in this regard. Both authors appeal to the reader in all regards to decide for him/herself.

Logical positivists, such as Carnap and Ayer, say Existentialists frequently are confused about the verb "to be" in their analyses of "being". They argue that the verb is transitive, and pre-fixed to a predicate (e.g., an apple *is red*): without a predicate, the word is meaningless. Another alleged confusion, in existentialist metaphysical literature, is that existentialists try to understand the meaning of the word "nothing" (the negation of existence) by presuming it must refer to something. Borrowing Kant's argument against the ontological argument *for* the existence of God, logical positivists argue that existence is not a property. Existentialists would respond to both claims by an appeal to the reader's intuitive understanding on the matter, which is guided to this end through the descriptive content of their works. They treat the matter as beyond the scope of argument and logic.

CULTURAL MOVEMENT AND INFLUENCE

The term *existentialism* was first adopted as a self-reference in the 1940s and 1950s by Jean-Paul Sartre, and the widespread use of literature as a means of disseminating their ideas by Sartre and his associates meant existentialism "was as much a literary phenomenon as a philosophical one." Among existentialist writers were Parisians Jean Genet, André Gide, André Malraux, and playwright Samuel Beckett, the Norwegian Knut Hamsun, and the Romanian friends Eugène Ionesco and Emil Cioran. Prominent artists such as the Abstract Expressionists Jackson Pollock, Arshile Gorky, and Willem de Kooning have been understood in existentialist terms, as have filmmakers such as Jean-Luc Godard and Ingmar Bergman. Also, existential theological influence is apparent in *Angel's Egg*, a Japanese anime feature film produced by Tokuma Shoten in 1985 which blends surrealistic and existentialist qualities.

The French director Jean Genet's 1950 fantasy-erotic film *Un chant d'amour* shows two inmates in solitary cells whose only contact is through a hole in their cell wall, who are spied on by the prison warden. Reviewer James Travers calls the film a "...visual poem evoking homosexual desire and existentialist suffering" which "... conveys the bleakness of an existence in a godless universe with painful believability"; he calls it "... probably the most effective fusion of existentialist philosophy and cinema."

Stanley Kubrick's 1957 anti-war film *Paths of Glory* "illustrates, and even illuminates...existentialism" by examining the "necessary absurdity of the human condition" and the "horror of war". The film tells the story of a fictional World War I French army regiment which is ordered to attack an impregnable German stronghold; when the attack fails, three soldiers are chosen at random, court-martialed by a "kangaroo court", and executed by firing squad. The film examines existential ethics, such as the issue of whether objectivity is possible and the "problem of authenticity".

On the lighter side, the British comedy troupe Monty Python have explored existential themes throughout their works, from many of the sketches in their original television show, the *Flying Circus*, to their last major release and the 1983 film *The Meaning of Life*. Of the many adjectives (some listed in the introduction above) that might indicate an existential tone, the one utilized the most by the group is that of the absurd. Some contemporary films dealing with existential issues include *Fight Club*, *Waking Life*, and *Ordinary People*.

Jean-Paul Sartre wrote *No Exit* in 1944, an existentialist play originally published in French as *Huis Clos* (meaning *In Camera* or "behind closed doors") which is the source of the popular quote, "Hell is other people." (In French, "l'enfer, c'est les autres"). The play begins with a Valet leading a man into a room that the audience soon realizes is in hell. Eventually he is joined by two women. After their entry, the Valet leaves and the door is shut and locked. All three expect to be tortured, but no torturer arrives. Instead, they realize they are there to torture each other, which they do effectively, by probing each other's sins, desires, and unpleasant memories.

Existentialist themes are displayed in the Theatre of the Absurd, notably in Samuel Beckett's *Waiting for Godot*, in which two men divert themselves while they wait expectantly for someone (or something) named Godot who never arrives. They claim Godot to be an acquaintance but in fact hardly know him, admitting they would not recognize him if they saw him. Samuel Beckett, once asked who or what Godot is, replied, "If I knew, I would have said so in the play." To occupy themselves they eat, sleep, talk, argue, sing, play games, exercise, swap hats, and contemplate suicide—anything "to hold the terrible silence at bay". The play "exploits several archetypal forms and situations, all of which lend themselves to both comedy and pathos."

The play also illustrates an attitude toward man's experience on earth: the poignancy, oppression, camaraderie, hope, corruption, and bewilderment of human experience that can only be reconciled in mind and art of the absurdist. The play examines questions such as death, the meaning of human existence and the place of God in human existence. Tom Stoppard's *Rosencrantz & Guildenstern Are Dead* is an absurdist tragicomedy first staged at the Edinburgh Festival Fringe in 1966. The play expands upon the exploits of two minor characters from Shakespeare's *Hamlet*. Comparisons have also been drawn to Samuel Beckett's *Waiting For Godot*, for the presence of two central characters who almost appear to be two halves of a single character.

Many plot features are similar as well: the characters pass time by playing Questions, impersonating other characters, and interrupting each other or remaining silent for long periods of time. The two characters are portrayed as two clowns or fools in a world that is beyond their understanding. They stumble through philosophical arguments while not realizing the implications, and muse on the irrationality and randomness of the world.

Jean Anouilh's *Antigone* also presents arguments founded on existentialist ideas. It is a tragedy inspired by Greek mythology and the play of the same name (Antigone, by Sophocles) from the 5th century B.C. In English, it is often distinguished from its antecedent by being pronounced in its original French form, approximately "Ante-GÔN." The play was first performed in Paris on 6 February 1944, during the Nazi occupation of France. Produced under Nazi censorship, the play is purposefully ambiguous with regards to the rejection of authority (represented by Antigone) and the acceptance of it (represented by Creon).

The parallels to the French Resistance and the Nazi occupation have been drawn. Antigone rejects life as desperately meaningless but without affirmatively choosing a noble death. The crux of the play is the lengthy dialogue concerning the nature of power, fate, and choice, during which Antigone says that she is "... disgusted with [the]...promise of a humdrum happiness"; she states that she would rather die than live a mediocre existence. Critic Martin Esslin in his book *Theatre of the Absurd* pointed out how many contemporary playwrights such as Samuel Beckett, Eugène Ionesco, Jean Genet, and Arthur Adamov wove into their plays the existential belief that we are absurd beings loose in a universe empty of real meaning.

Esslin noted that many of these playwrights demonstrated the philosophy better than did the plays by Sartre and Camus.

Though most of such playwrights, subsequently labeled "Absurdist" (based on Esslin's book), denied affiliations with existentialism and were often staunchly anti-philosophical (for example Ionesco often claimed he identified more with 'Pataphysics or with Surrealism than with existentialism), the playwrights are often linked to existentialism based on Esslin's observation.

Many solo artists and bands have released existentially themed works ranging from single songs to entire albums. Some of these artists have focused and built their entire careers exploring these themes. Notable examples include Jim Morrison of The Doors, Scott Walker, Roger Waters of Pink Floyd, Trent Reznor of the industrial band Nine Inch Nails among others. Also in Electronica style, a good example is Enigma for the albums MCMXC a.D., Le Roi Est Mort, Vive Le Roi! and The Screen Behind the Mirror.

Christ's teachings had an indirect style, in which his point is often left unsaid for the purpose of letting the single individual.confront the truth on their own. This is evident in his parables, which are a response to a question he is asked. After he tells the parable, he returns the question to the individual. An existential reading of the Bible demands that the reader recognize that he is an existing subject studying the words more as a recollection of possible events.

This is in contrast to looking at a collection of "truths" which are outside and unrelated to the reader, but may develop your reality/God. Such a reader is not obligated to follow the commandments as if an external agent is forcing them upon him, but as though they are inside him and guiding him from inside.

This is the task Kierkegaard takes up when he asks: "Who has the more difficult task: the teacher who lectures on earnest things a meteor's distance from everyday life-or the learner who should put it to use?" Existentially speaking, the Bible doesn't become an authority in a person's life until they authorize the Bible to be their personal authority. Existentialism has had a significant influence on theology, notably on postmodern Christianity and on theologians and religious thinkers such as Nikolai Berdyaev, Karl Barth, Paul Tillich, Wilfrid Desan and John Macquarrie.

EXISTENTIALISTIC ATHEISM

In opposition to theology exists an atheist existentialism that is running ways totally different from those theological ones. One of the major offshoots of existentialism as a philosophy is existential psychology and psychoanalysis, which first crystallized in the work of Ludwig Binswanger, a clinician who was influenced by both Freud, Edmund Husserl, Heidegger and Sartre. A later figure was Viktor Frankl, who had studied with Freud and Jung as a young man. His logotherapy can be regarded as a form of existential therapy.

An early contributor to existential psychology in the United States was Rollo May, who was influenced by Kierkegaard. One of the most prolific writers on techniques and theory of existential psychology in the USA is Irvin D. Yalom.

The person who has contributed most to the development of a European version of existential psychotherapy is the British-based Emmy van Deurzen. With complete freedom to decide, and complete responsibility for the outcome of decisions, comes anxiety (angst). Anxiety's importance in existentialism makes it a popular topic in psychotherapy. Therapists often use existential philosophy to explain the patient's anxiety. Psychotherapists using an existential approach believe that a patient can harness his anxiety and use it constructively.

Instead of suppressing anxiety, patients are advised to use it as grounds for change. By embracing anxiety as inevitable, a person can use it to achieve his full potential in life. Humanistic psychology also had major impetus from existential psychology and shares many of the fundamental tenets. Terror management theory is a developing area of study within the academic study of psychology. It looks at what researchers claim to be the implicit emotional reactions of people that occur when they are confronted with the knowledge they will eventually die.

EDUCATION FOR GOOD LIFE TO EVERY INDIVIDUAL

Education is a necessity for every human on this earth. Throughout the centuries man has evoloved through different stages of learning and this has made man more aware and conscious of his own self, his rights, his duties as a citizen and moreover, he has acquired a vast knowledge about God through the teachings of various religeons.

This has become possible only through acquiring knowledge and learning through out life without which man is like without mind, without self awareness.

Therefore every individual on this earth should have acess to quality education with ease so that he may know the truth of life and his own being. We all know that the world has advanced in various educational fields and particulary the west has been able to setup a smart education system, along with easy acess.

The literacy rate has reached a high level which outranks the eastern part of the world. They provide free seconday education to their people which make it easy for the whole population to acquire quality education.

Therefore, the citizens are much aware and consious of their rights an duties and thus they are able to enjoy a high standard of living.

In contrast, the eastern part of the world particularly the asian and african countries are facing high rate of illiteracy and backwardnes.

This is particularly due to poor education system and lack of education facilities.

This lackness has deprived the people from acquiring knowledge which has made them unaware and backward from the modern day society. They don't have any awareness about how to live a civilized society.

They are just following old customs and tradition and following the footsteps of their predecessors.

This is so unjust. It is so unfair that man is left with no option to change himself but just to follow the way of living of their ancestors like a robot. As they don't have knowledge of what is happening in the world and they are not aware of their rights and duties, therefore, leaders and high class of people in these countries exploit this illiterate class for their vested interest.

We need to look in to it and extend cooperation with them, in this regard, so that they become able to overcome their backwardness by following the footsteps of the successful western people. It is only us who can help them.

It's only us who has the responsibility. It is only us who should be held responsible for not providing support to these people. Therefore, I would like to request those who possess power and fortune in their hands to support the poor regions of the world and lead them towards progress.

Unit III

Contributions of Educational Thinkers

INDIAN THINKERS: SWAMI VIVEKANANDA

Vivekananda was a renowned thinker in his own right. One of his most important contributions was to demonstrate how Advaitin thinking is not merely philosophically far-reaching, but how it also has social, even political, consequences. One important lesson he claimed to receive from Ramakrishna was that "Jiva is Shiva " (each individual is divinity itself). This became his Mantra, and he coined the concept of *daridra narayana seva* - the service of God in and through (poor) human beings. If there truly is the unity of Brahman underlying all phenomena, then on what basis do we regard ourselves as better or worse, or even as better-off or worse-off, than others? - This was the question he posed to himself. Ultimately, he concluded that these distinctions fade into nothingness in the light of the oneness that the devotee experiences in Moksha. What arises then is compassion for those "individuals" who remain unaware of this oneness and a determination to help them.

Swami Vivekananda belonged to that branch of Vedanta that held that no-one can be truly free until all of us are. Even the desire for personal salvation has to be given up, and only tireless work for the salvation of others is the true mark of the enlightened person. He founded Sri Ramakrishna Math and Mission on the principle of Atmano Mokshartham Jagad-hitaya cha (for one's own salvation and for the welfare of the

World). However, Vivekananda also pleaded for a strict separation between religion and government ("church and state"). Although social customs had been formed in the past with religious sanction, it was not now the business of religion to interfere with matters such as marriage, inheritance and so on.

The ideal society would be a mixture of Brahmin knowledge, Kshatriya culture, Vaisya efficiency and the egalitarian Shudra ethos. Domination by any one led to different sorts of lopsided societies. Vivekananda did not feel that religion, nor, any force for that matter, should be used forcefully to bring about an ideal society, since this was something that would evolve naturally by individualistic change when the conditions were right.

The turban that Vivekananda used to wear is generally believed to be suggested by Maharaja of Khetri. But some followers of Ayyavazhi claim that Vivekananda visited the Swamithope Pathi during his visit to Kanyakumari in December 1892 and believe that he was impressed by the principles behind rituals of this monistic faith, such as wearing a head gear during worship in temple, worshipping in front of mirror etc., and started wearing a turban then on. Some also suggest that Vivekananda received some spiritual instructions from the disciples of Ayya Vaikundar.

There is no mention of this in Vivekananda's biographies or works. It is also said that while he was a child, he was impresssed by the turban of the horse cab driver, who used to ferry his father on his daily work. Subsequently when he renounced the world and took to sanyasa, he started using one himself. *Though it may not be obvious but Swami Vivekananda inspired India's (whom he loved so dearly) freedom struggle movement. His writings inspired a whole generation of freedom fighters in Bengal in particular and India at large. Most prominent were Subhas Chandra Bose, Aurobindo and countless others.*

His books (compiled from lectures given around the world) on the four are very influential and still seen as fundamental texts for anyone interested in the Hindu practice of Yoga. His letters are of great literary and spiritual value.

He was also a very good singer and a poet. He had composed many songs including his favourite "Kali the Mother". He used humour for his teachings and was also an excellent cook. His language is very free flowing and much of the charms of his original English letters have been destroyed by copybookish translation into Bengali. His own Bengali writings stand testimony to the fact that he believed that words - spoken or written should be for making things easier to understand rather than show off the speaker or writer's knowledge.

Many years after his death, Rabindranath Tagore (a prominent member of the Brahmo Samaj) had said: *If you want to know India, study Vivekananda. In him everything is positive and nothing negative.* Incidentally, in the earlier years Tagore did not have much respect for Swami Vivekananda for his idol-worshipping. On the other hand, *Swamiji* was not particularly impressed by Tagore, though he had been interacting with Tagore's father Maharshi Debendra Nath. *Swamiji* was a very good singer and used to sing lots of *Bhajans,* including about twelve written and composed by Tagore. Another contemporary Sri Aurobindo, actually considered *Swamiji* as his mentor. While in Alipore Jail, Sri Aurobindo used to be visited by Swami Vivekananda in his meditation. *Swamiji* guided Sri Aurobindo's yoga.

Mahatma Gandhi who strived for a lot of reform in Hinduism himself, said: *Swami Vivekananda's writings need no introduction from anybody. They make their own irresistible appeal.* Abroad, he has had some interactions with Max Mueller and Romain Rolland. The latter also wrote a book in 1930 entitled *Vie de Vivekananda (Life of Vivekananda).*

SRI AUROBINDO

Sri Aurobindo has been variously described as the greatest Indian philosopher of modern times, an outstanding leader of India's freedom movement, an astute political and social thinker, an inspired poet and a towering spiritual personality. For his contribution to a rational and scientific approach to knowledge, he can appropriately be thought of as an Evolutionary or Integral Scientist. His entire thought and work were an endeavor to integrate all aspects of life based on the evolution of consciousness. The research activities of MSS are based on Sri Aurobindo's integral conception of human personality, social development and evolution.

"Of all modern Indian writers Aurobindo – successively poet, critic, scholar, thinker, nationalist, humanist – is the most significant and perhaps the most interesting. Yet few have heard of him in England or America. This is a pity, for he should make a special appeal to the intelligent Anglo-Saxon. He is not an arm-chair philosopher, but a man who, having led a life of intense activity, has retired to brood over it, if one may say so of a Hindu, in the dim light of Gothic cathedral. In fact, he is a new type of thinker, one who combines in his vision the alacrity of the West with the illumination of the East. To study his writings is to enlarge the boundaries of one's knowledge.

"..... He gave up everything, and withdrew to Pondicherry to follow the new light that had been vouchsafed to him. What was this light? To be of active help to the new world which, in his opinion, was struggling to be born. To achieve this aim he had, first, to make of his body, mind and spirit a delicate and precise instrument, and then to learn to draw from this instrument the maximum of its possibilities.

Aurobindo cannot be dismissed as one who happens to have written a few fine books. He..... writes as though he were standing among the stars, with the constellations for his companions. "That he is a great idealist goes without saying; but he is not an idealist in the Shankaran or Berkeleian manner. He has achieved a reconciliation between matter and spirit. They are, in his opinion, one and indivisible. It is not necessary, he says, to prove the existence of God. He is: in Him we live and move and have our being. The world is His manifestation, and so is as real as God.

If it is a dream, it is a dream in Reality and made of the same stuff as this Reality. If the gold is real, Aurobindo tells us, the vessel of gold is as real and can never be a figment of the brain. "Aurobindo is no visionary. He has always acted his dreams. 'Truth of philosophy,' he has said, 'is of a merely theoretical value unless it can be lived'..... an internationalist, not in a dreamy nor yet in a conventional manner, but by inner compulsion – the compulsion of thought leading to an inevitable conclusion. Long before others, he spoke of 'one world.' His final word is that we are, whether we like it or not, 'members one of another.' Unless we realize this truth, and act upon it, we shall never have peace and goodwill on earth."

RABINDRANATH TAGORE

The tendency towards a newer and fresher reconstruction of Indian Philosophic thought has been noticeable during the past two decades. In India the impetus was given by the fresh thought infused by Christian Civilization. At times such an infusion has the effect of annihilating the original thought of the country wherever such thought is weak and irrational. At other times and places, it has the opposite effect of provoking fresh thought conflict. Every conflict has also the effect of making one probe deeper into one's own thought, and when this conflict is intellectual, without being dogmatic, it stimulates assimilation. This has been the case wherever the thought which was provoked by this Christian conflict was strong and profound-as in India. Thus stimulated and thrown on the defensives the Indian philosopher diving deep into his own culture and thought, brought to the surface several tendencies, quite old but now re-lived in his own being thought that soared without a material foundation now tried to find its bed-rock in human life and being.

It is characteristic of Rabindranath's philosophy to call it the 'Religion of Man'. In his Religion of Man, Rabindranath sketches beautifully and arrestingly the way of expression of the Universal Spirit—within the conditions of space and time. He shows that the Spirit had at first taken the quantitative direction and found at last a quantitative mass-infinity undoubtedly an infinity but as far from real infinity of Spirit. Mere mass without integral organization leads of to disruption and results in the giving -up of beauty and simplicity for the sake of gorgeousness and unnecessary, unwieldy and uncouth decoration. This could be seen in forms of the pre—historic mosters. Their very size prevented them form protecting themselves against attacks from less massive and more lithe and better organized creatures.

Spirit bloated and grew vast as it were misinterpreting its own fundamental nature of intensive infinity. But checked and prevented from growing vaster by the very fact of the survival of the fittest and made to recognize that size by no means makes for efficiency in deference, there originated an orientation towards real evolution of spirit which is conscious interiority and intelligent adjustment. Man's evolution as a spiritual being was assured thereafter and coherent organization became the chief character of evolutionary history. Real power consists not in size but in organization and intelligent direction. As this development progressed, we may say that the unfolding of the main purpose now pronouncedly became human instead of remaining natural.

The natural passes over in its conscious character into the human. Therefore does man start with the artificial by reconstructing conditions far from those of the animal (for that has been civilization) only shows that the spiritual end has been the transformation of the unconscious organization into the conscious. It is not true to say that human destiny is at cross-purposes with that of Nature. Natural process and human organization are but one continuous enfoldment of the self-same purpose of Spiritual Life. The natural process and human organization tend to the expression of the Divine- God.

The highest truth of man is the full creative expression of himself in the light of eternal Life of Man, the man himself universalized. From the repetitive and the imitative instinctive-life, through all the sorrows and defeats, the spirit in nature tries to follow this trend up towards the complete exemplification of this purpose of Spirit is Man (purushottama) who is the goal of individual human beings. If we are confronted with the question whether or not we should take present human beings as representative, in however little measure of the universal, we must admit that man is yet unborn, but thought unborn he is yet with us in our inmost purposes, and wherever man has caught the purpose of universal life, he has to that extent become the true man-a universal being.

Not in his primitive desires which are as yet animal because unconscious expressions of an urge towards his true nature, (every urge within the human breast and animal life but the expression of the spirit within, struggling to release its meaning and life), but in his rationalized consciousness which recognizes the greater and the All – 'surplus'. This is the purpose and goal of individual life. Reason is universal and truly spiritual, and reason in man is the sure code guide towards universal Life. This Reason, however, is not the intellect which tries to thwart the main ends of universality but confines itself to particular ends, but it is intuition which is the appreciator of the harmony of life and its meaning and which guides the conduct of man accordingly.

We find, thus, that Rabindranath holds the humanistic thesis that the goal of the world or cosmos is human and that its realization is a possibility only when the individuals act consciously towards the fullest exemplification of the Universal Man. This inner realization or consciousness of Man is essentially the recognition of oneself. Some people hold that evolutionary history is a fantasy and an illusion. It has no reality. It is mere appearance. In fact, they even go to the extent of saying that the individual human being himself is an illusion, caught up in an illusion, trying to reach an illusion. Rabindranath holds that the individual souls are not illusion, that the world of which we know is certainly not an illusion, though it is an appearance-quite a different thing.

It is an intimation of the more real thought by itself and in itself if it is as yet understandable. To deprive truth of its appearance is to deprive it of its best part. "When you deprive truth of its appearance, it loses the best part of its reality. For appearance is a personal relationship, it is for me ... "This appreciation which seems to be the surface but which carries the message of the inner spirit" is something that cannot be denied reality because it is the only manner we can know the real at all. To create an opposition between reality and appearance is to misjudge the nature of reality. It is due to the perversity of intellectual obscurantists and abstractionists turned mystical, that such a change has been maintained and human values sacrificed. Rabindranath, though an intuitionist, does not sacrifice, as pseudo—mistics have done, the world of values.

To him the human values are absolute truth. He does not join the intuitionists who maintain that in some sense the reality which is experiences or the appearance is a distorted or segmented reality. The charge which Bergson levels against intellect as the fundamental instrument of mind which has an innate separate and utilitarian bent and which therefore distorts reality to further the ends of practical life is only partially true. Bergson has greater influence on modern thought. His intuition resembles superficially the integrative consciousness of Hindu thought, and facile writers on Indian Philosophy have adapted his description without looking deeper into it. Intellect has the primary and inevitable tendency to abstract experience and to contemplate on those abstracted experiences, which also abstracted, lose life and movement, their peculiar individuality and completeness.

When it is exercised to its fullest, it becomes a satisfying instrument neither valuable nor practicable. But when it is used within limits for the purpose of understanding, it becomes defining and analyzing activity. But such a definition and analysis can be valuable only when one has complete knowledge of the object. The real then has to be understood as a whole and not in segments. Knowledge of it can be complete only when its unique character is realized. To enter into the object and understand it as a whole is the way of intuition. The whole is a definite uniqueness, not a vague undefined experience, though to describe it by words may not be possible. When Bergson calls Intuition 'intellectual sympathy', he means intellect as limited in its tendency and as having for its main purpose wholeness and completeness, and as characterized by emotion or instinctive dynamism.

Bergson intellect can be abused as much as intuition can be. Everything is sanctified or defiled by the goal to which it tends. Instincts are proclaimed holy when they aim at the liberation of true values within the individual life. Reason, then must apply to experience and evaluable it, draw out its significance and express its inmost aspiration. It is only then that it becomes truly spiritual. To hold that intellect and intuition are opposities, emergents out of life which contradict and thwart the purpose of each other, is to hold a view which is damaging to philosophy and to life alike. Nor are action and thought contradictories. Pragmatism is perfectly right when it affirms this criterion of workability.

Only it fails to see the real springs of practical action. Ultimate knowledge is really a synthesis, a synthesis of thought and action. This knowledge will lead not to the abstract impersonality of knowledge and reality but to the concrete personality of reality. Reality is a synthesis, a whole that ought to be apprehended as a Whole – not merely as nature, nor merely as spirit but as a unity comprising both the subjective and the objective. In man as a psycho-physical being, it finds its first resolution of this dualism of the subjective and the objective. The objective - view of the scientist is a partial representation of the whole. The Scientist is too preoccupied with the constancies in nature, its laws of causality and regular occurrence. He tries to discover those impersonal principles of nature that order it.

He certainly does not know the future but he can deduce or calculate the chances. But the fact of chance always makes him uncertain as to the individual events happening one way or the other. The past is capable of exact determination but the future is pregnant with the impossibilities of today and of the past. The nature of the world seems therefore incapable of any purely mechanical explanation. The subjective world-view on the other hand depends only upon one's personal whims and fancies. Having constructed a world of imagination the individual seeks to live in his own creation. The individual thus concentered in his own person, living an isolated life, unrelated to other lives ends in a life of glorified fantasy of egoistc existence.

The world, according to the subjective thinker is

individual creation, having no objective or trans-subjective reference. But even he finds that there is such a thing as objective commonness in existence, which is referred to as identical by all beings, even if such an identity is only for the sake of practical life. This objectivity is affirmed of the world with respect to the individual selves who experience it, because it is obvious that the individual knowledge is too little and narrow to enable him to create a universe more than himself. Even subjective Idealists like Berkeley also maintain that there must be a Spiritual Being greater then the individual whose creative fancy this world is. This they call God.

All who alone fashions and creates this world, and has as his fundamental nature creative activity. Before His manifestation we are nothing, and our understanding of Him fails to grasp the plan of the unfoldment of His Nature. The objective world also strives to gain significance through subjective life that so fashions it as to express the sure purpose of Spirit.

There is an inner pulsation within it that seems to vibrate in unison with the purpose of human Life: else it would not be possible to organize it. Within it Spirit is struggling to express itself. Its very orderliness (which some idealists think is imposed by man's schematizing mind) suggests the organized nature of its being.

The world, therefore, is spiritual not because its substance is spirit (spirit is no substance here but purposive governing activity), but because its order and unfoldment are coterminous with the world of the subject and his ideals. The world is ideal because its ground is in something which is forcing expression in and though its texture.

This ethical trend within its being is what makes even the most hardened realists affirm the ideal character of reality. Idealism is true only when we understand it in terms of ethical life, not in terms of the philosophers of Absolutistic schools of thought who somehow call themselves idealists. This possible organization of the objective world by the subject is a conscious process – a process which is planned by the individuals who have recognized this ideal as the goal of Man. In personality, then, the resolution of subjective individualism and objective impersonalism take place.

The Personality of Man attains its fullest scope and measure when its infinity is realized within the finite, when the absolute values of Spirit are adequately represented and assured within the relative. For, "Man has found out the great paradox that what is limited is not imprisoned within its limits; it is ever moving and therefore shedding its finitude every moment. In fact, imperfection is not a negation of perfection; finitude is not contradictory to infinity; they are but completeness manifested in parts, infinity revealed within limits." What exactly is this ideal nature? Is it something that is far- off and somehow influencing the world-process?

Rabindranath holds the view that the Ideal Man is constantly immanently sustaining the process of the revelation of His Being in terms of the relative and the finite. Such sustaining may be compared to the teleological immanence of Spirit of Aristotle' theory. We are conscious of this Ideal in our most lucid moments, in our appreciation of art and nature, in Beauty, in other words, in the sacrificial moment when we offer ourselves entirely for the person we love, in the expression of our truth which is direct and unequivocal, and in the just acts of equity. We cannot deny that which we feel so surely. Even the most extreme of the a moralists and immoralists cannot deny that life is governed by such principles as beauty, truth and equity, because we know in the depths of our being that we are thoroughly governed by such Ideals. We even affirm that the Ideal is immanent within us sustaining our very life.

The more consciously we express and the more consciously we are guided by this ideal power, the more we become men, or as Tagore would express it, Man. The arguments of Tagore therefore, for the existence of God are cosmo— teleological as well as ontological. But to be able to express our faith in God we have to be conscious of our real Self. "We have our personal self. It has desires which struggle to create a world where they could have their unrestricted activity and satisfaction. While it goes on, we discover that our self-realization reaches its perfection in the abnegation of self. This fact has made us aware that the individual finds his meaning in a fundamental reality comprehending all individuals – the reality which is the moral and spiritual basis of human values. This belongs to our religion.

As science is the liberation of our knowledge in universal reason, which cannot be other than human reason, religion is the liberation of our individual personality in the universal person who is human all the same." Thus the ideal of reason which science lays down, is the liberation of itself from finite and relativity; the ideal of love is the liberation of the individual love from the finitude of its individual relations or selfishness. Sometimes one feels that this must be a progressive process—this release of the individual love from the bond of individual relationship, even as the body of scientific laws goes on liberating itself from the relativity to which it is restricted by the very nature of experience.

It must, however, be remembered that in Science there is an objective impersonality which integrates itself with other laws of science, equally impersonal. But the movement of love is, on the other hand, personal; and its enlargement does not lead to impersonal contemplation but to concrete expression towards all. There is an ascent to perfection – a gradual liberation by the submission of our wills to the sovereignty of the Universal will, which is universal Love. There is a gradual submission of our desires to the happiness of the family; the family is sacrificed for the happiness of the nation, the race, and finally, Man. All sacrifice is inevitably attended with pain. But even pain becomes a valuable asset, it becomes the measure of our Love. All suffering is due to the inability to sacrifice oneself –or rather to adjust oneself to the perfect Ideal which constantly seeks expression through us.

This pain is the intrinsic quality of sacrifice, is indeed, the joy of love and giving for the sake of Man. Humanity must realize this Universal will and submit to its greatest expression which cannot be expressed in terms of human experience. The voice of Conscience might be considered to be the chord which catches the rhythmic vibrations of the Universal Mind. The voice of beauty, the call of Truth, is the same for all, in the sense that it manifests the universality of its nature. So, it is absolutely certain that there is a universal Mind which works through the relative finite centres or selves. No less imperative is the call of Love. "Want of love is a degree of callousness: for love is the perfection of consciousness. We do not love because we do not comprehend, or rather we do not comprehend because we do not love".

The private individual has to shed his privateness and assume universal significance which is that of the Universal Person. The Upanishad says "Know thou the one soul. It is the bridge leading to the Immortal Being. This is the ultimate end of man, to find the One which is in him; which is his truth, which is his Soul; the key with which he opens the gate of spiritual life, the heavenly Kingdom." The freedom which characterizes moral life is really the freedom of the Spirit which has assumed several modes of expressing the infinite in terms of the finite. To ask why there is so much suffering if there is a God or a universal Being is to ask a question of inconsequence. The freedom of the individual is a condition necessary for the creative life of spirit. Craving for uniformity, men create a state of uniformity, but it has not attraction of distinction nor the richness of beauty, nor the rhythm of music. All true love is characterized by joy, and that is because all love is soul-offering.

All true co-operation is based on the free acceptance of love which cannot be brought into being by force. If there is freedom which sometimes ends in severance of relations-independence-it is because there is another element which forces the individual into loving and union. But the element of severance is, according to Tagore, only an appearance, and the element of union is the ultimate truth. Anarchy that regions in the moral life of the individual are a condition precedent to real co-operative life, the life of love. Just as we have to pass though 'the valley of the shadow of death' to attain to Happiness, we have to pass through the stage of saverance ere we attain to Love.

The more we adjust our ends to the universal goal as

revealed by our conscience (which is not to be mistaken with the norms and standards of life but which in some measure expresses the fundamental universality of the values of truth, love and beauty) the more we become truly free. Then the Godhead becomes one with the individual, the infinite is revealed in the finite mind. This could be possible only if the universal Being is really human and not the phantom of intellectual philosophy. God is a person of universal significance, whose nature is Love and Beauty. His relation to men is integral, or organic. "It is only the Vaishnava religion that has boldly declared that God has bound himself to man, and in that consists the greatest glory of human existence.

In the spell of the wonderful rhythm of the finite he fetters himself at every step and thus gives his love out in music in his most perfect lyrics of beauty.' It is because the personality of God is human, there is possible the rapport with the Infinite All. It only means that God's Personality is superior to the impersonality of the logical Absolute. The impersonality of God is his Truth-aspect. God interpreted through Logic appears to be an abstraction, a concept. But God understood in terms of value, of moral life and religion is personality. "Some modern philosophers of Europe who are directly or indirectly indebted to the Upanishads, far from realizing their debt, a negation of all that is in the world. In a word, that the infinite being is to be found nowhere else except in metaphysics. It may be that such a doctrine is to be is found and still is prevalent with a section of our countrymen. But that is certainly not in accord with a pervading spirit of the Indian Mind".

The metaphysical Absolute is a result of pure scholasticism. It is a tenet held by none except the intellectualist thinkers. All religious thinkers accept no such description of God. Nor is the destination of man the abstraction of the Absolute. There is not the slightest evidence to support the view that increasing understanding, sympathy and co-operation tend to make real personalities disappear. It is only those who have developed the fundamental persistence of immortal existence. "It is precisely the stability and originality of people of character that keeps the world from stagnation," say Rabindranath.

The truth of our private selves does not lie in our idiosyncracies but in the moral nature of the freedom that we possess and exercise. Rabindranath believes in the Joy of existence. He accepts the Unity of all things, Advita the Absolute Divine All. In God according to Rabindranath the super-personal God en rapport with individual God manifests himself in the parts. But no part can absorb the whole. The part cannot defeat the ends of the whole by the accentuation of itself. It must subordinate its individuality to the whole; if it does not, it perishes. Civilization is the continual discovery of the transcendental Humanity or God. All men, therefore should try to live for Man, for it is His Joy that the world reveals. Therefore is the significance of the parts and the snatches of finite experience realised only when we go beyond the purely partial, and investigate the purpose for which the parts stands, not merely in order to plan out the whole as the metaphysician or the geographer does. It is only the artist who sees the All and the One, and understands the goal of human existence.

Without the vision of the All, we are certain to sink down in the morass of internecine quarrels, and Civilization would become nothing other then selfish enterprise. The Artist is the real Seer,' he has sees beyond the temporal and the fragmentary and the temporal. The Poets and the Artists alone can save the world, for theirs is the Vision of Beauty, Truth and Bliss. They alone can plan the future with sympathy and true Love. They alone, having intuition, perceive the Man sub specie eternitatis, whilst the individual beings look at it in fragments. Rabindranath has taken uponhimself the task of planning such an education and his International University at Bolpur aspires to bring into being a culture which shall reflect the Man and not any particular individual or nation or race. Not the renunciation of life but the fulfillment of Life is immortal Joy and unending beauty. That should be the main aim of Knowledge. The world is the Creative Excellence of the Man, the Lila, play of Divine Perfection.

In evaluating Rabindranath's Philosophy, at the very outset, it must be said that it makes no pretence at offering a complete exposition of the moot-points of intellectual philosophers. In spite of its poetic character, there are certain features that demand attention and appreciation even, from the intellectualists. There is a spiritual purpose, says Rabindranath, that runs through the ages. This Purpose is Man. Rabindranath's theory does not, however, clearly explain how the Divine Mind finds projection in the individual. Rebindranath assumes that this perfection of Man will find its fullest expression in an altogether utopian order of existence where the intellectual and the intuitive cooperation of all the several peoples of the world shall reign supreme and the peoples shall give to one another their particular riches of spiritual experience. Thus the completest Deity comes into being.

Man, then is the whole Universe of existence come to complete expression in human terms. Two interpretations are possible here. We may conceive of the whole universe as the One Purushottama appeating diversified but yet holding the unity which is the very nature of His Spiritual existence. The several individuals, then, are parts somehow, reaching beyond themselves, even as our individual organs strive for the maintenance of the unity of the body,— to express the infinite purpose of the Deity, whose instruments they become. A more conscious realization of the interdependence of the parts and the whole makes for complete Oneness. It is necessary in the case of human beings that the unconsciousness that is a characteristic of functioning of the organs of the body must give place of the conscious and deliberate offering of the several parts of the life of the whole which is Man.

The other alternative is the Divine expresses Himself fully each of His perfections 3 Plato affirms that the world only mirrors the eternal Ideas and this mirroring is an imperfect and unreal manifestation. Rabindranath is a realist and does not accept that the world is illusory. Plato holds that the individually, and in each individual he is complete and full. The Goal of the Process is then Society. Rabindranath inclines to the former view. The Goal is Man. Here again we have two alternatives. Should the surrender of the parts to the whole be made once and forever? This course has a parallel in the Social contract theory of Hobbes or should the surrender be a conscious endeavour at every moment of individual existence? The former surrender becomes nugatory after a time for there is no love and real affection but mere habit, the latter love and real affection but mere habit, the latter becomes the real revealing affection to the unity of the whole.

The description of evolution by Rabindranath has novel reatures. It is quite distinct from anything that we know of in India or western thought, and effectively reconciles several western theories. Evolution of Spirit into Matter and a return to itself through its texture is the real though of the East. The summit of this return is Man.

The immanent urge within matter is Spirit. How this urge expresses itself through extension at first and then by a return to its intensive character has been explained. Rabindranath Pure Idea God, the Highest Essence can be known only by discovering the essences in existence and subsuming then under the most universal Being. Rabindranath affirms the realization of the pure Being in the values of the universe, of space and time. It is not through intellectual generalization that will lead to the Concrete Universal Being, Man, but the loving that surrender to the All. This concept is the most intriguing in Rabindranath. Whatever he means this to be identical with the Leviathan of Hobbes or with the Utopia of the Anarchists; whether the Absolute of Bosanquet or the World of souls who have attained co-operative freedom is not quite clear. Concurs with the view of those thinkers who have been deeply influenced by Aristotle, viz Bergson, Lloyd Morgan, and General Smuts.

That Spirit as vital energy fashions and creates now forms or patterns of life for the purpose of expressing itself adequately and that the progress of evolution is guided by the principle of adequate expression of Spirit is the main thesis of these thinkers. Lioyed Morgan and Bergson agree in so far as they posit new forms of spirit as reflex, instinct, intellect, and intuition. We cannot derive any one of these forms from the rest, though they are equally manifestation of the identical Elan. Tagore does not however, visualize the emergence of these forms clearly. He seems to follow Bergson in so far as the impeding of one form of Spirit by another is concerned, though not with respect to all forms of Spirit. The quantitative movement of Spirit impedes the qualitative.

He follows more closely Yadava Prakasa's cleavage theory of evolution. Originally spirit began to function in the direction of quantitative infinity- and matter was the result. When it began its movement towards intensity and qualitative infinity, it created Life and man. Its final expression through Man is the transcendent – over humanity—God. The original matrix of existence is the Absolute Undifferentiated Spirit. In the theory of Yadava, the cosmic process is immediate, and sudden. In Rabindranath it is closely linked with time. In both theories, the identity of the One Spirit becomes the unity of the three in relative existence, and by becoming such it reveals an intenser harmony and humanity. More so in Rabindranath's Philosophy.

The theory of Raabindranath does not account for the nature of the many-ness of the individuals as fully and satisfactorily as maybe desired. But his theory of sacrifice of less perfect individuals for the purpose of the most perfect being, Man, deserves consideration. General Smut explains that in evolution less perfect wholes are subsumed under larger and more perfect wholes. The completer whole reveals some peculiar characteristic over and above the qualities of lesser wholes that compose it if not altering them. There is visible a newer function emerging from such an interrelation of wholes. Functionally, its activity is not the mere sum of the functions of the units which from it.

At first, in evolution, small cells (unicellular organisms) are independent units. Later they group themselves to form more complex bodies with diversified functions. These groupings brings into being functional characteristics like instinct, intellect, consciousness, and intuition. These functional characteristics are therefore the quality of the wholes, the more complex and diversified, and the more dominant and delicate are these forms of spiritual activity. The highest is the organization on the physical basis of wholeness is the human body. These units now progress towards the still more complex spiritual units, the family, Society, community, State, and finally, Deity.

The last is the completes personally, the most real and perfect whole. Its nature is transcendent to anything contained in the several units. In an ideal sense the Deity as the spirit moving towards the whole is immanent at every stage of the process. In Rabindranath's theory, however, the Ideal is more powerfully present. His idealistic tendency is greater, and resembles strongly the Hegelian. If we can compare this Ideal Deity with Man, Narayana, we have not only the explanation. Of Evolution but also the realization of the Most perfect whole, the Supreme Personality, God who is organic with the world. It is not clear in Rabindranath's philosophy whether humans the ideal implication of the parts in the whole, or the natural biological implication of the units in the whole as in Smuts' theory.

Ranbindranath speaks about the sacrifice of the individual units for the gradual realization of the unity of the family, community, nation, state, universe, each in turn being sacrificed for the sake of MAN. Rabindranath does not mean to annual the individuals or communities, but he intends to make them whole, so as to bring into being the Ideal expression of MAN. As a Seer, Rabindranath sees this ideal purpose of Man, as a poet he sings about Him, for this perfect being is not a mere emergent possibility but an actual fact when we Love deeply, truly and spontaneously. Evil andchance are not the truth of existence. Despair is not the last word; tragedy is not the highest summit of spirituality. Delight through sacrifice is the highest truth of existence. This entire world is the Lila, the creative Delight of Man – to Him who sees this within Himself.

MAHATAMA GANDHI

Given Gandhi's values and his vision of what constituted

a truly civilized and free India, it was not surprising that he developed firm views on education. Education not only moulds the new generation, but reflects a society's fundamental assumptions about itself and the individuals which compose it. His experience in South Africa not only changed his outlook on politics but also helped him to see the role education played in that struggle. He was aware that he had been a beneficiary of Western education and for a number of years while he was in South Africa he still tried to persuade Indians to take advantage of it. However, it was not until the early years of this century, when he was in his middle thirties, that he became so opposed to English education that he could write about 'the rottenness of this education' and that 'to give millions a knowledge of English is to enslave them... that, by receiving English education, we have enslaved the nation'.

He was enraged that he had to speak of Home Rule or Independence in what was clearly a foreign tongue, that he could not practice in court in his mother tongue, that all official documents were in English as were all the best newspapers and that education was carried out in English for the chosen few. He did not blame the colonial powers for this. He saw that it was quite logical that they would want an elite of native Indians to become like their rulers in both manners and values. In this way, the Empire could be consolidated. Gandhi blamed his fellow Indians for accepting the situation. Later in his life he was to declare that 'real freedom will come only when we free ourselves of the domination of Western education, Western culture and Western way of living which have been ingrained in us... Emancipation from this culture would mean real freedom for us'.

As we have seen, Gandhi had not only rejected colonial education but also put forward a radical alternative. So what was this alternative? What was so radical about it? First of all, I need to say a word about Gandhi's attitude to industrialization. He was, in fact, absolutely opposed to modern machinery. In his collected works, he refers to machinery as having impoverished India, that it was difficult to measure the harm that Manchester had done to them by producing machine-made cloth which, in turn, ruined the internal market for locally produced handwoven goods. Typically of Gandhi, however, he does not blame Manchester or the mill owners. 'How can Manchester be blamed?' he writes. 'We wore Manchester cloth and this is why Manchester wove it'. However, he notes that where cloth mills were not introduced in India, in places such as Bengal, the original hand-weaving occupation was thriving.

Where they did have mills e.g. in Bombay, he felt that the workers there had become slaves. He was shocked by the conditions of the women working in the mills of Bombay and made the point that before they were introduced these women were not starving. He maintained that 'if the machinery craze grows in our country, it will become an unhappy land'. What he wanted was for Indians to boycott *all* machine-made goods not just cloth. He was quite clear when he asked the question 'What did India do before these articles were introduced?' and then answered his own question by stating 'Precisely the same should be done today.

As long as we cannot make pins without machinery, so long will we do without them. The tinsel splendour of glassware we will have nothing to do with, and we will make wicks, as of old, with home-grown cotton and use hand-made earthen saucers or lamps. So doing, we shall save our eyes and money and support *swadeshi* and so shall we attain Home Rule'. Within this context of the need for a machine-less society, Gandhi developed his ideas on education. The core of his proposal was the introduction of productive handicrafts in the school curriculum. The idea was not simply to introduce handicrafts as a compulsory school subject, but to make the learning of a craft the centrepiece of the entire teaching programme.

It implied a radical restructuring of the sociology of school knowledge in India, where productive handicrafts had been associated with the lowest groups in the hierarchy of the caste system. Knowledge of the production processes involved in crafts, such as spinning, weaving, leather-work, pottery, metal-work, basket-making and book binding, had been the monopoly of specific caste groups in the lowest stratum of the traditional social hierarchy. Many of them belonged to the category of 'untouchables'. India's own tradition of education as well as the colonial education system had emphasized skills such as literacy and acquisition of knowledge of which the upper castes had a monopoly.

Gandhi's proposal intended to stand the education system on its head. The social philosophy and the curriculum of what he called 'basic education' thus favoured the child belonging to the lowest stratum of society. In such a way it implied a programme of social transformation. It sought to alter the symbolic meaning of 'education' and to change the established structure of opportunities for education. Why Gandhi proposed the introduction of productive handicrafts into the school system was not really as outrageous as may appear. What he really wanted was for the schools to be self-supporting, as far as possible.

There were two reasons for this. Firstly, a poor society such as India simply could not afford to provide education for all children unless the schools could generate resources from within. Secondly, the more financially independent the schools were, the more politically independent they could be. What Gandhi wanted to avoid was dependence on the state which he felt would mean interference from the centre. Above all else, Gandhi valued self-sufficiency and autonomy. These were vital for his vision of an independent India made up of autonomous village communities to survive. It was the combination of *swaraj* and *swadeshi* related to the education system.

A state system of education within an independent India would have been a complete contradiction as far as Gandhi was concerned. He was also of the opinion that manual work should not be seen as something inferior to mental work. He felt that the work of the craftsman or labourer should be the ideal model for the 'good life'. Schools which were based around productive work where that work was for the benefit of all were, therefore, carrying out education of the whole person - mind, body and spirit. The right to autonomy that

Gandhi's educational plan assigns to the teacher in the context of the school's daily curriculum is consistent with the libertarian principles that he shared with Tolstoy.

Gandhi wanted to free the Indian teacher from interference from outside, particularly government or state bureaucracy. Under colonial rule, the teacher had a prescribed job to do that was based on what the authorities wanted the children to learn. Textbooks were mandatory so that Gandhi found that 'the living word of the teacher has very little value. A teacher who teaches from textbooks does not impart originality to his pupils'.

Gandhi's plan, on the other hand, implied the end of the teacher's subservience to the prescribed textbook and the curriculum. It presented a concept of learning that simply could not be fully implemented with the help of textbooks. Of equal, if not more importance, was the freedom it gave the teacher in matters of curriculum. It denied the state the power to decide what teachers taught and what they did in the classroom. It gave autonomy to the teacher but it was, above all, a libertarian approach to schooling that transferred power from the state to the village.

Gandhi's basic education was, therefore, an embodiment of his perception of an ideal society consisting of small, self-reliant communities with his ideal citizen being an industrious, self-respecting and generous individual living in a small co-operative community. For informal educators, we can draw out a number of useful pointers. First, Gandhi's insistence on autonomy and self-regulation is reflected in the ethos of informal education. Gandhi's conception of basic education was concerned with learning that was generated within everyday life which is the basis on which informal educators work. It was also an education focused on the individual but reliant on co-operation between individuals. There is also a familar picture of the relationships between educators and students/learners:

A teacher who establishes rapport with the taught, becomes one with them, learns more from them than he teaches them. He who learns nothing from his disciples is, in my opinion, worthless. Whenever I talk with someone I learn from him. I take from him more than I give him. In this way, a true teacher regards himself as a student of his students. If you will teach your pupils with this attitude, you will benefit much from them. Lastly, it was an education that aimed at educating the whole person, rather than concentrating on one aspect. It was a highly moral activity.

RADHAKRISHNAN

Radhakrishnan argued that Western philosophers, despite all claims to objectivity, were biased by theological influences of their own culture. He wrote books on Indian philosophy according to Western academic standards, and made Indian philosophy worthy of serious consideration in the West. In his book "Idealist View of Life" he has made a powerful case for the importance of intuitive thinking as opposed to purely intellectual forms of thought. He is well known for his commentaries on the Prasthana Trayi namely, the Bhagavadgita, the Upanishads and the Brahma Sutra. He was elected as a Fellow of the British Academy in 1938. He was awarded the Bharat Ratna in 1954, and the Order of Merit in 1963.

He received the Peace Prize of the German Book Trade in 1961, and the Templeton Prize in 1975, a few months before his death. He donated the entire Templeton Prize amount to Oxford University. The Oxford University instituted the Radhakrishnan Scholarships in 1989 which was later renamed the Radhakrishnan Chevening Scholarships in his memory.

"It is not God that is worshipped but the authority that claims to speak in His name. Sin becomes disobedience to authority not violation of integrity."

KRISHNAMURTI

As much will be said throughout this paper on Krishnamurti's perspective on education, I can confine my summary comments here to saying simply that education was seen as towards the fullest development of the full human being. From the full body of his work, we can conclude that, for Krishnamurti, education is 1.) educating the whole person (all parts of the person), 2.) educating the person as a whole (not as an assemblage of parts), and 3.) educating the person within a whole (as part of society, humanity, nature, etc.) from which it is not meaningful to extract that person. From the above it probably goes without saying, though it can not be said often enough, education is not about preparation for only a part of life (like work) but is about preparation for the whole of life and the deepest aspects of living.

Now that some attempt has been made at summarising Jiddu Krishnamurti's approach to the nature of religiousness/religiosity, the nature of human beings, and the nature of education, I will try to support the main theme of this paper by presenting what Krishnamurti said about 1.) the intentions of education, 2.) the physical nature of the places in which education occurs, and 3.) the participants in education - the students and staff. I use the expression 'educational centres' instead of 'schools' as this is often the expression that Krishnamurti used, and because the educational centres that he founded were also meant to be places for adults to learn.

In English, or rather in the English of England, schools are specifically places for younger students. To support my theme I will show how Krishnamurti described the three elements mentioned above (the intentions, the places, and the participants) in religious terms, which has the added benefit of seeing the relationship they have with one another. I believe these three elements are the focus of much, if not most, of Krishnamurti's work on education.

THE INTENTIONS OF EDUCATION

Krishnamurti repeatedly stated the intentions of the education centres he founded in very unequivocal terms, and in very religious ones.... children... must be educated rightly... educated so that they become religious human beings. (Krishnamurti 1979)

Surely they must be centres of learning a way of life which is not based on pleasure, on self-centered activities, but on the understanding of correct action, the depth and beauty of relationship, and the sacredness of a religious life. (Krishnamurti 1981b) (Letter dated 15th October 1980)

These places exist for the enlightenment of man (Krishnamurti 1981b) (letter of 15th October 1979) Part of what is religious (as stated previously) is having a consciousness that sees reality, that sees 'what is'.

The difference between understanding what one is and striving to become something that one isn't is mirrored in the difference between wanting to discover 'what is' and striving to change 'what is'. Jiddu Krishnamurti didn't deny growth or change, in fact he applauded it. But meaningful growth and real material change without the all too frequent unfortunate side effects cannot be produced by just ensuring young people acquire knowledge and skills, and teaching them to conform to the strictures and demands of society in order to get on in life. In emphasising the latter, parents may comfort themselves that they are helping their children have material security, and schools may congratulate themselves on their examination results, but in Krishnamurti's view they are only adding to the sorrows and violence of the world. He decries the fact that most education is to......acquire a job or use that knowledge for self-satisfaction, for self-aggrandisement, to get on in the world.

Merely to cultivate technical capacity without understanding what is true freedom leads to destruction, to greater wars; and that is actually what is happening in the world. (Krishnamurti 1953a)

Merely to stuff the child with a lot of information, making him pass examinations, is the most unintelligent form of education. Krishnamurti often stated that the purpose of education is to bring about freedom, love, "the flowering of goodness" and the complete transformation of society. He specifically contrasts this to what he feels are the intentions of most schools which emphasise preparing young people to succeed materially in the society that exists (or a slightly altered one). Even though it is fashionable for schools to declare loftier goals, it is instructive to examine how much undivided attention is dedicated during the day to such lofty goals and how much time is given to preparation for earning a living. It is also instructive to examine what are felt to be the imperatives that shape the educational experience - things like the use of space, who and what determines pedagogic activities, the use of time, and what is assessed, by whom and for what.

As previously mentioned, a constant theme in Jiddu Krishnamurti's declarations of the intentions of education is freedom, but freedom for Krishnamurti is more inner in character than political. Of course, there is a connection between psychological freedom and outward compulsion - it is difficult to help a student find the former in a climate dominated by the latter - but it is not political freedom that interests Krishnamurti. Rather he is interested in the deeper freedom of the psyche and the spirit, the inner liberation that he felt was both the means and the ends of education. Freedom is at the beginning, it is not something to be gained at the end. There is no freedom at the end of compulsion; the outcome of compulsion is compulsion.

If you dominate a child, compel him to fit into a pattern, however idealistic, will he be free at the end of it? If we want to bring about a true revolution in education, there must obviously be freedom at the very beginning, which means that both the parent and the teacher must be concerned with freedom and not with how to help the child to become this or that. For Jiddu Krishnamurti, the intentions of education must be the inner transformation and liberation of the human being and, from that, society would be transformed. Education is intended to assist people to become truly religious. These intentions must not be just pleasant sounding ideals to which one pays lip service, and they are not to be arrived at by their opposites. And the religious intentions are not for some eventual goal, but for life in educational centres from moment to moment.

THE PHYSICAL NATURE OF THE PLACES OF EDUCATION

Krishnamurti felt that the physical nature of educational

centres was very important. He maintained that we are affected or informed by and therefore educated by far more than we suspect, and this is especially true of young impressionable minds. I will focus on what I believe to be the three elements that Krishnamurti spoke of most concerning the physicality of educational centres - 1.) the aesthetics, which includes order, 2.) special areas that Jiddu Krishnamurti felt should exist in the centres he founded, and by extension we can assume he would feel should exist in all schools, and 3.) the atmosphere he felt should prevail and which he usually spoke of as part of the physical nature of the centres, though one can argue that they are material only in a very special sense. Again, in keeping with the theme of my paper, I will show that Krishnamurti spoke of these four elements in religious terms.

- Aesthetics. The schools Krishnamurti founded are very beautiful places, and this is not by accident. Beauty is important, not just because it is pleasing, but because sensitivity to beauty is related to being religious and indispensable to the healthy growth of a child.

To be religious is to be sensitive to reality. Your total being - body, mind, and heart - is sensitive to beauty and ugliness, to the donkey tied to a post, to the poverty and filth in this town, to laughter and tears, to everything about you. From this sensitivity for the whole of existence springs goodness, love.

He himself was extremely attentive to details and critical of things that were badly done. He very understood if things could not be better because of real constraints, and he never pushed the administrators of his schools to produce anything that was beyond their means. However, if things were not good through slipshod handling, neglect or lack of sensitivity, then he felt it ran counter to an essential element in education as it ran counter to the religious life that the staff is meant to be living. To expect sensitivity to develop in a child when the staff is insensitive is to teach a very strong lesson in hypocrisy. Like several holistic educators before him (i.e. Rousseau,

Pestalozzi, and Fröbel) Jiddu Krishnamurti felt that some very important things could not be taught by proscription, these things need to be lived in the presence of the learner for them to be learned. And, like Keats, whose poetry he greatly admired, Krishnamurti felt that beauty was related to truth.

Perhaps we should include in this discussion on aesthetics what Krishnamurti felt about nature and education. This makes sense in that for Krishnamurti, nature was both beautiful and a demonstration of order. The educational centres Krishnamurti founded are invariably in parks or countryside. This was not just because he felt that nature was pleasing, but because he felt that a relationship with nature had important implications for living sanely and to a relationship with the sacred. He would not, however, condemn as hopeless, inner-city schools that don't have such luxuries, because nature was wholly available in the smallest part; a blade of grass, a house plant, or a gold fish.

That healing [of the mind] gradually takes place if you are with nature, with that orange on the tree, and the blade of grass that pushes through the cement, and the hills covered, hidden, by the clouds. This is not sentiment or romantic imagination but a reality of a relationship with everything that lives and moves on the earth. If you establish a relationship with it [nature] then you has relationship with mankind... But if you have no relationship with the living things on this earth you may lose whatever relationship you have with humanity, with human beings.

- Special areas that should exist in educational centres. Another physical aspect of the educational centres Jiddu Krishnamurti created, and another indication of the religiousness of education, was his insistence that the schools have special places for silence. He often spoke to the students of the importance of a quiet mind or silence so that they could observe their thoughts.

You see meditation means to have a very quiet, still mind, not a chattering mind; to have a really quiet body, quiet mind so that your mind becomes religious. The mind of a religious man is very quiet, sane, rational, logical- and one needs such a mind...

Jiddu Krishnamurti usually asked that these special places not be on the periphery of the schools, but in the centre of the them. Like a sanctum sanctorum, they were to be the heart, the space that generated the rest of the school. Contrary to most conceptions of schools, Krishnamurti felt that action was to be on the periphery and the insight born of silence was to be at the centre.

- Atmospheres. While atmospheres are generated by aesthetics, the setting, and the effect of special areas in educational centres, there are also atmospheres that are generated by the participants. At least part of the atmospheres generated by people can be deliberately generated. This atmosphere is. another link in understanding the religiousness of education. At Brockwood (the school that Krishnamurti founded in England) Krishnamurti frequently talked about the importance of generating an atmosphere that would itself have an effect on students the moment they arrived. Long discussions were held with the staff at Brockwood about the nature of such an atmosphere and how it might come about.

Jiddu Krishnamurti had no doubt that it was possible and necessary. It had more the ring of something religious than anything commonly associated with a school. It was something sacred that worked its own magic on people in a profound and transforming way. Without that real religious atmosphere, he felt that a school was empty, or worse, it was a parody of itself, a kind of Disneyesque impression of something real but with no real substance. Such an atmosphere, though distinct from the people in the schools, could not be separated from the people. A place may carry an atmosphere, but it is the people who create it or destroy it. To illustrate this he would cite places that at one time were known to have had very special and powerful atmospheres but which were destroyed through neglect, incompetence or corrupt behaviour.

Examples of this are some of the great cathedrals or

temples that have become tourist industries or money making enterprises, and so have lost any sense of religiousness. They became lifeless and without meaning even though they maintained all the physical appearance of their former selves. There was a very memorable discussion with Jiddu Krishnamurti at the end of his life when several representatives of different schools he founded in India, America, and England went for a walk with him.

He asked us all what would be left in his schools to indicate that they were Krishnamurti schools if the name Krishnamurti was removed and if all his books, audio tapes and video tapes were gone; and if something was still there, what would sustain it. It was a question about the all important ineffable qualities, the atmospheres of the educational centres, and it was a question about what we were generating; and it was a question answered by a very uncomfortable and telling silence.

THE PARTICIPANTS IN EDUCATION

There are, generally speaking, two kinds of participants in educational centres: staff and students. Jiddu Krishnamurti felt that any adult that was regularly in one of the centres was a staff member (regardless of function) and because of their regular contact with at least the educational environment if not the students, then they were in the position of educators. Everyone, staff and students, had something religious about their natures just by virtue of being human, but they had something more than that by virtue of their being in education. Krishnamurti didn't speak of them as religious figures (such as priests or accolades) but one thing that distinguishes participants in education from participants in some other social organizations (i.e. police officers, nurses, bankers, etc.) is that people in education must have religiousness central to their overall intention and central to the nature of the life they lived on a daily basis.

As this is equally necessary to both staff and students, there can be no real hierarchy between them. There are, of course, differences between staff and students in their responsibilities and experience; but in all that is most important in education the staff and students are really in the same boat. Staff members may know more about academic subjects, or gardening, or administration and therefore have a certain authority in those areas, but these are not the central concerns of education. In the central concerns of education, which is to do with inner liberation, both the students and the teachers are learners and therefore equal, and this is untouched by functional authority.

Therefore I say, authority has its place as knowledge, but there is no spiritual authority under any circumstances... That is, authority destroys freedom, but the authority of a doctor, mathematics teacher and how he teaches, that doesn't destroy freedom.

In thus helping the student towards freedom, the educator is changing his own values also; he too is beginning to be rid of the "me" and the "mine", he too is flowering in love and goodness. This process of mutual education creates an altogether different relationship between the teacher and the student.

Jiddu Krishnamurti felt that the over-riding quality of an educator should be religiosity. Because he is devoted solely to the freedom and integration of the individual, the right kind of educator is deeply and truly religious. He does not belong to any sect, to any organised religion; is free of beliefs and rituals...

Because the educator is religious; he is concerned first with 'being', and then right 'doing' will follow from it. Krishnamurti describes this relationship between 'being' and 'doing' frequently, but perhaps nowhere more succinctly than in one of his talks in Bombay,... it is not 'doing is being' but 'being is doing'.

For Jiddu Krishnamurti, 'doing' derived from 'being' rather than 'being' deriving from 'doing' - the reverse of convention. Much more needs to be said than this paper permits about the consequences of reversing the roles of 'being' and 'doing', or even worse, of confusing them. Note the modern convention of a question like, "Who are you?" (a question about being) which is answered by, "I'm a lawyer, engineer, etc." (a statement about doing). Suffice it to say that this reversal or confusion usually leads to a highly developed 'doing' (which is easier to accomplish) with impoverished 'being,' and Krishnamurti felt that dysfunction was the usual consequence of such imbalance.

When discussing the selection process for students and staff at his English educational centre, Krishnamurti always stressed the importance of the candidate's 'being' - their deepest sensitivities, their goodness and intelligence (in his definitions of those words which had nothing to do with conventional morality or IQ), the depth of their questions about themselves and the world. Although he wanted both staff and students to be intellectually sound, he never stressed academic prowess, cultural abilities, or capacities as being more important than the willingness and ability to lead what he called a religious life'. In one memorable discussion, Jiddu Krishnamurti questioned the staff about all the qualities they looked for in prospective students (as it was all the staff together who chose new students and staff members). Krishnamurti then described himself as a boy.

He said he had been vague, shy, dreamy and bad at all academics, but sensitive, full of wonder, trusting, and affectionate; and Krishnamurti asked if, according to the criteria the staff had just enunciated, they would have accepted him as a child. Again, a painful silence. Our description of the students we were seeking for a Krishnamurti school seemed not to include the young Krishnamurti. How was this possible? It was because we as staff members were thinking too conventionally and traditionally, we were more interested in 'doing' than 'being', more interested in the measurable than the immeasurable; we were choosing what most like us was, we were again choosing Barabbas.

Earlier on in this paper, I tried to give a summary of Jiddu Krishnamurti's view of the nature of a human being. It now remains to say just a few things about the relation of this view to what he felt were the consequences for education. I will concentrate on only two elements as they most directly support my contention that for Krishnamurti education was a religious activity. These two elements are: 1.) the distinction between mind and brain, and 2.) people need to be revealed to themselves not shaped by others. Krishnamurti's view that a human has both a brain and a mind puts him at odds with most modern perspectives and most learning theory. Although this article is too short to do justice to this topic, we can simplify the difference as follows: the brain is the material centre of the nervous system and the organ of cognition. It is therefore responsible for co-ordination of the senses, memory, rationality, intellectual knowledge, etc.

The mind, which is not material, is related to insight (non-visual perception), compassion, and the profound intelligence that Jiddu Krishnamurti held as the real goal of life and therefore of education. Obviously one needs a brain that functions well (like one needs a heart or a liver that functions well) but the real source of acting rightly, of goodness, and of a religious life is the mind. In this unequal relationship between the two, a good brain can not ameliorate a mind, but a good mind does ameliorate the brain. The brain has an important role to play with the mind, and that role is freeing itself from its conditioning and from activities that inhibit the mind's healthy functioning (i.e. hate, fear, pride, etc.); and helping the brain do this is one of the main functions of education (not accumulating knowledge).

The real issue is the quality of our mind: not its knowledge but the depth of the mind that meets knowledge. Mind is infinite, is the nature of the universe which has its own order, has its own immense energy. It is everlastingly free. The brain, as it is now, is the slave of knowledge and so is limited, finite, fragmentary. When the brain frees itself from its conditioning, then the brain is infinite, then only there is no division between the mind and the brain. Education then is freedom from conditioning, from its vast accumulated knowledge as tradition. This does not deny the academic disciplines which have their own proper place in life.

Contrary to the perspective that has shaped much in conventional education, Jiddu Krishnamurti felt that each person needs to explore themselves and reveal themselves to themselves rather than be shaped into something by others. This is not a new perspective, and again has links to the educational theories of Rousseau, Pestalozzi, Fröbel, and Montessori. The function of education, then, is to help you from childhood not to imitate anybody, but to be yourself all the time. So freedom lies...in understanding what you are from moment to moment. You see, you are not [normally] educated for this; your education encourages you to become something or other...

To understand life is to understand ourselves, and that is both the beginning and the end of education. Krishnamurti felt that not only was a person's nature and deepest aspects to be uncovered, but each person also has a unique vocation that needs to be discovered; what he/she really loves to do has to be found and pursued, and to do anything else is a deprivation of the worst kind, especially if such deprivation is in order to pursue success or other such cultural aspirations. The discovery of the natural vocation for an individual student and the student's understanding what he really loves to do may not fit into the plans of the parents or society, but it is an important part of understanding oneself and, consequently, of education.

Modern education is making us into thoughtless entities; it does very little towards helping us to find our individual vocation. To find out what you really love to do is one of the most difficult things. That is part of education. Right education is to help you to find out for yourself what you really, with all your heart, love to do. It does not matter what it is, whether it is to cook, or to be a gardener, but is something in which you have put your mind, your heart.

I realize I have not said anything about how Jiddu Krishnamurti felt that any of the above could be put into practice. The theme of this paper is too small to attempt that, and yet still I feel I have bitten off more than I can chew - or perhaps it is just more than I could present in a digestible form. I have wanted to show that for Krishnamurti education was first and foremost a religious activity. In 1929 he stated what he felt was the central intention in his life, I want to do a certain thing in the world and I am going to do it with unwavering concentration. I am concerning myself with only one essential thing; to set man free.

For this Krishnamurti started schools, and for this reason only. We read the words of the young seventeen year old Krishnamurti who wrote, If the unity of life and the oneness of its purpose could be clearly taught to the young in schools, how much brighter would be our hopes for the future!

Forty one years later he wrote, If one becomes aware that there can be peace and harmony for man only through right education, then one will naturally give one's whole life and interest to it. And that is exactly what he did.

WESTERN THINKERS: PLATO, ROUSSEAU, FROEBEL, DEWEY AND MONTESSORI

PLATO

Plato is the earliest important educational thinker. He saw education as the key to creating and sustaining his *Republic*. He advocated extreme methods: removing children from their mothers' care and raising them as wards of the state, with great care being taken to differentiate children suitable to the various castes, the highest receiving the most education, so that they could act as guardians of the city and care for the less able. Education would be holistic, including facts, skills, physical discipline, and music and art, which he considered the highest form of endeavor.

For Plato the individual was best served by being subordinated to a just society. Plato's belief that talent was distributed non-genetically and thus must be found in children born in any social class. His belief moves us away from aristocracy as a political system. He builds on this by insisting that those suitably gifted are to be trained by the state so that they may be qualified to assume the role of a ruling class. What this establishes is essentially a system of selective public education premised on the assumption that an educated minority of the population are, by virtue of their education (and inborn educability), sufficient for healthy governance. Today's tracking systems could be justified with Plato's ideas.

Plato should be considered foundational for democratic philosophies of education both because later key thinkers treat him as such, and because, while Plato's methods are autocratic and his motives leaned toward a meritocracy, he nonetheless prefigures much later democratic philosophy of education. This is different in degree rather than kind from most versions of, say, the American experiment with democratic education, which has usually assumed that only some students should be educated to the fullest, while others may, acceptably, fall by the wayside.

Plato's writings contain some of the following ideas: Elementary education would be confined to the guardian class till the age of 18, followed by two years of compulsory military training and then by higher education for those who qualified. While elementary education made the soul responsive to the environment, higher education helped the soul to search for truth which illuminated it. Both boys and girls got the same kind of education. Elementary education consisted of music and gymnastics, designed to train and blend gentle and fierce qualities in the individual and create a harmonious person.

At the age of 20, a selection was made. The best one would take an advanced course in mathematics, geometry, astronomy and harmonics. The first course in the scheme of higher education would last for ten years. It would be for those who had a flair for science. At the age of 30 there would be another selection; those who qualified would study dialectics and metaphysics, logic and philosophy for the next five years. They would study the idea of good and first principles of being. After accepting junior positions in the army for 15 years, a man would have completed his theoretical and practical education by the age of 50.

JEAN-JACQUES ROUSSEAU

Rousseau, though he paid his respects to Plato's philosophy, rejected it as impractical due to the decayed state of society. Rousseau also had a different theory of human development; where Plato held that people are born with skills appropriate to different castes (though he did not regard these skills as being inherited), Rousseau held that there was one developmental process common to all humans. This was an intrinsic, natural process, of which the primary behavioral manifestation was curiosity. This differed from Locke's 'tabula rasa' in that it was an active process deriving from the child's nature, which drove the child to learn and adapt to its surroundings.

Rousseau wrote in his book *Emile* that all children are perfectly designed organisms, ready to learn from their surroundings so as to grow into virtuous adults, but due to the malign influence of corrupt society, they often fail to do so. Rousseau advocated an educational method which consisted of removing the child from society—for example, to a country home—and alternately conditioning him through changes to environment and setting traps and puzzles for him to solve or overcome.

Rousseau was unusual in that he recognized and addressed the potential of a problem of legitimation for teaching. He advocated that adults always be truthful with children, and in particular that they never hide the fact that the basis for their authority in teaching was purely one of physical coercion: "I'm bigger than you." Once children reached the age of reason, at about 12, they would be engaged as free individuals in the ongoing process of their own.

FRIEDRICH FRÖBEL

Friedrich Wilhelm August Fröbel (or Froebel) (April 21, 1782 – June 21, 1852) was a German pedagogue, a student of Pestalozzi who laid the foundation for modern education based on the recognition that children have unique needs and capabilities. He created the concept of the "kindergarten", and also coined the word now used in German and English. Friedrich Fröbel was born at Oberweißbach in the Principality of Schwarzburg-Rudolstadt in Thuringia. His father, who died in 1802, was the pastor of the orthodox Lutheran (alt-lutherisch) parish there. The church and Lutheran Christian faith were pillars in Fröbel's own early education. Oberweibach was a wealthy village in the Thuringian Forest and had been known centuries long for its natural herb remedies, tinctures, bitters, soaps and salves. Families had their own inherited areas of the forest where herbs and roots were grown and harvested.

Each family prepared, bottled, and produced their individual products which were taken throughout Europe on trade routes passed from father to son, who were affectionately called "Buckelapotheker" or *Rucksack Pharmacists*. They adorned the church with art acquired from their travels, many pieces of which can still be seen in the renovated structure. The pulpit from which Fröbel heard his father preach is the largest in all Europe and can fit a pastor and 12 men, a direct reference to Christ's apostles.

Shortly after Fröbel's birth, his mother's health began to fail. She died when he was nine months old, profoundly influencing his life. In 1792, Fröbel went to live in the small town of Stadt-Ilm with his uncle, a gentle and affectionate man. At the age of 15 Fröbel, who loved nature, became the apprentice to a forester. In 1799, he decided to leave his apprenticeship and study mathematics and botany in Jena. From 1802 to 1805, he worked as a land surveyor. On 11 September 1818, Fröbel wed Wilhelmine Henriette Hoffmeister (b. 1780) in Berlin. The union was childless. Wilhelmine died in 1839, and Fröbel married again in 1851. His second wife was Louise Levin.

He began as an educator in 1805 at the *Musterschule* (a secondary school) in Frankfurt, where he learnt about Johann Heinrich Pestalozzi's ideas. He later worked with Pestalozzi in Switzerland where his ideas further developed. From 1806 Fröbel was the live-in teacher for a Frankfurt noble family's three sons. He lived with the three children from 1808 to 1810 at Pestalozzi's institute in Yverdon-les-Bains in Switzerland. In 1811, Fröbel once again went back to school in Göttingen and Berlin, eventually leaving without earning a certificate. He became a teacher at the *Plamannsche Schule* in Berlin, a boarding school for boys, and at that time also a pedagogical and patriotic centre.

During his service in the Lützow Free Corps in 1813 and 1814 – when he was involved in two campaigns against Napoleon – Fröbel befriended Wilhelm Middendorf, a theologian and fellow pedagogue, and Heinrich Langethal, also a pedagogue. After Waterloo and the Congress of Vienna, Fröbel found himself a civilian once again and became an assistant at the Museum of Mineralogy under Prof. Weiß. This did not, however, last very long, and by 1816 he had quit and founded the *Allgemeine Deutsche Erziehungsanstalt* ("German General Education Institute") in Griesheim near Arnstadt in Thuringia. A year later he moved this to Keilhau near Rudolstadt. In 1831, work was continued there by the other cofounders Wilhelm Middendorf and Heinrich Langethal.

In 1820, Fröbel published the first of his five Keilhau pamphlets, *An unser deutsches Volk* ("To Our German People"). The other four were published between then and 1823. In 1826 he published is main literary work, *Die Menschenerziehung* ("The Education of Man") and founded the weekly publication *Die erziehenden Familien* ("The Educating Families"). In 1828 and 1829 he pursued plans for a people's education institute (*Volkserziehungsanstalt*) in Helba (nowadays a constituent community of Meiningen), but they were never realized. From 1831 to 1836, Fröbel once again lived in Switzerland. In 1831 he founded an educational institute in Wartensee (Lucerne). In 1833 he moved this to Willisau, and from 1835 to 1836, he headed the orphanage in Burgdorf (Berne), where he also published the magazine *Grundzüge der Menschenerziehung* ("Features of Human Education"). In 1836 appeared his work *Erneuerung des Lebens erfordert das neue Jahr 1836*.

He returned to Germany, dedicated himself almost exclusively to preschool child education and began manufacturing playing materials in Bad Blankenburg. In 1837 he founded a "care, playing and activity institute for small children in Bad Blankenburg. From 1838 to 1840 he also published the magazine *Ein Sonntagsblatt für Gleichgesinnte.* In 1840 he coined the word kindergarten for the Play and Activity Institute he had founded in 1837 at Bad Blankenburg for young children, together with Wilhelm Middendorf and Heinrich

Langethal. These two men were Fröbel's most faithful colleagues when his ideas were also transplanted to Keilhau near Rudolstadt.

He designed the educational play materials known as Froebel Gifts, or *Fröbelgaben*, which included geometric building blocks and pattern activity blocks. A book entitled *Inventing Kindergarten*, by Norman Brosterman, examines the influence of Friedrich Fröbel on Frank Lloyd Wright and modern art. Friedrich Fröbel's great insight was to recognise the importance of the activity of the child in learning. He introduced the concept of "free work" (*Freiarbeit*) into pedagogy and established the "game" as the typical form that life took in childhood, and also the game's educational worth. Activities in the first kindergarten included singing, dancing, gardening and self-directed play with the Froebel Gifts. Fröbel intended, with his *Mutter- und Koselieder* – a songbook that he published – to introduce the young child into the adult world.

These ideas about childhood development and education were introduced to academic and royal circles through the tireless efforts of his greatest proponent, the Baroness (Freiherrin) Bertha Marie von Marenholtz-Bülow. Through her Fröbel made the acquaintance of the Royal House of the Netherlands, various Thuringian dukes and duchesses, including the Romanov wife of the Grand Duke von Sachsen-Weimar. Baroness von Marenholtz-Bülow, Duke von Meiningen and Fröbel gathered donations to support art education for children in honour of the 100th anniversary of the birth of Goethe. The Duke of Meiningen granted the use of his hunting lodge, called Marienthal (the Vale of Mary) in the resort town of Bad Liebenstein for Fröbel to train the first women as Kindergarten teachers (called *Kindergärtnerinnen*). Fröbel died on 21 June 1852 in Mariental. His grave is still found at the cemetery at Schweina, where his widow, who died in Hamburg, was also buried on 10 January 1900.

Legacy

Fröbel's idea of the kindergarten found appeal, but its spread in Germany was thwarted by the Prussian government, whose education ministry banned it on 7 August 1851 as "atheistic and demagogic" for its alleged "destructive tendencies in the areas of religion and politics". Other states followed suit. The reason for the ban, however, seems to have been a confusion of names. Fröbel's nephew Karl Fröbel had written and published *Weibliche Hochschulen und Kindergärten* ("Female Colleges and Kindergartens"), which apparently met with some disapproval. To quote Karl August Varnhagen von Ense, "The stupid minister von Raumer has decreed a ban on kindergartens, basing himself on a book by Karl Fröbel. He is confusing Friedrich and Karl Fröbel."

Fröbel's student Margarethe Schurz founded the first kindergarten in the United States at Watertown, Wisconsin in 1856, and she also inspired Elizabeth Peabody, who went on to found the first English-speaking kindergarten in the United States – the language at Schurz's kindergarten had been German, to serve an immigrant community – in Boston in 1860. This paved the way for the concept's spread in the USA. The German émigré Adolph Douai had also founded a kindergarten in Boston in 1859, but was obliged to close it after only a year. By 1866, however, he was founding others in New York City.

The pedagogue August Köhler was the initiator and cofounder in 1863 of the *Deutscher Fröbelverein* ("German Fröbel Association"), first for Thuringia, out of which grew the *Allgemeiner Fröbelverein* ("General Fröbel Association") in 1872, and a year later the *Deutscher Fröbelverband* ("German Fröbel Federation"). August Köhler critically analyzed and evaluated Fröbel theory, adopted fundamental notions into his own kindergarten pedagogy and expanded on these, developing an independent "Köhler Kindergarten Pedagogy". He first trained kindergarten teachers in Gotha in 1857. In the beginning, Köhler had thought to engage male educators exclusively, but far too few applied.

Thekla Naveau founded in October 1853 the first kindergarten in Sondershausen and on 1 April 1867 the first kindergarten after the Prussian ban was lifted in Nordhausen. Angelika Hartmann founded in 1864 the first kindergarten after Fröbel's model in Köthen, Anhalt. In 1908 and 1911, kindergarten teacher training was recognized in Germany through state regulatory laws. In the meantime, there are many kindergartens in Germany named after Fröbel that continue his pedagogy. Many of them have sprung from parental or other private initiatives. The biggest Fröbel association, *Fröbel e.V.*, today runs more than 100 kindergartens and other early childhood institutions throughout the country through the *Fröbel-Gruppe*.

Committed to Fröbel's legacy is also the *Neuer Thüringer Fröbelverein* (NTFV; "New Thuringian Fröbel Association"), and in particular to protecting the legacy's business receipts. As well, the Association runs a school museum and the Fröbel Archive in Keilhau.

Furthermore it engages itself in Fröbel institutions worldwide (United States, United Kingdom, Japan). Through this network, the NTFV further continues one of the most prominent lines of modern pedagogy from the authentic "Fröbel town" of Keilhau. The Fröbel Diploma, now conferred by the Fröbel Academy in Rudolstadt, can also be traced back to the NTFV. All this ensures that Fröbel's ideas will live on into the future. Fröbel's building forms and movement games are also forerunners of abstract art as well as a source of inspiration to the Bauhaus movement. In Fröbel's honour, Walter Gropius designed the *Friedrich Fröbel Haus*.

JOHN DEWEY

In *Democracy and Education: An Introduction to the Philosophy of Education*, New York: Macmillan. (1916), Dewey stated that in its broadest sense education is the means of the "social continuity of life" given the "primary ineluctable facts of the birth and death of each one of the constituent members in a social group". Education is therefore a necessity, for "the life of the group goes on." Dewey was a relentless campaigner for reform of education, pointing out that the authoritarian, strict, pre-ordained knowledge approach of modern traditional education was too concerned with delivering knowledge, and not enough with understanding students' actual experiences.

MARIA MONTESSORI

Maria Montessori (August 31, 1870 – May 6, 1952) was an Italian physician, educator, philosopher, humanitarian and devout Catholic; she is best known for her philosophy and the Montessori method of education of children from birth to adolescence. Her educational method is in use today in a number of public as well as private schools throughout the world. Maria Montessori was born in Chiaravalle (Ancona), Italy to Alessandro Montessori, and Renilde Stoppani (niece of Antonio Stoppani). At the age of thirteen she attended an all-boy technical school in preparation for her dreams of becoming an engineer.

Montessori was the first woman to graduate from the University of Rome La Sapienza Medical School, becoming the first female doctor in Italy. She was a member of the University's Psychiatric Clinic and became intrigued with trying to educate the "mentally retarded or "unhappy little ones" and the "uneducatable" in Rome. In 1896, she gave a lecture at the Educational Congress in Torino about the training of the disabled. The Italian Minister of Education was in attendance, and was impressed by her arguments sufficiently to appoint her the same year as director of the Scuola Ortofrenica, an institution devoted to the care and education of the mentally retarded. She accepted, in order to put her theories to proof. Her first notable success was to have several of her 8 year old students apply to take the State examinations for reading and writing.

The "defective" children not only passed, but had above-average scores, an achievement described as "the first Montessori miracle." Montessori's response to their success was "if mentally disabled children could be brought to the level of normal children then (she) wanted to study the potential of 'normal' children". "Scientific observation has established that education is not what the teacher gives; education is a natural process spontaneously carried out by the human individual, and is acquired not by listening to words but by experiences upon the environment. The task of the teacher becomes that of preparing a series of motives of cultural activity, spread over a specially prepared environment, and then refraining from obtrusive interference. Human teachers can only help the great work that is being done, as servants help the master. Doing so, they will be witnesses to the unfolding of the human soul and to the rising of a New Man who will not be a victim of events, but will have the clarity of vision to direct and shape the future of human society".

Because of her success with these children, she was asked to start a school for children in a housing project in Rome, which opened on January 6, 1907, and which she called "Casa dei Bambini" or Children's House. Children's House was a child care centre in an apartment building in the poor neighborhood of Rome. She was focused on teaching the students ways to develop their own skills at a pace they set, which a principle Montessori was called "spontaneous self-development".

A wide variety of special equipment of increasing complexity is used to help direct the interests of the child and hasten development. When a child is ready to learn new and more difficult tasks, the teacher guides the child's first endeavors in order to avoid wasted effort and the learning of wrong habits; otherwise the child learns alone. It has been reported that the Montessori method of teaching has enabled children to learn to read and write much more quickly and with greater facility than has otherwise been possible.

The Montessori Method of teaching concentrates on quality rather than quantity. The success of this school sparked the opening of many more, and a worldwide interest in Montessori's methods of education. After the 1907 establishment of Montessori's first school in Rome, by 1917 there was an intense interest in her method in North America, which later waned, in large part due to the publication of a small booklet entitled "The Montessori System Examined" by Kirkpatrick- a follower of John Dewey. (Nancy McCormick Rambusch contributed to the revival of the method in America by establishing the American Montessori Society in 1960); at the same time Margaret Stephenson came to the US from

Europe and began a long history of training Montessori teachers under the auspices of the Association Montessori Internationale (AMI).

Montessori was exiled by Mussolini mostly because she refused to compromise her principles and make the children into soldiers. She moved to Spain and lived there until 1936 when the Spanish Civil War broke out. She then moved to the Netherlands until 1939. In the year 1939, the Theosophical Society of India extended an invitation asking Maria Montessori to visit India. She accepted the invitation and reached India the very same year accompanied by her only son, Mario Montessori Sr. This heralded the beginning of her special relationship with India. She made the international Headquarters of the Theosophical Society at Adyar, Chennai, her home. However the war forced her to extend her stay in India. With the help of her son, Mario, she conducted sixteen batches of courses called the Indian Montessori Training Courses.

These courses laid a strong foundation for the Montessori Movement in India. In 1949 when she left for The Netherlands she appointed Albert Max Joosten as her personal representative, and assigned him the responsibility of conducting the Indian Montessori Training Courses. Joosten along with Swamy S R, another disciple of Dr. Maria Montessori, continued the good work and ensured that the Montessori Movement in India was on a sound footing. During a teachers conference in India she was interned by the authorities and lived there for the duration of the war. Montessori lived out the remainder of her life in the Netherlands, which now hosts the headquarters of the AMI, or *Association Montessori Internationale.* She died in Noordwijk aan Zee. Her son Mario headed the AMI until his death in 1982.

Maria Montessori died in the Netherlands in 1952, after a lifetime devoted to the study of child development. Her early work centered on women's rights and social reform and evolved to encompass a totally innovative approach to education. Her success in Italy led to international recognition, and for over 40 years she traveled all over the world, lecturing, writing and establishing training programs. In later years, 'Educate for Peace' became a guiding principle, which underpinned her work.

Pedagogy

Aside from a new pedagogy, among the premier contributions to educational thought by Montessori are:

- Instruction of children in 3-year age groups, corresponding to sensitive periods of development (example: Birth-3, 3-6, 6-9, 9-12, 12-15 year olds with an Erdkinder (German for "Land Children") Programme for early teens
- Children as competent beings, encouraged to make maximal decisions
- Observation of the child in the prepared environment as the basis for ongoing curriculum development (presentation of subsequent exercises for skill development and information accumulation)
- Small, child-sized furniture and creation of a small, child-sized environment (microcosm) in which each can be competent to produce overall a self-running small children's world
- Creation of a scale of sensitive periods of development, which provides a focus for class work that is appropriate and uniquely stimulating and motivating to the child (including sensitive periods for language development, sensorial experimentation and refinement, and various levels of social interaction)
- The importance of the "absorbent mind," the limitless motivation of the young child to achieve competence over his or her environment and to perfect his or her skills and understandings as they occur within each sensitive period. The phenomenon is characterized by the young child's capacity for repetition of activities within sensitive period categories (Example: exhaustive babbling as language practice leading to language competence).

- Self-correcting "auto-didactic" materials (some based on work of Jean Marc Gaspard Itard and Edouard Seguin)

A conference in Rome on 6/7th January 2007 heralded the start of a year of celebrations for children and schools around the world. Dr. Maria Montessori's innovative approach was that "Education should no longer be mostly imparting of knowledge, but must take a new path, seeking the release of human potentialities." What followed worldwide has been called the "discovery of the child" and the realization that: "...mankind can hope for a solution to its problems, among which the most urgent are those of peace and unity, only by turning its attention and energies to the discovery of the child and to the development of the great potentialities of the human personality in the course of its formation."

The efficacy of Montessori teaching methods has most recently been demonstrated by the results of a study published in the US journal, Science (29 September 2006) which indicates that Montessori children have improved behavioral and academic skills compared with a control group from the mainstream system. The authors concluded that "when strictly implemented, Montessori education fosters social and academic skills that are equal or superior to those fostered by a pool of other types of schools."

The Montessori method of education that she derived from this experience has subsequently been applied successfully to children and is quite popular in many parts of the world. Despite much criticism of her method in the early 1930s-1940s, her method of education has been applied and has undergone a revival. It can now be found on six continents and throughout the United States, but is still subject to some criticism. The Association Montessori Internationale is member of the International Coalition for the Decade for the Culture of Peace and Nonviolence.

Unit IV

Sociology and Education

MEANING AND NATURE OF SOCIOLOGY OF EDUCATION AND EDUCATIONAL SOCIOLOGY; SOCIAL ORGANIZATIONS

The sociology of education is the study of how public institutions and individual experiences affects education and its outcome. It is most concerned with the public schooling systems of modern industrial societies, including the expansion of higher, further, adult, and continuing education. Education has always been seen as a fundamentally optimistic human endeavour characterised by aspirations for progress and betterment. It is understood by many to be a means of overcoming handicaps, achieving greater equality and acquiring wealth and status. Education is perceived as a place where children can develop according to their unique needs and potential. It is also perceived as one of the best means of achieving greater social equality.

Many would say that the purpose of education should be to develop every individual to their full potential and give them a chance to achieve as much in life as their natural abilities allow(meritocracy). Few would argue that any education system accomplishes this goal perfectly. Some take a particularly negative view, arguing that the education system is designed with the intention of causing the social reproduction of inequality. A systematic sociology of education began with Émile Durkheim's work on moral education as a basis for organic solidarity and that by Max Weber, on the Chinese literati as an instrument of political control. It was after the Second World War, however, that the subject received renewed interest around the world: from technological functionalism in the US, egalitarian reform of opportunity in Europe, and human-capital theory in economics.

These all implied that, with industrialization, the need for a technologically-skilled labour force undermines class distinctions and other ascriptive systems of stratification, and that education promotes social mobility. However, statistical and field research across numerous societies showed a persistent link between an individual's social class and achievement, and suggested that education could only achieve limited social mobility. Sociological studies showed how schooling patterns reflected, rather than challenged, class stratification and racial and sexual discrimination. After the general collapse of functionalism from the late 1960s onwards, the idea of education as an unmitigated good was even more profoundly challenged. Neo-Marxists argued that school education simply produced a docile labour-force essential to late-capitalist class relations.

THEORETICAL PERSPECTIVES

The sociology of education contains a number of theories. Thc work of each theory is presented below.

STRUCTURAL FUNCTIONALISM

Structural functionalists believe that society leans towards equilibrium and social order. They see society like a human body, in which institutions such as education are like important organs that keep the society/body healthy and well. Social health means the same as social order, and is guaranteed when nearly everyone accepts the general moral values of their society. Hence structural functionalists believe the aim of key institutions, such as education, is to socialise children and teenagers. Socialisation is the process by which the new generation learns the knowledge, attitudes and values that they will need as productive citizens.

Although this aim is stated in the formal curriculum, it is

mainly achieved through *"the hidden curriculum"*, a subtler, but nonetheless powerful, indoctrination of the norms and values of the wider society. Students learn these values because their behaviour at school is regulated [Durkheim in] until they gradually internalise and accept them. Education must, however perform another function. As various jobs become vacant, they must be filled with the appropriate people. Therefore the other purpose of education is to sort and rank individuals for placement in the labour market. Those with high achievement will be trained for the most important jobs and in reward, be given the highest incomes. Those who achieve the least, will be given the least demanding (intellectually at any rate, if not physically) jobs, and hence the least income.

According to Sennet and Cobb however, "to believe that ability alone decides who is rewarded is to be deceived". Meighan agrees, stating that large numbers of capable students from working class backgrounds fail to achieve satisfactory standards in school and therefore fail to obtain the status they deserve.

Jacob believes this is because the middle class cultural experiences that are provided at school may be contrary to the experiences working-class children receive at home. In other words, working class children are not adequately prepared to cope at school. They are therefore "cooled out" from school with the least qualifications, hence they get the least desirable jobs, and so remain working class. Sargent confirms this cycle, arguing that schooling supports continuity, which in turn supports social order.

Talcott Parsons believed that this process, whereby some students were identified and labelled educational failures, "was a necessary activity which one part of the social system, education, performed for the whole". Yet the structural functionalist perspective maintains that this social order, this continuity, is what most people desire. The weakness of this perspective thus becomes evident. Why would the working class wish to stay working class? Such an inconsistency demonstrates that another perspective may be useful.

EDUCATION AND SOCIAL REPRODUCTION

The perspective of conflict theory, contrary to the structural functionalist perspective, believes that society is full of vying social groups with different aspirations, different access to life chances and gain different social rewards. Relations in society, in this view, are mainly based on exploitation, oppression, domination and subordination. Some conflict theorists believe education is controlled by the state which is controlled by the powerful, and its purpose is to reproduce existing inequalities, as well as legitimise 'acceptable' ideas which actually work to reinforce the privileged positions of the dominant group. Connell and White state that the education system is as much an arbiter of social privilege as a transmitter of knowledge.

Education achieves its purpose by maintaining the status quo, where lower-class children become lower class adults, and middle and upper class children become middle and upper-class adults. This cycle occurs because the dominant group has, over time, closely aligned education with middle class values and aims, thus alienating people of other classes. Many teachers assume that students will have particular middle class experiences at home, and for some children this assumption isn't necessarily true. Some children are expected to help their parents after school and carry considerable domestic responsibilities in their often single-parent home. The demands of this domestic labour often make it difficult for them to find time to do all their homework and thus affect their academic performance.

Where teachers have softened the formality of regular study and integrated student's preferred working methods into the curriculum, they noted that particular students displayed strengths they had not been aware of before. However few teacher deviate from the traditional curriculum, and the curriculum conveys what constitutes knowledge as determined by the state - and those in power [Young in]. This knowledge isn't very meaningful to many of the students, who see it as pointless. Wilson & Wyn state that the students realise there is little or no direct link between the subjects they are doing and their perceived future in the labour market.

Anti-school values displayed by these children are often derived from their consciousness of their real interests. Sargent believes that for working class students, striving to succeed and absorbing the school's middle class values, is accepting their inferior social position as much as if they were determined to fail. Fitzgerald states that "irrespective of their academic ability or desire to learn, students from poor families have relatively little chance of securing success". On the other hand, for middle and especially upper-class children, maintaining their superior position in society requires little effort. The federal government subsidises 'independent' private schools enabling the rich to obtain 'good education' by paying for it. With this 'good education', rich children perform better, achieve higher and obtain greater rewards. In this way, the continuation of privilege and wealth for the elite is made possible.

Conflict theorists believe this social reproduction continues to occur because the whole education system is overlain with ideology provided by the dominant group. In effect, they perpetuate the myth that education is available to all to provide a means of achieving wealth and status. Anyone who fails to achieve this goal, according to the myth, has only themself to blame. Wright agrees, stating that "the effect of the myth is to...stop them from seeing that their personal troubles are part of major social issues". The duplicity is so successful that many parents endure appalling jobs for many years, believing that this sacrifice will enable their children to have opportunities in life that they did not have themselves.

These people who are poor and disadvantaged are victims of a societal confidence trick. They have been encouraged to believe that a major goal of schooling is to strengthen equality while, in reality, schools reflect society's intention to maintain the previous unequal distribution of status and power [Fitzgerald, cited in]. This perspective has been criticised as deterministic, pessimistic and allowing no room for the agency of individuals to improve their situation. It should be recognised however that it is a model, an aspect of reality which is an important part of the picture.

STRUCTURE AND AGENCY

Bourdieu and Cultural Capital

This theory of social reproduction has been significantly theorised by Pierre Bourdieu. However Bourdieu as a social theorist has always been concerned with the dichotomy between the objective and subjective, or to put it another way, between structure and agency. Bourdieu has therefore built his theoretical framework around the important concepts of habitus, field and cultural capital. These concepts are based on the idea that objective structures determine individuals' chances, through the mechanism of the habitus, where individuals internalise these structures. However, the habitus is also formed by, for example, an individual's position in various fields, their family and their everyday experiences. Therefore one's class position does not determine one's life chances, although it does play an important part, alongside other factors.

Bourdieu used the idea of cultural capital to explore the differences in outcomes for students from different classes in the French educational system. He explored the tension between the conservative reproduction and the innovative production of knowledge and experience. He found that this tension is intensified by considerations of which particular cultural past and present is to be conserved and reproduced in schools. Bourdieu argues that it is the culture of the dominant groups, and therefore their cultural capital, which is embodied in schools, and that this leads to social reproduction.

The cultural capital of the dominant group, in the form of practices and relation to culture, is assumed by the school to be the natural and only proper type of cultural capital and is therefore legitimated. It demands "uniformly of all its students that they should have what it does not give" [Bourdieu]. This legitimate cultural capital allows students who possess it to gain educational capital in the form of qualifications. Those lower-class students are therefore disadvantaged. To gain qualifications they must acquire legitimate cultural capital, by exchanging their own (usually working-class) cultural capital. This exchange is not a straight forward one, due to the class ethos of the lower-class students.

Class ethos is described as the particular dispositions towards, and subjective expectations of, school and culture. It is in part determined by the objective chances of that class. This means that not only do children find success harder in school due to the fact that they must learn a new way of 'being', or relating to the world, and especially, a new way of relating to and using language, but they must also act against their instincts and expectations. The subjective expectations influenced by the objective structures found in the school, perpetuate social reproduction by encouraging less-privileged students to eliminate themselves from the system, so that fewer and fewer are to be found as one journeys through the levels of the system.

The process of social reproduction is neither perfect nor complete, but still, only a small number of less-privileged students achieve success. For the majority of these students who do succeed at school, they have had to internalise the values of the dominant classes and use them as their own, to the detriment of their original habitus and cultural values. Therefore Bourdieu's perspective reveals how objective structures play an important role in determining individual achievement in school, but allows for the exercise of an individual's agency to overcome these barriers, although this choice is not without its penalties.

CHARACTERISTICS; SOCIAL GROUPS; SOCIAL CHANGE; SOCIAL MOBILITY

Social mobility is the degree to which an individual's family or group's social status can change throughout the course of their life through a system of social hierarchy or stratification. Subsequently, it is also the degree to which an individual's or group's descendants move up and down the class system. The individual or family can move up or down the social classes based on achievements or factors beyond their control. It is a sociological concept. Intra-generational mobility ("within" a generation) is defined as changes in social status over a single life-time. Inter-generational mobility ("across" generations) is defined as changes in social status that occur from the parents' to the children's generation.

These definitions are particularly useful when analyzing how social status changes from one time period to another, and if a person's parents' social status influences that of their own. Sociologists usually focus on intergenerational mobility because it is easier to depict changes across generations rather than within one. This information helps sociologists determine whether inequality in a culture changes over time. Intra-generational mobility occurs when a person strives to change his or her own social standing. In some societies, this type of change is not possible. In social systems where people are divided into castes, social mobility cannot occur. Whatever caste a person is born into, is what they will remain for the entirety of their life. However, in cultures based on merit, like the United States or the United Kingdom, people are free to move up and down the social ladder.

Intra-generational mobility can move a person either higher or lower in the social ladder. If one starts at a low level, they can improve their status by working hard, getting a better job, or becoming more culturally sound, to name a few. Pierre Bordieu describes three types of capital that place a person in a certain social category. These are economic capital, social capital, and cultural capital. Economic capital is command over economic resources such as money and assets. Social capital is resources one achieves based on group membership, relationships, networks of influence, and support from other people. Cultural capital is any advantage a person has that gives them a higher status in society, such as education, skills, and any other form of knowledge. Usually, people with all three types of capital have a high status in society.

Inter-generational mobility occurs across generations. This mobility is both merit- and non-merit-based. Ability and hard work affect social mobility, but so does parents' wealth, race, gender, and luck. Fiona Devine wrote a book, *Class practices: how parents help their children get good jobs*, specifically on intergenerational mobility and how parents' influence can affect the child's social mobility. Nearly every chapter emphasizes the importance of a good education in order to be successful. Parents also help children make important connections with people in order to expand their social network. Parents that can create social capital for their children tend to increase their child's social mobility.

Recent researchers collecting data on the economic mobility of families across generations, looked at the probability of reaching a particular income distribution in regards to where their parents were ranked and found that 42 per cent of those whose parents were in the bottom quintile ended up in the bottom quintile themselves, 23 per cent of them ended in the second quintile, 19 per cent in the middle quintile, 11 per cent in the fourth quintile and 6 per cent in the top quintile. These data indicate the difficulty of upward intergenerational mobility. Annette Lareau makes a compelling argument regarding child-raising in her book, *Unequal Childhoods: Class, Race, and Family Life*. She describes two different ways to raise children: concerted cultivation and natural growth. Concerted cultivation, normally used by middle-class families, incorporates scheduling many structured, organized activities for the child. They are taught to use their language to reason with parents and other adults, and often the child adopts a sense of entitlement. Natural growth is almost the exact opposite of concerted cultivation.

Occurring mainly in poor or working-class families, this style of childrearing does not include organized activities, and there is a clear division between the adult and the child. Children usually spend large amounts of their day creating their own activities, and they hardly ever speak with adults. In fact, adults use language in order to direct or order the children, never to negotiate with them. These two different types of childrearing can affect inter-generational mobility. Children who grow up with a concerted cultivation style of childrearing learn from their parents how to talk with adults as equals and negotiate to get favorable outcomes in any situation. This skill helps them create powerful social networks, which can improve their social standing. Children with natural growth accomplishment tend to have a more difficult time improving their social standing.

They lack the social skills and sense of entitlement that children raised with the concerted cultivation method have, and therefore are less likely to acquire good jobs (and therefore, improve their social standing). Children who have been raised with natural growth do learn to comply with authority figures, instead of argue with them, which gives them an advantage over concerted cultivated children in certain fields of employment. However, those are generally the entry-level fields where you are paid to follow orders and not to think, and are therefore the lower-paying ones, whereas the middle-class concertedly cultivated children's reasoning skills aid them in attaining the higher-paying, higher-prestige white collar jobs.

ABSOLUTE AND RELATIVE MOBILITY

Absolute mobility means that living standards are increasing in absolute terms: You are better off than your parents, and your children will be better off than you. Structural changes, such as changes in occupational structure rates, means that there is more room at the top, which leads to high absolute mobility rates. For example, suppose a person begins his working career with an income of $32,000. If a decade later his income is $36,000 (adjusting for inflation), he has experienced upward absolute income mobility.

Relative mobility refers to the degree to which individuals move up or down compared to others in their cohort. In other words, relative mobility means that if your family is poor, you have a decent chance of moving up the relative income ladder. That is, the rank order of people in society is malleable. Relative mobility relates to the openness or fluidity of society and is insensitive to the impact of structural changes. For example, suppose a person's income increases from $32,000 at the start of his working career to $36,000 a decade later, but most people who began their work life around the same time experience a larger increase. The person has experienced upward absolute mobility but downward relative mobility. Because relative mobility depends on one's place in the distribution, it is a zero-sum phenomenon. In other words, if one person moves up in relative terms, another by definition must have moved down. In contrast, absolute mobility is not zero-sum.

Although both absolute and relative mobility are both forms of intragenerational mobility, these two have very little to do with each other. High absolute mobility rates can co-exist with highly unequal relative mobility chances. Thus, you can have an economy with a lot of absolute mobility, and little relative mobility or an economy with a lot of relative mobility, and little absolute mobility. Social mobility is an act of moving from one social class to another. The amount of movement up and down the class structure would indicate the extent of social mobility prevalent in the society.

The social mobility is greatly influenced by the level of openness of the society. Open society is the one where people attain their status primarily by their own efforts. In fact the extent of mobility may be taken as an index of openness of a society indicating how far talented individuals born into lower strata can move up the socioeconomic ladder. In this respect, social mobility is an important political issue, particularly in countries committed to liberal vision of equality of opportunity to all citizens. In this perspective industrial societies are mostly open societies portraying high social mobility. Compared with them, pre-industrial societies have mostly been found to be closed societies where there has been low social mobility. People in such societies have been confined to their ancestral occupations and their social status has mostly been ascribed.

Social mobility can be classified as: Vertical mobility: The movement of individuals and groups up or down the socioeconomic scale. Those who gain in property, income, status, and position are said to be upwardly mobile, while those who move in the opposite direction are downwardly mobile. Horizontal mobility: The movement of individuals and groups in similar socioeconomic positions, which may be in different work situations. This may involve change in occupation or remaining in the same occupation but in a different organization, or may be in the same organization but at a different location. Lateral mobility: It is a geographical movement between neighborhoods, towns or regions. In modern societies there is a great deal of geographical mobility. Lateral mobility is often combined with vertical as well as horizontal mobility.

The movement of people up or down the social hierarchy can be looked at either within one generation called intra-generational mobility or between generations labeled as inter-generational mobility. Intra-generational mobility consists of movement up and down the stratification system by members of a single generation (the-social class in which you began life compared with your social class at the end of your life). Inter-generational mobility consists of movement up and down the stratification system by members of successive generations of a family (your social class location compared with that of your parents, for example). Comparison is usually made between social class status of son and father. Mobility is functional. Open societies provide opportunities to its members for the development of their talents and working toward their individual fulfillment. At the same time a person can select the best person for doing a particular job.

RULES OF STATUS: ASCRIPTION AND ACHIEVEMENT

Achieved status is a position gained based on merit, or achievement (used in an open system). An open system describes a society with mobility between different social classes. Individuals can move up or down in the social rankings; this is unlike closed systems, where individuals are set in one social position for life despite their achievements. Ascribed status is a position based on who a person is, not what they can do (used in a closed system).

When this ascriptive status rule is used (Medieval Europe), people are placed in a position based on personal traits beyond their control. Mobility is much more frequent in countries that use achievement as the basis for status (U.S. &

Canada). However, societies differ on the amount of mobility that occurs due to the direction of structural changes in their overall status systems. The process by which an individual *alters* the ascribed social status of their parents into an achieved social status for themselves is called Social Transformation.

STRUCTURAL AND EXCHANGE MOBILITY

Structural mobility is a type of forced vertical mobility that results from a change in the distribution of statuses in a society. It occurs when the demands of a particular occupation reach its max and more people are needed to help fill the positions. Exchange mobility is that which is not structural. The key word "exchange" means trade-off. This means instead of positions reaching the max and more people are needed, positions are dropped and someone else must step up to fill the position. When ascriptive status is in play, there is not much exchange mobility occurring.

UPWARD AND DOWNWARD MOBILITY

Upward social mobility is a change in a person's social status resulting in that person receiving a higher position in their status system. Likewise, downward mobility results in a lower position. A prime example of an opportunity for upward mobility nowadays is athletics. There is an increased number of minorities seeking careers as professional athletes which can either lead to improved social status or could potentially harm them due to neglecting other aspects of their life (ex. education). Transformative assets would also allow one to achieve a higher status in society, as they increase wealth and provide for more opportunity. A transformative asset could be a trust fund set up by family that allows you to own a nice home in a nice neighborhood, instead of an apartment in a down trodden community. This type of move would allow the person to develop a new circle of friends of the same economic status.

MOBILITY IN THE AMERICAN WORKFORCE

Intra-generational mobility refers to the social mobility

within a single generation. It measures shifts in career at some point in the individual's lifetime, where your occupational status is determined by individual merit. Thus, irrespective of family background, one can move from being an unskilled blue collar worker to becoming a CEO of a multi-million dollar corporation. Intra-generational mobility within the work force is a concept that has been heavily influenced by the American dream. Meritocracy, the idea that everybody who has a good work ethic can succeed and move up in class, is a notion that has been put into question using statistics through sociological research. There are several factors which complicate a strictly meritocratic view of an individual's ability to "climb the corporate ladder." These factors primarily include education, gender and race, and social networks.

Sociologists Blau and Duncan collected mobility data along with the U.S. Bureau of the Census in 1962. The data included information on occupational family backgrounds. In 1962, 56.8% of son's with fathers who occupations in upper nonmanual had ended up with occupations in the same level. Only 1.2% of sons with fathers who had farming occupations ended up in upper nonmanual occupations.

In 1973, these differences increased. 59.4% of sons with fathers in upper nonmanual occupations achieved occupations of this same level and.9% of sons with fathers in farming occupations ended up in upper nonmanual occupations. However, the occupational structure is more rigid towards the top and bottom. Those in lower nonmanual occupations, and upper and lower manual occupations were more likely to be vertically mobile. Upper nonmanual occupations have the highest level of occupational inheritance.

EDUCATIONAL FACTOR

Wages and earnings tend to correlate with the amount of education a person has obtained. In 2003, those workers with less than a high school diploma, earned a median income of $21,000; while those workers with a four year college degree earned a median income of $53,000 (James 2005). The poverty line in 2005 according to the U.S. Department of Health and

Human Services was $19,350 for a four-person household; therefore, those with less education are more likely to be bordering on this line than those with more education. With a college degree, it is more likely for one to attain a professional-level job wherein he or she may earn a higher salary in comparison to someone working in a secondary, service-based job.

Higher educational opportunities are necessary in order to pull away from the poverty line. Of the 30 fastest growing occupations, more than half require an associates degree or higher. Yet, these jobs are less likely to supply additional jobs to the labour market; meaning, the majority of job growth is found in low-wage jobs. These low-wage jobs are associated with those people who have less education. Workers in these areas are deemed unskilled because it does not require a great amount of education in order to perform these jobs, so the stereotype goes. White collar jobs, however, necessitate more human capital and knowledge and therefore produce higher earnings and require greater education. Therefore, it can be understood that education is a main determinant for potential social mobility in the American workforce.

GENDER AND RACE FACTOR

When examining status mobility within the American labour force, race and gender inevitably come into play. History has shown that women and minorities have a disadvantage in earning promotions; thus, being a woman or minority is one of the main determinants in hindering status mobility within the labour market. Women and minorities hold jobs with less rank, authority, opportunity for advancement, and pay than men and whites. This concept is considered to be the "glass ceiling" effect. Despite the increased presence of blacks and women in the work force over the years, there remains a very small percentage that holds top managerial positions, implying the "glass ceiling."

One explanation is seen in the networks of different genders and minorities. The more managers that are in employees' immediate work environment, the higher their chances are of interacting and spending time with high status employees. The race and sex composition of employees' immediate work environment should indirectly affect the status of their network members. For instance, the more women with whom employees work, the more women with whom they will interact, and thus the more women they will have in their networks. The more women and minorities that employees have in their networks, the more low-status network members they should have because women and minorities tend to occupy low-level positions in work organizations.

Less than half of all managers are women, whereas the vast majority of all clerical and office workers are women. Furthermore, less than fifteen per cent of all managers were minorities, whereas roughly a quarter of all clerical and office employees were minorities. The networks of women and minorities are simply not as strong as those of males and whites. Therefore, women and minorities have a clear disadvantage in status mobility from the beginning. In regards to women, another explanation for this "glass ceiling" effect in the American work force is due to the job-family trade off that women face compared to men. Data from the 1996 General Social Survey examined the trade-offs that women and men made as they attempted to balance their employment and family obligations, and the multiple ways that gender affects those trade-offs.

Evidence suggests that both parents face job-family conflict, but that men and women are almost equivalent in feeling like such a conflict exists. However, there is information that suggests women adjust their jobs around their family responsibilities more than men do. Some of these adjustments include adding flex-time, changing jobs, or creating part-time work. Women with children, particularly married women, are more likely to either temporarily leave the labour force or cut back on employment by working part-time or part of the year.

Unfortunately, part time employment generally applies to lower paying jobs. When women with children remain in these jobs, it takes out any chance they have of being promoted into a higher status job. Also, research shows that after a woman has had children and gone to part-time employment, she is not very likely to return to full-time employment for at least a few years. This gap of time can often lead to a decrease in the number of jobs that will become available to her. Taking a break from the work force tends to decreases human capital when it comes to find a job. Women are also more likely than men to take leave from their jobs to care for others rather than themselves.

This evidence makes employers wary of hiring and promoting women in the work force. Others have pointed out that men have statistically been willing to accept job conditions that women were not, such as working outside in extreme weather, working where you can become physically dirty on a regular basis, working more hours, etc. This is based on survey information, not speculation or stereotype, and shows that it is difficult to make direct comparisons ('apples to apples'). Economically, if it were less expensive to hire women for exactly the same duties, then every business interested in increasing profit margins would try to hire women exclusively; so it seems paradoxical that women have a harder time getting a job and also get paid less. This leaves doubt about the objectivity of the allegations.

Social mobility is especially difficult for immigrants in the United States. As George J. Borjas explains in his paper, *Social Mobility in the Immigrant Population*, the first generation of immigrants has the most difficult time adjusting to American society. They have to deal with language barriers in addition to trying to adjust to the new environment and culture. Second generation immigrants (those with at least one parent not born in the United States) adjust to life in the United States more easily. "There is significant economic 'catching up' between the first and second generations, with the relative wage of the second generation being, on average, about 5 to 10 per cent higher than that of the first generation" states Borjas. Since the second generation has access to American schools, they typically learn English in addition to their native language and understand the culture of their society better than their parents do. Borjas also argues that social mobility across generations depends on "ethnic capital," characteristics of the ethnic environment where children are raised.

"A highly advantaged ethnic environment—where most parents are college graduates, for example—imbues the children who grow up in that environment with valuable characteristics that enhance the children's socioeconomic achievement later in life," Borjas explains. Especially true for immigrant families, ethnic capital largely affects the second generation's social mobility. Intergenerational mobility is particularly apparent in immigrant households.

Every generation following the original immigrants appears to increase their income by 5 to 10 per cent, thus creating social mobility. Thus, if a family started out very poor when it migrated to the United States, they will improve their position in society substantially with every generation. However, Borjas noticed a trend known as regression towards the mean. It "acts like a double-sided magnet," pulling both extremes (very poor and very rich) towards the middle. For example, if parents in a family are very successful, it is likely that the children will also be successful but unlikely that they will be as successful as their parents were. Regression towards the mean creates more equality in the United States, regardless of where the parents start out.

THE NEGATIVE IMPACT OF INCARCERATION ON SOCIAL MOBILITY

Within the United States the prison population has been steadily increasing since the early 1970s and has now surpassed two million. This is the highest per capita rate in the world. This boom is largely fueled by the "War on Drugs" that was started with President Nixon in 1971 as an effort to help Vietnam vets recover from their addictions. It wasn't until Ronald Reagan that the "War on Drugs" took on its modern meaning. This war has had the effect of effectively creating an underclass by providing a number of ways to deny one of the most important tools for social mobility, Education.

- The drug war has combined with public school zero-tolerance policies to remove tens of thousands of adolescents from their public schools.

- Denial of higher education has been adopted as an additional punishment for drug offenders.
- The war on drugs siphons drug users out of society and into prison.

The lack of education for convicted felons is compounded with difficulties in finding employment. These two factors contribute towards a high recidivism rate and downward social mobility.

CLASS CULTURES AND NETWORKS

Cultural capital, a term first coined by French sociologist Pierre Bourdieu is the process of distinguishing between the economic aspects of class and powerful cultural assets. Bourdieu found that the culture of the upper social class is oriented more toward formal reasoning and abstract thought. The lower social class is geared more towards matters of facts and the necessities of life. He also found that the environment that a person is developed in has a large affect on the social class that a person will have.

SOCIAL SYSTEM

Societies which use slavery are an example of low social mobility because, for the enslaved individuals, upward mobility is practically nonexistent, and for their owners, downward mobility is practically outlawed. Social mobility is normally discussed as "upward only", but it is a two-sided phenomenon - where there is upward mobility, there can also be relative downward mobility. If merit and fortune play a larger role in life chances than the luck of birth, and some people can manage a relative upward shift in their social status, then some people can also move downward relative to others.

This is the risk that motivates people in power to increasingly devise and commission political, legal, education, and economic mechanisms that permit them to fortify their advantages. However, by controlling that inclination, it is possible in a growing economy for there to be greater upward mobility than downward - as has been the case in Western Europe. Official or legally recognized class designations do not exist in modern western democracies and it is considered possible for individuals to move from poverty to wealth or political prominence within one generation. Despite this formal opportunity for social mobility, recent research suggests that Britain and particularly the United States have less social mobility than the Nordic countries and Canada. These authors state that "the idea of the US as 'the land of opportunity' persists; and clearly seems misplaced."

Not only does social mobility vary across types of countries, it can also change over time. Comparing the United States to the United Kingdom, there was social mobility of different degrees existing between the two countries during different historical periods. In the United States in the mid-19th century inequality was low and social mobility was high. In the late 19th century, the U.S. had much higher social mobility than in the UK, due to the common school movement and open public school system, a larger farmer sector, as well as higher geographic mobility in the United States. However, during the latter half of the 20th and early 21st centuries, the difference between the social mobilities of the two countries has declined, as social inequality has grown in both countries, but particularly in the United States. In other words, the individual's family background is more predictive of social position today than it was in 1850.

In market societies like the modern United States, class and economic wealth are strongly correlated. However, in some societies, such as feudal societies transitioning to market societies, there is a reduced probability that class status and wealth overlap. Usually, though, membership in a high social class provides more opportunities for wealth and political power, and therefore economic fortune is often a lagging indicator of social class. In newly-formed societies with little or no established tradition (such as the American West in the 19th century) the reverse is true: Made wealth precipitates the elite of future generations.

Popular examples of upward social mobility from

America include Abraham Lincoln and Bill Clinton, who were born into working-class families yet achieved high political office in adult life, and Andrew Carnegie, who arrived in the U.S. as a poor immigrant and later became a steel tycoon. Examples from other countries include Pierre Bérégovoy who started working at the age of 16 as a metal worker and later became Prime Minister of France, Ramsay MacDonald the illegitimate son of a farm labourer and a housemaid who became Prime Minister of the United Kingdom, and Sir Joseph Cook, an Englishman who had no schooling and worked as a coal miner at the age of nine and went on to become Prime Minister of Australia.

SOCIAL SCIENCE AND UNDERSTANDING SEGMENTATION

Theory suggests that there is a connection between Social Psychologists understanding of collective identity and the way sociologists conceive it. Individuals are always seeking ways to define themselves with regard to the world around them and they can do this with the meaning given to community and the concept that people are different from others because of arbitrary differences. Boundaries could be sexual, racial, or lingual, or they could look at other definitions of boundaries. Geographical boundaries are an example that is strongly reinforced but not as apparent without extra symbols.

Sports teams are an excellent example of symbols that define geographic boundaries. When people place themselves, they must find a balance between their community or subgroup and larger communities and out groups (which are groups that can be perceived as having a distinct difference). Scientists "have been studying the segmentation between 'us' and 'them.'"

The social definition of groups creates entry and exit barriers that can help us understand the reasons that social mobility across group boundaries can be difficult. With symbols ranging from tattoos to elite prep schools, the concept of a boundary is readily apparent and seems to be instinctual. The interplay of 'achievement' with status with actual economic success depends largely on the way that the in-group perceives these values.

The nonparallel views of different groups at different point on the economic scale mean that advancement in some groups could be counter to the goals and directions of another group. High-income urban culture can define itself with multiple symbolic boundaries stemming from prejudice against other groups that they perceive to be of a different economic status. These actions make it difficult for others to interact with people who may be geographically very close. When groups consider themselves mutually exclusive, it is unlikely that they will worry about the well being of the others and are unwilling to share resources.

AN URBAN PLANNING PERSPECTIVE ON GROUP BOUNDARIES

Kevin A. Lynch touches on the concept of geographic boundaries and their social impact, as well as ways they can be manipulated in his book Image of the City. This work addresses the visible and invisible boundaries that are created in urban environments from an urban planners perspective. The spatial information people use to create boundaries can be as important to perception as other more culturally entrenched symbols. To use some of Lynch's own terms, the Paths that people use dictate their flow in every day behaviour, and what is accessible to them easily. Districts are large sections of the city that have some specific character; these create a means of building individual identity that is shared by those who live and work inside them, and felt by those that must cross Edges for various reasons. When seeking jobs or healthcare for instance.

According to Sampson, Morenoff, and Gannon-Rowley's article Assessing "Neighborhood Effects": Social Processes and New Directions in Research on the relationship between adolescent behaviour and indicators of residential differentiation, "Robert Park and Ernest Burgess laid the foundation for urban sociology by defining local communities as 'natural areas' that developed as a result of competition between businesses for land use and between population groups for affordable housing." This indicates that resources that are available to the community will largely be affected by the wealth of the population. There is change that happens in communities however, and they evolve over time.

This study suggests that longitudinal studies could observe trends in the community over time. As neighborhood dynamics change, there could be a movement of social groups into proximity with other similar groups creating a hybrid of the two cultures. Another possibility is that the groups in an area move around, but do not intermingle, and when they feel pressure that threatens their hold of an area, they could fight back at the local level, or choose to relocate to a place where economic conditions restrict entry.

The benefits of having symbols that define social boundaries work to keep people from falling down as much as they can prevent others from moving up. The value of work ethic that is shared in many cultures maintains an individual's drive and prompts them to seek out and hold employment. Symbols of social status such as leadership roles are important for developing role models, and leadership models are often seen by children as bridging the more detrimental class boundaries. As shown here: "There are also cross-cultural differences in how symbolic boundaries are linked to social boundaries. The same social boundary can be coupled with different symbolic boundaries as class distinctions in Europe are tied to the symbolic boundary between high culture and popular culture."

The ability for an individual to become wealthy out of poverty does *not* necessarily indicate that there is social mobility in his or her society. Some societies with low or nonexistent social mobility afford free individuals opportunities to initiate enterprise and amass wealth, but wealth fails to "buy" entry into a higher social class. In feudal Japan and Confucianist China, wealthy merchants occupied the *lowest* ranks in society (at least in theory). In pre-revolutionary France, a nobleman, however poor, was from the "second estate" of society and thus superior, at least in theory, to a wealthy merchant (from the "third estate"). In recent decades, new status hiearchies has emerged, leading to new opportunities for competition. India has seen a recent boom in employment, communication, distribution of goods, centralized administration, and urban living. This urbanization provides an escape from the ties of memberships in rural based communities. Factors that would predetermine an individual's status are not as effective in urban areas. According to Harold Gould, the criteria for determining occupations in India are a person's skill and quality of performance rather than place of birth. The status of any given role is based on its economic rewards and mobility.

Studies have also shown that technological advances have both displaced certain groups as well as offered the chance for upward mobility. Some groups find themselves displaced by developing technology because their economic and social status have declined (ex. water carriers in parts of Northern India have been displaced by the introduction of handpumps). In other cases, individuals are finding new occupation with the opportunity for upward mobility. Most advances, however, appear to coincide with the opportunity for enhancement of social status. According to sociologist John H. Goldthorpe, social mobility is normally seen in two ways. The first being that it is a basic source of social "structuration." The second is that the extent of mobility may be a strong indicator to the balance of power and different characteristics within a society.

CULTURE - MEANING, NATURE, CONSERVATION, DEVELOPMENT AND TRANSMISSION

Culture (from the Latin *cultura* stemming from *colere*, meaning "to cultivate") is a term that has different meanings. For example, in 1952, Alfred Kroeber and Clyde Kluckhohn compiled a list of 164 definitions of "culture" in *Culture: A Critical Review of Concepts and Definitions*. However, the word "culture" is most commonly used in three basic senses:

- Excellence of taste in the fine arts and humanities, also known as high culture

- An integrated pattern of human knowledge, belief, and behaviour that depends upon the capacity for symbolic thought and social learning
- The set of shared attitudes, values, goals, and practices that characterizes an institution, organization or group.

When the concept first emerged in eighteenth- and nineteenth-century Europe, it connoted a process of cultivation or improvement, as in agriculture or horticulture. In the nineteenth century, it came to refer first to the betterment or refinement of the individual, especially through education, and then to the fulfillment of national aspirations or ideals. In the mid-nineteenth century, some scientists used the term "culture" to refer to a universal human capacity. In the twentieth century, "culture" emerged as a concept central to anthropology, encompassing all human phenomena that are not purely results of human genetics. Specifically, the term "culture" in American anthropology had two meanings:

- The evolved human capacity to classify and represent experiences with symbols, and to act imaginatively and creatively; and
- The distinct ways that people living in different parts of the world classified and represented their experiences, and acted creatively.

Following World War II, the term became important, albeit with different meanings, in other disciplines such as sociology, cultural studies, organizational psychology and management studies. The term "cultural transmission" does not appear in Sigmund Freud's work, but the idea is implicit in such notions as *cultural heritage* and *phylogenetic inheritance*. Freud believed that the (since abandoned) biological precept, according to which "ontogenesis recapitulates phylogenesis," could be applied to human psychic development. The notion of cultural transmission refers to the possibility that the acquisitions of an individual or of a culture can be transmitted to descendents and form the basis of cultural development.

Freud addressed the topic for the first time in *Totem and Taboo* (1912-13a), where he advanced the hypothesis that the feeling of guilt over the murder of the primal father had persisted over the centuries and still affected generations that could know nothing directly about it. In Freud's later works, the main mechanism of transmission was said to be identification, which ensconced the lost object in the ego, as described in "Mourning and Melancholia", and finally produced an alteration in the ego that gave rise to the superego, as described in *The Ego and the Id* (1923b).

In the *New Introductory Lectures* (1933 [1932]) Freud observed that the superego could be viewed as the outcome of successful identification with the parental agency, and as the natural and legitimate heir to the Oedipus complex. As the bearer of tradition, the superego was a true agent of cultural transmission from one generation to the next. In *Moses and Monotheism* Freud returned to the idea of an archaic heritage and compared such inherited acquired characteristics to instincts in animals—an inheritance on par with symbolism. After Freud, the idea of phylogenetic transmission was seemingly relegated to the background, as an explanation of last resort, and the emphasis shifted toward a detailed and expanded study of identifications.

The point of departure for this was Freud's remark in the *New Introductory Lectures,* in which he observed that the child's superego was not formed in the image of the real or imaginary parents, but instead modeled on the parents' superego. The main focus soon moved beyond direct parental and intergenerational identifications to more distant identifications, such as those with grandparents, ancestors, or mythical characters in family history, who re-emerge amid the descendents as a kind of actualization of family prehistory. The theme of the intergenerational (or transgenerational) appears in psychotherapeutic work with families, children, and adolescents, and sometimes gives the impression that this sphere of observation is being invaded by the study of archaic identifications.

The other area where this theme comes to the fore is work with survivors or descendents of survivors of the Holocaust or other genocides, such as those committed by Latin American dictatorships. In these two areas, the importance of secrets, the unspoken, or ancestral crimes that the family has decided to bury, is much in evidence. In the case of the survivors of genocide, there is an attempt to make the traumatic situation disappear by denying it representation. But the buried material reappears two or three generations later, as a ghost that occupies the place where the concealment of important aspects of the ancestor's life has produced a "blank" in the descendant's psyche. In such cases, we speak of "alienating identifications." A particular aspect of this type of intergenerational transmission was studied by Nicolas Abraham and Maria Torok (1972/1978), in relation to the problem of grief.

We thus see that a number of ideas are related: in Freud's work we encountered identification, phylogenetic heritage, and intergenerational process; in other authors, the notions of transgenerational transmission, "fantasies of identification", and "alienating identifications." In summary, we may say that the concept of phylogenetic heritage has gradually been reconsidered, to the benefit of more detailed study of the mechanisms of possible transmission, notably identification, the core of the issue.

The uncovering of alienating factors in the subject's prehistory, factors that can go back several generations, has come to the fore, replacing the ideas of "family romance" and "mythical descent," so well known to us since Freud. But emphasis on the intergenerational may push analytic work in the direction of applied psychoanalysis, so distancing it from a deeper understanding of the configurations and processes of the analytic situation, which is the prime locus of psychoanalytic discovery. This danger may even be exploited by the ever-renewed faces of resistance to psychoanalysis.

SOCIAL DEVIANTS - INFLUENCES ON PERSONALITY DEVELOPMENT

An individual's personality is the complex of mental characteristics that makes them unique from other people. It includes all of the patterns of thought and emotions that cause us to do and say things in particular ways. At a basic level, personality is expressed through our temperament or emotional tone. However, personality also colors our values, beliefs, and expectations. There are many potential factors that are involved in shaping a personality. These factors are usually seen as coming from heredity and the environment. Research by psychologists over the last several decades has increasingly pointed to hereditary factors being more important, especially for basic personality traits such as emotional tone. However, the acquisition of values, beliefs, and expectations seem to be due more to socialization and unique experiences, especially during childhood.

Some hereditary factors that contribute to personality development do so as a result of interactions with the particular social environment in which people live. For instance, your genetically inherited physical and mental capabilities have an impact on how others see you and, subsequently, how you see yourself. If you have poor motor skills that prevent you from throwing a ball straight and if you regularly get bad grades in school, you will very likely be labeled by your teachers, friends, and relatives as someone who is inadequate or a failure to some degree. This can become a self-fulfilling prophesy as you increasingly perceive yourself in this way and become more pessimistic about your capabilities and your future.

Likewise, your health and physical appearance are likely to be very important in your personality development. You may be frail or robust. You may have a learning disability. You may be slender in a culture that considers obesity attractive or vice versa. These largely hereditary factors are likely to cause you to feel that you are nice-looking, ugly, or just adequate. Likewise, skin colour, gender, and sexual orientation are likely to have a major impact on how you perceive yourself. Whether you are accepted by others as being normal or abnormal can lead you to think and act in a socially acceptable or marginal and even deviant way. There are many potential environmental influences that help to shape personality.

Child rearing practices are especially critical. In the dominant culture of North America, children are usually raised in ways that encourage them to become self-reliant and independent. Children are often allowed to act somewhat like equals to their parents. For instance, they are included in making decisions about what type of food and entertainment the family will have on a night out. Children are given allowances and small jobs around the house to teach them how to be responsible for themselves. In contrast, children in China are usually encouraged to think and act as a member of their family and to suppress their own wishes when they are in conflict with the needs of the family. Independence and self-reliance are viewed as an indication of family failure and are discouraged. It is not surprising that Chinese children traditionally have not been allowed to act as equals to their parents.

Despite significant differences in child rearing practices around the world, there are some similarities. Boys and girls are socialized differently to some extent in all societies. They receive different messages from their parents and other adults as to what is appropriate for them to do in life. They are encouraged to prepare for their future in jobs fitting their gender. Boys are more often allowed freedom to experiment and to participate in physically risky activities. Girls are encouraged to learn how to do domestic tasks and to participate in child rearing by baby-sitting. If children do not follow these traditional paths, they are often labeled as marginal or even deviant. Girls may be called "tomboys" and boys may be ridiculed for not being sufficiently masculine.

There are always unique situations and interpersonal events that help to shape our personalities. Such things as having alcoholic parents, being seriously injured in a car accident, or being raped can leave mental scars that make us fearful and less trusting. If you are an only child, you don't have to learn how to compromise as much as children who have several siblings. Chance meetings and actions may have a major impact on the rest of our lives and affect our personalities. For instance, being accepted for admission to a prestigious university or being in the right place at the right time to meet the person who will become your spouse or life partner can significantly alter the course of the rest of your life. Similarly, being drafted into the military during wartime, learning that you were adopted, or personally witnessing a tragic event, such as the destruction of the World Trade Centre towers in New York, can change your basic perspective.

We often share personality traits with others, especially members of our own family and community. This is probably due largely to being socialized in much the same way. It is normal for us to acquire personality traits as a result of enculturation. Most people adopt the traditions, rules, manners, and biases of their culture. Given this fact, it is not surprising that some researchers have claimed that there are common national personality types, especially in the more culturally homogenous societies. During the 1940's, a number of leading anthropologists and psychologists argued that there are distinct Japanese and German personalities that led these two nations to view other countries as trying to destroy them.

The concept of national personality types primarily had its origins in anthropology with the research of Ruth Benedict beginning in the 1920's. She believed that personality was almost entirely learned. She said that normal people acquire a distinct *ethos*, or culturally specific personality pattern, during the process of being enculturated as children. Benedict went on to say that our cultural personality patterns are assumed to be "natural" by us and other personality patterns are viewed as being "unnatural" and deviant. She said that such feelings are characteristic of all people in all cultures because we are ethnocentric. Benedict compared the typical personalities of the 19th century North American Plains Indians with those of the farming Pueblo Indians of the Southwest.

She said that the bison hunting Plains Indians had personalities that could be typified as being aggressive, prone to violence, and seeking extreme emotional states. In contrast, she said that the typical Pueblo Indian was just the opposite—peaceful, non-aggressive, and sobre in personality. Benedict's views were especially popular in the 1930's among early feminists such as her student Margaret Mead. This was because if personality is entirely learned, it means that feminine and masculine personality traits are not biologically hard-wired in. In other words, culture rather than genes, makes women nurturing towards children and passive in response to men.

Likewise, culture makes men aggressive and domineering. If this is true, these stereotypical behaviors can be altered and even reversed. Mead carried out ethnographic field work among the Polynesian and Melanesian peoples of the South Pacific to find examples of societies in which femininity and masculinity have very different and even opposite characteristics from those found in the Western World. She began her research in Samoa in 1925 where she discovered a relaxed adolescence in which sex is talked about freely by boys and girls rather than hidden or suppressed.

Most anthropologists today believe that Benedict and her students went too far in their assertions about the influence of culture on personality formation and in discounting heredity. They also tended to over simplify by defining people who did not share all of the traits of the "national personality type" as being deviants. It is more accurate to see the members of a society as having a range of personality types. What Benedict was describing was actually the modal personality. This is the most common personality type within a society. In reality, there is usually a range of normal personality types within each society.

In the early 1950's, David Riesman proposed that there are three common types of modal personality that occur around the world. He called them tradition oriented, inner-directed, and other directed personalities. The tradition-oriented personality is one that places a strong emphasis on doing things the same way that they have always been done. Individuals with this sort of personality are less likely to try new things and to seek new experiences. Those who have inner-directed personalities are guilt oriented. That is to say, their behaviour is strongly controlled by their conscience. As a result, there is little need for police to make sure that they obey the law. These individuals monitor themselves.

If they break the law, they are likely to turn themselves in for punishment. In contrast, people with other-directed personalities have more ambiguous feelings about right and wrong. When they deviate from a societal norm, they usually don't feel guilty. However, if they are caught in the act or exposed publicly, they are likely to feel shame. Advocates of Riesman's concept of three modal personalities suggest that the tradition-oriented personality is most common in small-scale societies and in some sub-cultures of large-scale ones. Inner-directed personalities are said to be more common in some large-scale societies, especially ones that are culturally homogenous. In contrast, the other-directed personality is likely to be found in culturally diverse large-scale societies in which there is not a uniformity in socialization processes and there is considerable anonymity for city dwellers.

While Riesman's analysis of personalities was insightful, critics have pointed out that individuals may have characteristics of all three of his identified modal types. For instance, most North Americans probably do not feel guilty about exceeding speed limits when they are driving on freeways, however, they would feel very guilty hitting someone with their car and would likely call the police. In other words, for some infractions of the law they are other-directed (or shame-controlled), and for others they are inner-directed (or guilt-controlled).

Likewise, many people like to do some things in the same way every day but seek new experiences in other areas of their lives. You may like to wear the same style of clothes and spend your leisure time at the same place with your friends most days. However, you may easily get bored eating the same kinds of food every day and regularly try new restaurants when you go out to eat. In other words, you are tradition-oriented for some things but not others.

Unit V

Process of Socialisation

AGENTS OF SOCIALIZATION - FAMILY, SCHOOL, RELIGION, COMMUNITY; EDUCATION AS A SOCIAL SYSTEM, AS A SOCIAL PROCESS AND A PROCESS OF SOCIAL PROGRESS

Socialization may be defined as the totality of processes which a society uses to make young and new members learn the language, religion, norms and values of that society. Socialization can also be defined as the process by which an individual, born with potentialities of enormously wide range, is led to develop actual behaviour which is confined within a much narrower range- the range of what is customary and acceptable for him according to the standards of his groups. It is the acquisition of the ability to behave in accordance with expected social expectations.

In essence it is the totality of processes which a society uses to prepare its young and new members for a meaningful social living. It is germane to know that man is a social animal. We therefore learn to be human through meaningful social relationship with other members of the society. Being solitary is considered at all times is considered as an act of anti-socialism. When an adult leaves his immediate society for another, he will have to learn the culture of his new society. This process of being acquainted with the culture of the new society is called re-socialization.

THE PROCESS OF SOCIALIZATION

Socialization involves: proper performance behaviour;

playing of approved social role; and development of social attitudes. The two main types of socialization are formal and informal socialization. Formal Socialization involves the preparation of young and new members of a society for future careers. It is the kind of learning we receive in the school for social preparation of young and new members of a society for future careers. It is the kind of learning we receive in the school for social perpetuation and development. Formal Socialization provides members of the society with adequate knowledge and skills for the development of the society.

It also creates employment opportunities for members of the society. Informal Socialization on the other hand is the kind of learning we receive at home or from members of the society which is meant to prepare young and new members of the society for a meaningful social living. A child usually learns the language, religion, norms and values of the society from his family. This is why a family is considered as the primary agent of socialization. A child can also learn the norms and values of the society from his peer groups, neighbour and media. Agents of Socialization Agents of socialization are social systems and institutions which help in initiating young and new members into the way of life of the society. These agents are the family, the school, religious institutions, media, legal and political systems.

THE FAMILY SYSTEM

A family is a person's origin either by blood, marriage or adoption. Family is so important in a person's life that one cannot claim to have passed through it. It is the primary agent of socialization because a child learns his social responsibilities first from his family. Whatever value a child has is believed to be a reflection of his family. Types of Family Natal Family: This is the family to which a child is born or adopted. Conjugate Family: This is the family in which one is a spouse. Nuclear Family: This is the type of family that is made up of husband, wife and children.

It is also known as monogamous family. Joint Family: This type of family consists of a group of related families living together in a geographical area under the authority of a head. "Agbo-ile" in Yoruba community of Nigeria is a good example of joint family. Extended Family: This is similar to joint family but members do not live in the same geographical location. Compound Family: This is a type of family in which a man has more than one wife or a woman having more than one husband, and they are all living together. A marriage involving a man and two wives or more is known as polygamy. However, when a woman customarily or legally marries more than one husband, it is known as polyandry.

Single-Parent Family: This is a type of family in which either the husband or wife takes responsibilities of the children alone. Social Functions of the Family The family gives every member of the society an identity making it possible to trace their origin or lineage. It is also a source of societal regeneration and a reservoir of values. The family keeps society alive by producing new generation.

EDUCATION AND SOCIALIZATION

Education is an important agent of socialization. Education has systems: formal education and informal education. Both Systems play a major role in initiating members of the society into the way of life of the society. Formal education equips learners with adequate knowledge and skills which are required for doing new things or doing old things in new ways.

This helps to promote novelty and invention which are the ingredients for social development in the society. It also helps to prepare young members of the society for future careers. Informal education lends hand to the learning of moral behaviour, language, religion, greetings and other social values in the family.

Informal education helps to prepare young members of the society for adulthood and enables them to see themselves as being responsible for the social progress or the social ills of the society. Finally, informal education promotes professional preparation. Needless to say: every profession has its ethos. For example, teachers are meant to be disciplined, courageous, firm and sympathetic. All these qualities are learnt informally during professional training and practice.

SOCIOLOGY OF THE SCHOOL

Sociology of the school involves various activities taking place in the school that can affect the social life of the learner. Peer groups, teachers, and associations can influence learner's behaviour. Some of the socializing influence that takes place in the school includes the following:

- Teacher's influence on learners.
- Learner's influence on teachers
- Teacher's influence on fellow teachers
- Learner's influence on fellow learners

SOCIETY AND SOCIALIZATION

According to Jean D. Grambs (1965), a society is defined as a group of people who share a common culture- a culture that includes the formal and informal social arrangements, the mores, the language, the religious institutions and the processes of government. The following are the main features of a society:

- A society is a group of people in meaningful social interaction or relationship. This social interaction is seen in their common language, belief, commerce, politics and social functions.
- A society lasts longer than its members.
- A society is functional and operative.
- Her members share compatible ways of life. These include their language, norms, and the type of food they eat.

Socialization is a central process in social life. Its importance has been noted by sociologists for a long time, but their image of it has shifted over the last hundred years. In the early years of American sociology, socialization was equated with civilization. The issue was one of taming fierce individualists so they would willingly cooperate with others on common endeavors. An unruly human nature was assumed to exist prior to an individual's encounter with society.

This nature had to be shaped to conform to socially acceptable ways of behaving. As time went on, however, socialization came to be seen more and more as the end result— that is, as internalization. Internalization means taking social norms, roles, and values into one's own mind. Society was seen as the primary factor responsible for how individuals learned to think and behave. This view is evident in the work of functionalist Talcott Parsons, who gave no hint that the result of socialization might be uncertain or might vary from person to person.

If people failed to play their expected roles or behaved strangely, functionalists explained this in terms of incomplete or inadequate socialization. Such people were said to be "unsocialized"—they had not yet learned what was expected of them. The trouble is, they might very well know what was expected but simply be rejecting it. Someone who runs a red light, for example, knows perfectly well that one is not supposed to do that but is doing it anyway.

The possibility that individuals might have needs, desires, values, or behaviors different from those that society expects (or demands) of them was not seriously considered by functionalists. As Parsons used the term "internalization," it referred to the tendency for individuals to accept particular values and norms and to conform to them in their conduct. Dennis Wrong (1961) deplored this view of internalization as being an "oversocialized" conception of human beings. It left no room for the "animal" or biological side of human existence, where motivational drives might conflict with the discipline of internalized social norms.

Functionalists deny the presence in humans "of motivational forces bucking against the hold that social discipline has over them". Individual drives do sometimes conflict with social expectations, however. For example, a common theme in movies and TV is that of married people becoming involved in sexual relationships with persons other than their spouses. They *know* they are not supposed to have an affair, but they do so anyway.

Undoubtedly as a reaction to the overly determined

Parsonian view of socialization, a group of interpretive sociologists has reasserted the independence of individuals. They reject Parsons's view of socialization as internalized values, norms, and habits, and they reject the notion of society as something out there (a given) that affects individuals the way Parsons suggested it did. The interpretive perspective sees socialization as an interactive process.

Individuals negotiate their definitions of the situation with others. A couple, for example, may negotiate between themselves a conception of marriage that is sharply different from the view of marriage held by people in the larger society. The interpretive view offers an "undersocialized" view of human behaviour, since it tends to minimize the importance of historical social structures and the deep internalization of social values and norms. But the innovative couple may find that their personally developed conception of marriage is challenged or undermined by friends, in-laws, legal systems, employers, or others.

Both the functionalist and the interpretive views of socialization are incomplete. Each is relevant for understanding some features, but both tend to ignore other important aspects of social life. It is useful to combine the helpful points of each approach into a more complete view of socialization. Wentworth (1980) proposes exactly such a synthesis. He suggests that an adequate view of socialization must leave room for free will and human autonomy, though noting the patterned social structures and processes that influence individuals.

Wentworth's combined view clarifies the socialization that occurs in families, schools, groups, sports teams, organizations, and societies. It may also explain why resocialization programs such as those designed to rehabilitate criminals, drug addicts, alcoholics, or sex offenders often have relatively low rates of success.

We can distinguish three major aspects of socialization:

- The *context* in which it occurs
- The actual *content and processes* people use to socialize others
- The *results* arising from those contexts and processes

The *context* is like the theater or stage in which socialization occurs. Social context includes culture, language, and social structures such as the class, ethnic, and gender hierarchies of a society. Context also includes social and historical events, power and control in social life, and the people and institutions with whom individuals come in contact in the course of their socialization.

The *content and process* of socialization is like the play, the lines, and the actors. It includes the structure of the socializing activity—how intense and prolonged it is, who does it, how it is done, whether it is a total experience or only a partial process, how aware the individual is of alternatives, and how attractive those alternatives are. *Content* refers specifically to what is passed from member to novice. *Processes* are those interactions that convey to new members how they are to speak, behave, think, and even feel.

The view of socialization as an interactive process stands in contrast to the deterministic views of how socialization occurs.Old and new members interact, and in the process exercise mutual influence on each other.

Outcomes may properly be defined as what happens later, after someone has been exposed to particular content and processes. New members may learn the behaviors, attitudes, and values that old members hoped they would learn. What do these include? First and foremost among humans is learning how to speak and to apply the rules of language to creating new sentences.

Like learning to play chess, learning a language involves being shown some of the ways vocabulary and grammar can be combined (like learning how the various pieces can be moved in a chess game), and then creating one's own combinations from those possibilities.Closely related to learning to use a language is gaining a sense of the rules underlying a society's culture. Even learning to walk in an upright position appears to be the result of socialization. Socialization occurs within biological, psychological, and social contexts. Each of these offers possibilities and limitations that may influence socialization.

The Biological Context

Biological features are regularly suggested as sources of human behaviour. Sociobiologists suggest that some human capacities may be "wired into" our biological makeup. For example, even newborn babies seem to strive for maximum social interaction.

They move their heads back and forth in burrowing or "rooting" motions looking for milk; they have powerful, grasping fingers that cling tightly to other human fingers or bodies; and they move so as to maximize body contact with their caregivers. These facts suggest that infants are born wanting human contact.

Sociobiologists argue that traits which aid survival and reproduction (like learning not to eat things that induce vomiting) will survive, whereas others (like unusual whiteness in certain animals, which makes them easier prey) will tend to die out. Although this evidence suggests that biological factors clearly play a role in development, it does not show that all human behaviour is biologically determined.

Biology sets the stage, on which a very broad range of human behaviour occurs. Most or all of the important differences between societies are due to social rather than biological factors. As educators have become more aware of children with "learning disabilities," they have begun to wonder if some conditions, such as those labeled "dyslexia" (that is, the inability to grasp the meaning of something one reads) are due to the incomplete development of certain nerve pathways in the brain that may scramble signals on the way to the brain, making it likely that children will "see" *bs* instead of *ds*, *qs* rather than *ps*, and so forth.

Such problems may be part of the biological context of socialization. They may interact in significant ways with psychological and social factors during socialization and have important effects on the outcomes— for example, if children are labeled retarded or develop a sense of worthlessness, they may be less likely to learn. In short, biology provides rich potential for becoming human and may present general tendencies, such as the tendency to seek out social interaction or to use language, but it does not determine the particular form such social development takes.

The Psychological Context

The primary factor in the psychological context of socialization is the psychological state of the person being socialized. Psychological states include feelings such as fear, anger, grief, love, and happiness or a sense of emotional deprivation. Strongly feeling one or more of these emotions might very well inhibit or promote socialization of a particular kind. Fear may make it difficult for young children to be socialized in school, whereas people in love may leant very quickly what makes their loved ones happy. Emotions can also influence how individuals perceive the content of socialization, whether in becoming a member of a family group or a religious sect. Knowing something about the feelings of the people involved (the psychological context) helps explain the results of the socialization process.

Cognitive Development Theories

A number of psychologists emphasize the series of stages through which humans progress. Although emotional concerns can be involved, these theorists focus on cognitive (intellectual) development, which occurs in a systematic, universal sequence through a series of stages. The most influential theorist of intellectual development was the Swiss psychologist Jean Piaget. A sharp observer of children's development, Piaget stressed that children need to master the skills and operations of one stage of intellectual development before they are able to learn something at the next stage.

Whether or not they all agree on the unfolding of specific stages, cognitive development theorists see children as increasingly trying to make sense of their social worlds as they grow up. Children try to see patterns in the way things happen. Social contexts influence individual development. Culture exists before the socialization of new members begins. Parents, for example, do not need to decide alone what they arc going to teach their children, since much of what they will pass along they have themselves learned through socialization. Besides culture, individuals are affected by social and historical events and by a number of individuals who actively try to socialize them.

Major social and historical events can be a force in socializing an entire generation. Such major events as the Great Depression of the 1930s, the Holocaust in Europe during World War II, or the civil rights movement that took shape in the United States in the 1960s have profound implications for individual socialization. Elder (1974) compared children whose families were very poor during the 1930s with others whose families were more comfortable. Those suffering greater deprivation depended less on formal education for their life achievements and more on effort and accomplishment outside of education. Their health as adults tended to be affected negatively by their economic hardships. Finally, they tended to value marriage and family more highly as a result of their economic deprivation (Elder, 1974). Thus individuals who live in extraordinary times appear to be influenced by the historical events around them.

Obviously, parents and the immediate family of infants are important to their early care and development. Major changes in the family are increasing the importance of other caregivers as well. Teachers and schools transmit formal skills, knowledge, and social values. As infants mature, they have more and more contact with other children their age, called peers. Inevitably, children are affected by the community and nation in which they are reared. Children in the United States today spend a great deal of time with the mass media. Radio, movies, and— most significantly—television have transformed the way we experience the world and what we know about it.

THE FAMILY

In rural societies, children have most of their early social contact with the family. Today, however, the family's importance in the child's life is changing. The American family no longer necessarily conforms to the stereotypical nuclear family with two parents and two or more dependent children.

Fewer than one family in five consists of a working father, full-time homemaker mother, and at least one child. There are more and more single-parent families, and 56 per cent of all mothers with children under 6 years old are working. More and more children are receiving their early and primary care from others in addition to their parents. What are the effects on young children of having only one parent in the home?

Of having a mother who works outside the home? One study suggests that single parents with adequate financial and emotional support are able to raise their children quite effectively. Although most children growing up in America today will spend a great deal of time with people other than members of their families, this does not mean that the participation of families in socialization has ended. On the contrary, the family continues to be a major means of passing on values, attitudes, and behaviors. In the case of Alex and Alice as compared to Albert and his wife, family origin does a great deal to shape a child's social opportunities, resources, and experience. Different social positions may be related to different socialization for children even when they live in the same society.

DAY CARE

Nearly 10 million children 5 years old or younger have mothers who work away from home. This includes 48 per cent of the mothers of children 3 years old or younger. For these children, day care is an important agent of socialization. In 1982 there were more than 30,000 day-care centers, ranging from informal arrangements at the home of a neighbour to large nurseries run by schools, churches, charities, corporations, and occasionally employers. When the ratio of staff to children is at least one to ten or lower, when the groups of children are not larger than 20, and when caregivers are trained in early childhood development and are attentive to the children, the children who attend day care do very well. Children from very low income families have benefited considerably over the long term as a result of federally financed Head Start and other early day-care programs.

SCHOOLS

As societies become more complex and there is a greater division of labour, family members cannot spend all day every day teaching children what they need to know to function effectively as adults in society. Therefore, most societies have established schools to teach youngsters certain skills. Schools teach values and attitudes as well. These values and attitudes include, for example, competitiveness or cooperation, conformity or innovation. Schools try to impress upon children the importance of working for rewards, and they try to teach neatness, punctuality, orderliness, and respect for authority. Teachers are called upon to evaluate how well children perform a particular task or how much skill they have. Thus, in school, children's relationships with adults move from nurture and behavioral concerns to performance of tasks and skills determined by others.

PEERS

A peer group consists of friends and associates who are about the same age and social status. As children get older, going to school brings them into regular contact with other children of their age. As early as first or second grade, children form social groups. In these early peer groups, children learn to share toys and other scarce resources (such as the teacher's attention). Peers may reinforce behaviors that are stressed by parents and schools—for example, whether it is all right to hit someone else and what arc acceptable behaviors for boys and girls. As children move through school, the interests of peer groups may diverge more and more from those of adults. This is particularly true of the United States but seems also to be the case in certain socialist societies today.

Youthful concerns may centre on popular music and movies, sports, sex, or illegal activities. Parents and teachers, on the other hand, want children to do schoolwork, help at home, and "stay out of trouble." Peer groups may provide social rewards—praise, prestige, and attention—to individuals for doing things adults disapprove of. In the Soviet Union the peer group is used by authorities to reinforce the behaviors and attitudes they desire. For example, if a child comes to school late, it is not only the teacher who notes this (perhaps by praising children who are on time) but also those in the child's row in the classroom, who may be enlisted to urge the child to come to school on time.

Peer sanctions (punishments) are particularly effective. In Israel, for instance, in a collective farm group, a child who breaks a rule such as using a tractor when it is not allowed and damaging the machine in the process may be formally ostracized for some time. During this period the other children will not speak to or play with the child. Although effective in achieving social goals, the united effect of peer and official authority is more powerful and painful than official authority alone for the individual who does not conform. In our society, adolescents are heavily influenced by their peers when it comes to dress, musical fads, cheating, and drug use. In making their future life plans, however, they are influenced more by their parents than by their peers. Girls seem to be somewhat more influenced in their future life plans by peers than are boys.

COMMUNITY AND COUNTRY

Every society tries to influence how young people grow up. Much of this influence is expressed through parents, schools, and peers, but it is worth considering for a moment how children become exposed to the political and economic ideas that are considered important for citizens of a particular country. Children learn political information and attitudes rapidly during the elementary school years, particularly between fourth and fifth grades. One of the first things they learn is that they belong to some kind of a political unit. Even very young children develop a sense of "we" in relation to their own country and learn to see other countries in terms of "they." Children also tend to believe that their own country and language are superior to others. This bond may be the most critical socialization feature relating to the political life of the nation.

The family helps provide this basic loyalty to country, but the school also shapes the political concepts that expand and develop children's early feelings of attachment. Political orientations develop early and reach nearly adult levels by the end of elementary school, but there are still some critical changes that occur at other points during the life cycle. High school students become more aware of differences between political parties and tend to become more active politically. In the first decade of adult life people modify their political orientations as they take on new occupational and family roles. Children form economic ideas fairly early in life. One study examined how youngsters are socialized into capitalism. When third-graders were compared with twelfth-graders, the older students were found to hold more negative attitudes toward labour unions and more favorable attitudes toward business than did the younger children, suggesting that, over time, they developed attitudes that were more favorable toward capitalism, perhaps because of what they learned at school, from the media, or at home.

MASS MEDIA

The mass media include many forms of communication—such as books, magazines, radio, television, and movies—that reach large numbers of people without personal contact between senders and receivers. In the last few decades, children have been dramatically socialized by one source in particular: television. Studies have found that children spend more time watching TV than they spend in school. It seems unbelievable that in 1945 the pollster George Gallup asked Americans, "Do you know what television is?" Now virtually every American home has at least one television set, and the average set is on almost 7 hours a day. How has this transformation affected children? Reports vary, but children in the fifth to eighth grades view an average of 4 to 6 hours daily.

Most of the research on the effects of television has been on the cognitive and behavioral results of TV watching. The topic most often studied has been the influence of television on antisocial behaviour, especially violence. Current research supports the view that seeing violence on television increases the chance that a child will be aggressive. No publicly available studies unambiguously relate changes in behaviour (such as food habits or drug use) to exposure to television advertising.

Research also suggests that young people obtain considerable political and social information from television, but that how they perceive the information depends largely on parental influence. For example, during the Vietnam War, television was the most important source of public information about the war. Yet how young people felt about it— whether they favored or opposed it—seemed to be influenced more by their parents than by the opinions presented on television. Those who opposed the war interpreted the news on TV as opposing the war, whereas those favoring it saw the news as favoring it. Most researchers studying the effects of television on children have focused on the content of the programs and not on the total experience of television watching. They argue that there is too much violence and sex on children's programs and those more good educational programs for children are needed.

Winn (1977) suggests that the experience of watching television itself is limiting. When people watch television, no matter what the Programme, they are simply watchers and are not having any other experience. According to Winn, and many agree, children need to develop family relationships, the capacity for self direction, and the basic skills of communication (reading, writing, and speaking); to discover their own strengths and limitations, and to learn the rules that keep social interaction alive. Television works against all these goals by putting children in a passive situation where they do not speak, interact, experiment, explore, or do anything else active because they are *watching* a small moving picture on a machine. This research shows the growing importance of television as a medium of socialization, although clearly it is only one among a number of important influences.

Your family's social class, economic position, and ethnic background—as well as your gender—can affect the ways in which you will be socialized. People in more advantageous positions, like Alice and Alex, tend to develop higher self-evaluations. As a result, they feel justified in having more resources. Similarly, those in less desired positions tend to have lower self-evaluations and may feel that their lower status is deserved. Sociologists ask if children in different social classes are socialized differently. For instance are middle-class children socialized differently from lower-class children? If so, why and how? Middle-class parents are slightly less likely to use physical punishment than are lower-class parents. Middle-class parents appear to be more concerned about their children's intentions than with the negative consequences of their actions. Thus, if a child breaks a dish a middle-class parent will be concerned with whether he or she did it "on purpose" or whether it was an accident, and the reaction will vary accordingly. Lower-class parents tend to react in about the same way whatever the intention of the child.

These differences in parental response may stem from the life situations of people in different classes. Different parental experiences in the occupational world colour the view of what children need to learn. Parents who are closely supervised on the job (more often blue-collar workers) value conformity more than do less supervised parents (usually white-collar workers). Both blue- and white-collar parents increasingly prefer more autonomy in their children, at least in the Detroit area. Cross-cultural studies show that members of agrarian and herding societies (where food can be accumulated and stored) tend to emphasize compliance in their socialization practices. In societies where food cannot be stored (as in hunting, gathering, or fishing economies), members more often stress individual achievement and self-reliance.

Political structure may also be related to socialization practices. Autocratic states tend to have more "severe" socialization, show clear power and deference relationships, and stress obedience. The Soviet Union, for example, works harder to socialize children to conformity than does the United States. By way of contrast, tribal societies that lack a centralized or autocratic political system allow children to be less obedient and less conforming.

All these studies suggest that parents value different traits for their children, depending on the economic, political, and social situations they face. In general, when adults have more opportunities for self-determination, they value and try to develop greater self-reliance in their children. All groups try to socialize their children as well as they can, but they stress different behaviors, depending on what they see as needed in their own situation. Just as different societies may see the need for different behaviors and skills in their children, subgroups within society may do the same thing. They try to prepare their children as well as possible for the positions they are likely to hold.

TECHNOLOGICAL CHANGE - INDUSTRIALISATION AND MODERNISATION

Industrialization in US and Oxford English, is the process of social and economic change whereby a human group is transformed from a pre-industrial society into an industrial one. It is a part of a wider modernization process, where social change and economic development are closely related with technological innovation, particularly with the development of large-scale energy and metallurgy production. It is the extensive organization of an economy for the purpose of manufacturing. Industrialization also introduces a form of philosophical change, where people obtain a different attitude towards their perception of nature. There is considerable literature on the factors facilitating industrial modernization and enterprise development. Key positive factors identified by researchers have ranged from favorable political-legal environments for industry and commerce, through abundant natural resources of various kinds, to plentiful supplies of relatively low-cost, skilled and adaptable labour.

One survey of countries in Africa, Asia, the Middle East, and Latin America and the Caribbean in the late 20th century found that high levels of structural differentiation, functional specialization, and autonomy of economic systems from government were likely to contribute greatly to industrial-commercial growth and prosperity. Amongst other things, relatively open trading systems with zero or low duties on goods imports tended to stimulate industrial cost-efficiency and innovation across the board. Free and flexible labour and other markets also helped raise general business-economic performance levels, as did rapid popular learning capabilities. Positive work ethics in populations at large combined with skills in quickly utilizing new technologies and scientific discoveries were likely to boost production and income levels – and as the latter rose, markets for consumer goods and services of all kinds tended to expand and provide a further stimulus to industrial investment and economic growth. By the end of the century, East Asia was one of the most economically successful regions of the world – with free market countries such as Hong Kong being widely seen as models for other, less developed countries around the world to emulate.

According to the original sector classification of Jean Fourastié, an economy consists of a "Primary sector" of commodity production (farming, livestock breeding, exploitation of mineral resources), a "secondary sector" of manufacturing and processing, and a "Tertiary Sector" of service industries. The industrialization process is historically based on the expansion of the secondary sector in an economy dominated by primary activities. The first ever transformation to an industrial economy from an agrarian one was called the Industrial Revolution and this took place in the late 18th and early 19th centuries in a few countries of Western Europe and North America, beginning in Great Britain. This was the first industrialization in the world's history.

The Second Industrial Revolution describes a later, somewhat less dramatic change which came about in the late 19th century with the widespread availability of electric power, internal-combustion engines, and assembly lines to the already industrialized nations. The lack of an industrial sector in a country is widely seen as a major handicap in improving a country's economy, and power, pushing many governments to encourage or enforce industrialization. Most pre-industrial economies had standards of living not much above subsistence, meaning that the majority of the population were focused on producing their means of survival. For example, in medieval Europe, 80% of the labour force was employed in subsistence agriculture.

Some pre-industrial economies, such as classical Athens, had trade and commerce as significant factors, so native Greeks could enjoy wealth far beyond a sustenance standard of living through the use of slavery. Famines were frequent in most pre-industrial societies, although some, such as the Netherlands and England of the seventeenth and eighteenth centuries, the Italian city states of the fifteenth century, the medieval Islamic Caliphate, and the ancient Greek and Roman civilizations were able to escape the famine cycle through increasing trade and commercialization of the agricultural sector. It is estimated that during the seventeenth century Netherlands imported nearly 70% of its grain supply and in the fifth century BC Athens imported three quarters of its total food supply.

During the Arab Agricultural Revolution from the 8th to 13th centuries, the agricultural sector was revolutionized by a wider economy established across the medieval Islam I Arab world. This enabled the diffusion of many crops and farming techniques between different regions within and beyond the medieval Islamic world. As a result, the Islamic Caliphate experienced major changes in its economy, population distribution, population vegetation cover, agricultural production, income, and urban growth. Industrialization through innovation in manufacturing processes first started with the Industrial Revolution in the north-west and midlands of England in the eighteenth century. It spread to Europe and North America in the nineteenth century, and to the rest of the world in the twentieth.

INDUSTRIAL REVOLUTION IN WESTERN EUROPE

In the eighteenth and nineteenth centuries, Great Britain experienced a massive increase in agricultural productivity known as the British Agricultural Revolution, which enabled an unprecedented population growth, freeing up a significant percentage of the workforce from farming, and helping to drive the Industrial revolution.

Due to the limited amount of arable land and the overwhelming efficiency of mechanized farming, the increased population could not be dedicated to agriculture. New agricultural techniques allowed a single peasant to feed more workers than previously; however, these techniques also increased the demand for machines and other hardware which had traditionally been provided by the urban artisans. Artisans, collectively called bourgeoisie, employed rural exodus' workers to increase their output and meet the country's needs. The growth of their business coupled with the lack of experience of the new workers pushed a rationalization and standardization of the duties the in workshops, thus leading to a division of work, that is, a primitive form of Fordism.

The process of creating a good was divided into simple tasks, each one of them being gradually mechanized in order to boost productivity and thus increase income. The accumulation of capital allowed investments in the conception and application of new technologies, enabling the industrialisation process to continue to evolve. The industrialisation process formed a class of industrial workers who had more money to spend than their agricultural cousins. They spent this on items such as tobacco and sugar; creating new mass markets which stimulated more investment as merchants sought to exploit them. The mechanization of production spread to the countries surrounding England in western and northern Europe and to British settler colonies, making those areas the wealthiest and shaping what is now know as the Western world.

Some economic historians argue that the possession of so-called 'exploitation colonies' eased the accumulation of capital to the countries that possessed them, speeding up their development. The consequence was that the subject country integrated a bigger economic system in a subaltern position, emulating the countryside who demands manufactured goods and offers raw materials, while the metropole stressed its urban posture, providing goods and importing food. A classical example of this mechanism is said to be the triangular trade, who involved England, southern United States and western Africa. Critics argue that this polarity still affects the world, and has deeply retarded the industrialization of what is now known as the Third World. Some have stressed the importance of natural or financial resources that Britain received from its many overseas colonies or that profits from the British slave trade between Africa and the Caribbean helped fuel industrial investment.

EARLY INDUSTRIALIZATION IN OTHER COUNTRIES

After the Convention of Kanagawa, which was issued by Commodore Matthew C. Perry, had forced Japan to open the ports of Shimoda and Hakodate to American trade, the Japanese government realized that drastic reforms were necessary in order to stave off Western influence. The Tokugawa shogunate abolished the feudal system. The government instituted military reforms to modernize the Japanese army and also constructed the base for industrialization. In the 1870s, the Meiji government vigorously promoted technological and industrial development which eventually brought Japan to become a powerful modern country. In a similar way, Russia suffered during the Allied intervention in the Russian Civil War.

The Soviet Union's centrally controlled economy decided to invest a big part of its resources to enhance its industrial production and infrastructures in order to assure its own survival, thus becoming a world superpower. During the cold war, the other European communist countries, organized under the Comecon framework, followed the same developing scheme, albeit with a less emphasis on heavy industry. Southern European countries saw a moderate industrialization during the 1950s-1970s, caused by a healthy integration of the European economy, though their level of development, as well as those of eastern countries, doesn't match the western standards.

THE THIRD WORLD

A similar state-led developing programme was pursued

in virtually all the Third World countries during the Cold War, including the socialist ones, but especially in Sub-Saharan Africa after the decolonisation period. The primary scope of those projects was to achieve self-sufficiency through the local production of previously imported goods, the mechanisation of agriculture and the spread of education and health care. However, all those experiences failed bitterly due to lack of realism: most countries didn't have a pre-industrial bourgeoisie able to carry on a capitalistic development or even a stable and peaceful state. Those aborted experiences left huge debts toward western countries and fueled public corruption.

PETROL PRODUCING COUNTRIES

Oil-rich countries saw similar failures in their economic choices. An EIA report stated that OPEC member nations were projected to earn a net amount of $1.251 trillion in 2008 from their oil exports. Because oil is both important and expensive, regions that had big reserves of oil had huge liquidity incomes. However, this was rarely followed by economic development. Experience shows that local elites were unable to re-invest the petrodollars obtained through oil export, and currency is wasted in luxury goods. This is particularly evident in the Persian Gulf states, where the per capita income is comparable to those of western nations, but where no industrialization has started. Apart from two little countries (Bahrain and the United Arab Emirates), Arab states have not diversified their economies, and no replacement for the upcoming end of oil reserves is envisaged.

INDUSTRIALIZATION IN ASIA

Apart from Japan, where industrialization began in the late 19th century, a different pattern of industrialization followed in East Asia. One of the fastest rates of industrialization occurred in the late 20th century across four countries known as the Asian tigers thanks to the existence of stable governments and well structured societies, strategic locations, heavy foreign investments, a low cost skilled and motivated workforce, a competitive exchange rate, and low custom duties. In the case of South Korea, the largest of the four Asian tigers, a very fast paced industrialization took place as it quickly moved away from the manufacturing of value added goods in the 1950s and 60s into the more advanced steel, shipbuilding and automobile industry in the 1970s and 80s, focusing on the high-tech and service industry in the 1990s and 2000s. As a result, South Korea became a major global economic power today and is one of the wealthiest countries in Asia.

This starting model was afterwards successfully copied in other larger Eastern and Southern Asian countries, including communist ones. The success of this phenomenon led to a huge wave of offshoring – i.e., Western factories or tertiary corporations choosing to move their activities to countries where the workforce was less expensive and less collectively organised. China and India, while roughly following this development pattern, made adaptations in line with their own histories and cultures, their major size and importance in the world, and the geo-political ambitions of their governments (etc.). Currently, China's government is actively investing in expanding its own infrastructures and securing the required energy and raw materials supply channels, is supporting its exports by financing the United States balance payment deficit through the purchase of US treasury bonds, and is strengthening its military in order to endorse a major geopolitical role.

Meanwhile, India's government is investing in specific vanguard economic sectors such as bioengineering, nuclear technology, pharmaceutics, informatics, and technologically-oriented higher education, openly overpassing its needs, with the goal of creating several specialisation poles able to conquer foreign markets. Both Chinese and Indian corporations have also started to make huge investments in Third World countries, making them significant players in today's world economy.

NEWLY INDUSTRIALISED COUNTRIES

In recent decades, a few countries in Latin America, Asia,

and Africa, such as Turkey, South Africa, Malaysia, and Mexico have experienced substantial industrial growth, fueled by exportations going to countries that have bigger economies: the United States, Japan, China, and the EU. They are sometimes called newly-industrialised countries. Despite this trend being artificially influenced by the oil price increases since 2003, the phenomenon is not entirely new nor totally speculative. Most analysts conclude in the next few decades the whole world will experience industrialization, and international inequality will be replaced with worldwide social inequality.

NEGATIVE CONSEQUENCES

The concentration of labour into factories has brought about the rise of large towns to serve and house the working population.

The family structure changes with industrialization. The sociologist Talcott Parsons noted that in pre-industrial societies there is an extended family structure spanning many generations who have probably remained in the same location for generations. In industrialised societies the nuclear family, consisting of only of parents and their growing children, predominates. Families and children reaching adulthood are more mobile and tend to relocate to where jobs exist. Extended family bonds become more tenuous.

Environment

Industrialization has spawned its own health problems. Modern stressors include noise, air, water pollution, poor nutrition, dangerous machinery, impersonal work, isolation, poverty, homelessness, and substance abuse. Health problems in industrial nations are as much caused by economic, social, political, and cultural factors as by pathogens. Industrialization has become a major medical issue world wide.

In 2005, the USA was the largest producer of industrial output followed by Japan and China, according to International Monetary Fund. Currently the "international development community" (World Bank, OECD, many United

Nations departments, and some other organisations) endorses development policies based on merely poverty reduction, and giving poor populations access to basic services like water purification or primary education.

The community does not recognise traditional industrialization policies as being adequate to the Third World or beneficial in the longer term, with the perception that it could only create inefficient local industries unable to compete in a free-trade dominated world.

Unit VI

Population and Education

CONCEPT OF POPULATION

In biology, a population is the collection of inter-breeding organisms of a particular species; in sociology, a collection of human beings. Individuals within a population share a factor may be reduced by statistical means, but such a generalization may be too vague to imply anything. Demography is used extensively in marketing, which relates to economic units, such as retailers, to potential customers. For example, a coffee shop that wants to sell to a younger audience looks at the demographics of an area to be able to appeal to this younger audience. According to papers published by the United States Census Bureau, the world population hit 6.5 billion (6,500,000,000) on February 24, 2006. The United Nations Population Fund designated October 12, 1999 as the approximate day on which world population reached 6 billion. This was about 12 years after world population reached 5 billion in 1987, and 6 years after world population reached 5.5 billion in 1993.

However, the population of some countries, such as Nigeria, is not even known to the nearest million, so there is a considerable margin of error in such estimates. Population growth increased significantly as the Industrial Revolution gathered pace from 1700 onwards. The last 50 years have seen a yet more rapid increase in the rate of population growth due to medical advances and substantial increases in agricultural productivity, particularly in the period 1960 to 1995 made by the Green Revolution. In 2007 the United Nations Population

Division projected that the world's population will likely surpass 10 billion in 2055. In the future, world population has been expected to reach a peak of growth, from there it will decline due to economic reasons, health concerns, land exhaustion and environmental hazards. There is around an 85% chance that the world's population will stop growing before the end of the century.

There is a 60% probability that the world's population will not exceed 10 billion people before 2100, and around a 15% probability that the world's population at the end of the century will be lower than it is today. For different regions, the date and size of the peak population will vary considerably. Population control is the practice of curtailing population increase, usually by reducing the birth rate. Surviving records from Ancient Greece document the first known examples of population control. These include the colonization movement, which saw Greek outposts being built across the Mediterranean and Black Sea basins to accommodate the excess population of individual states. Infanticide, including abortion, was encouraged in some Greek city states in order to keep population down.

An important example of mandated population control is People's Republic of China's one-child policy, in which having more than one child is made extremely unattractive. This has led to allegations that practices like forced abortions, forced sterilization, and infanticide are used as a result of the policy. The country's sex ratio at birth of 114 boys to 100 girls may be evidence that the latter is often sex-selective. However, other countries without a one-child policy also have similar sex ratios but for different reasons such as nutrition. It is helpful to distinguish between fertility control as individual decision-making and population control as a governmental or state-level policy of regulating population growth. Fertility control may occur when individuals or couples or families take steps to decrease or to regulate the timing of their own child-bearing.

In Ansley Coale's oft-cited formulation, three preconditions for a sustained decline in fertility are: (1)

acceptance of calculated choice (as opposed to fate or chance or divine will) as a valid element in fertility, (2) perceived advantages from reduced fertility, and (3) knowledge and mastery of effective techniques of control. In contrast to a society with natural fertility, a society that desires to limit fertility and has the means to do so may use those means to delay childbearing, space childbearing, or stop childbearing. Delaying sexual intercourse (or marriage), or the adoption of natural or artificial means of contraception are most often an individual or family decision, not a matter of a state policy or societal-wide sanctions. On the other hand, individuals who assume some sense of control over their own fertility can also accelerate the frequency or success of child-bearing through planning.

At the societal level, declining fertility is almost an inevitable result of growing secular education of women. However, the exercise of moderate to high levels of fertility control does not necessarily imply low fertility rates. Even among societies that exercise substantial fertility control, societies with an equal *ability* to exercise fertility control (to determine how many children to have and when to bear them) may display widely different *levels* of fertility (numbers of children borne) associated with individual and cultural preferences for the number of children or size of families. In contrast to *fertility control,* which is mainly an individual-level decision, governments may attempt to exercise *population control* by increasing access to means of contraception or by other population policies and programs.

The idea of "population control" as a governmental or societal-level regulation of population growth does not require "fertility control" in the sense that it has been defined above, since a state can affect the growth of a society's population even if that society practices little fertility control. It's also important to embrace policies favoring population *increase* as an aspect of population control, and not to assume that states want to control population only by limiting its growth. To stimulate population growth, governments may support not only immigration but also pronatalist policies such as tax benefits, financial awards, paid work leaves, and childcare to encourage the bearing of additional children. Such policies have been pursued in recent years in France and Sweden, for example.

With the same goal of increasing population growth, on occasion governments have sought to limit the use of abortion or modern means of birth control. An example was Romania's 1966 ban on access to contraception and abortion on demand. In ecology, population control is on occasions considered to be done solely by predators, diseases, parasites, and environmental factors. In a constant environment, population control is regulated by the availability of food, water, and safety. The maximum number of a species or individuals that can be supported in a certain area is called the carrying capacity.

At many times human effects on animal and plant populations are also considered. Migrations of animals may be seen as a natural way of population control, for the food on land is more abundant on some seasons. The area of the migrations' start is left to reproduce the food supply for large mass of animals next time around. India is another example where the government has taken measures to reduce the country's population. Concerns that the rapidly growing population would adversely affect economic growth and living standards caused India to implement an official family planning Programme in the late 1950s and early 1960s; it was the first country in the world to do so.

IMPACT OF POPULATION GROWTH ON - SOCIAL, ECONOMIC AND ENVIRONMENTAL RESOURCES

Agricultural shortages exist because the human population is increasing faster than the food production capability of the agricultural system. Uneven distribution of food, inability to afford food, and political unrest also threaten world food security for human society. Currently, more than three billion humans worldwide are malnourished; this is the largest number and proportion of hungry people ever recorded in history (WHO, 1996)! Based on current rates of increase, the world population is projected to double to more than 12 billion in less than 50 years (PRB, 1997). As the world population continues to expand at a rate of 1.5%/year—adding more than a quarter million people daily—the task of providing adequate food becomes an increasingly difficult problem. The number of malnourished people could conceivably reach four to five billion in future decades.

Reports from the Food and Agriculture Office (FAO) of the United Nations and the U.S. Department of Agriculture, as well as numerous other international organizations, further confirm the serious nature of the global food supply problem. For example, the per capita availability of world cereal grains, which make up 80% of the world's food supply, has been declining since 1983.

These shortages have economic consequences as well, as is reflected in recent major increases in the price of cereal grains. Because the world population continues to expand, more pressure than ever before is being placed on the basic resources that are essential for food production. Unfortunately, the human population is growing exponentially, whereas food production can only increase linearly. Furthermore, degradation of land, water, energy, and biological resources that are vital to a sustainable agriculture continues unabated.

AGRICULTURAL RESOURCES

More than 99% of the world's food supply comes from the land; less than 1% is obtained from oceans and other aquatic habitats. As mentioned previously, the continued production of an adequate food supply is directly dependent on the availability of ample quantities of fertile land, fresh water, energy, and natural biodiversity. And obviously, as the human population grows, the requirement for all these resources escalates. Even if these resources are never completely depleted, their supply, on a per capita basis, will decline significantly because they must be divided among more and more people.

Throughout the world, fertile cropland is being lost from production at an alarming rate. This is clearly illustrated by the diminishing amount of land now devoted to cereal grains. Soil erosion by wind and water, in addition to general overuse of the land, are responsible for the loss of about 30% of the world's cropland during the past 40 years). The natural reformation of a mere 25 mm (1 inch) of fertile soil takes 500 years; to sustain adequate crop production, a soil depth of 150 mm is needed. Most eroded and unproductive agricultural land is now being replaced with cleared forest land and/or marginal land.

Indeed, the urgent need for more cropland accounts for more than 60% of the world's deforestation. Despite such land replacement strategies, per capita world cropland is declining, currently standing at only 0.27 ha per capita. This is only about 50% of the 0.5 ha per capita that is considered the minimum land area needed for the production of a diverse diet similar to that of the United States and Europe. Other countries have even less land; for example, China now has only 0.08 ha available per capita, about 15% of the accepted minimum.

Rainfall, and its collection in rivers, lakes, and vast underground aquifers, provides the water needed by humans for their personal survival and diverse activities. Fresh water is critical for all vegetation, especially crops. All plants transpire massive amounts of water during the growing season. For example, a hectare of corn, producing about 8,000 kg, transpires more than five million liters of water during just one growing season. This means that more than eight million liters of water must reach each hectare during the growing season both as rainfall and irrigation, to provide the adequate water supply for crop production. In total, agricultural production consumes more fresh water than any other human activity. About 70% of the world's fresh water supply is consumed, or used up by agriculture, making it unavailable for other uses.

Water resources are continually stressed as populous cities, states, and countries increase their withdrawal of water from rivers, lakes, and aquifers every year. For example, by the time the Colorado River reaches Mexico it has dwindled down to a trickle. Also, the great Ogalla aquifer in the central

U.S. is suffering an overdraft rate that is about 140% above its natural recharge rate. Water shortages in the U.S. and elsewhere in the world are already reflected in the per capita decline in crop irrigation that has occurred during the past twenty years. To compound the water problem, about 40% of the world population lives in regions that directly compete for shared water resources. In China, for example, more than 300 cities already are short of water, and these shortages are intensifying as Chinese urban areas and industries expand. Serious competition for water resources among individuals, industries, and regions both within and between countries is growing throughout the world community.

In addition to the quantity of water available, water purity also is vitally important. Diseases associated with impure and unsanitary water systems rob people of their health, nutrients, and livelihood. These problems are most serious in developing countries, where about 90% of common diseases can be traced to a lack of pure water. Worldwide, about four billion cases of disease and approximately six million deaths are caused by impure water or are water-borne each year. Furthermore, when a person is stricken with diarrhea, malaria, or other serious disease, from 5% to 20% of an individual's food intake is used by the body to offset the stress of the disease, further diminishing the benefits of his/her food intake.

Disease and malnutrition problems appear to be particularly serious in the third world, where poverty and poor sanitation is endemic. Poverty, disease, and malnutrition are especially serious in cities, particularly third-world cities. The number of people living in urban areas currently doubles every 10 to 20 years, creating environmental problems that include a lack of water and sanitation, increased air pollution, and significant food shortages. For these reasons, the potential for the spread and increase of disease is especially great in urban areas.

Energy from many sources, most importantly fossil energy sources, is a prime resource used in food production. About 75% of the fossil energy used each year throughout the world is consumed by populations living in developed countries. Of this energy, about 17% is expended in the production, processing, and packaging of food products. In particular, the intensive farming technologies characteristic of developed countries rely on massive amounts of fossil energy for fertilizers, pesticides, irrigation, and machines that substitute for human labour. In contrast, developing countries use fossil energy primarily for fertilizers and irrigation to help maintain yields, rather than to reduce human labour inputs.

The present world supply of oil is projected to last approximately 50 years at current production rates. The world's natural gas supply is considered adequate for about 50 years, and the coal supply for about 100 years. These projections, however, are based on current consumption rates and current population numbers; if population and consumption levels continue to increase, these fossil energy stores could be depleted even faster. Youngquist (1997) reports that current oil and gas exploration drilling data has not borne out some of the earlier optimistic estimates of the amount of these resources projected to be in the United States. Both the production rate and proven reserves have continued to decline.

Reliable analyses suggest that by now (1999) the United States has consumed about three-quarters of the recoverable oil that was ever in the ground, and that we are currently consuming the last 25% of U.S. oil resources. Projections suggest that U.S. domestic oil and natural gas production will be substantially less in 20 years than it is today. Even now, U.S. oil supplies are not sufficient to meet domestic needs, and oil is imported in increasing yearly amounts. Importing 60% of its oil puts the United States economy at risk, due to fluctuating oil prices and difficult political situations, such as occurred during the 1973 oil crisis and the 1991 Gulf War.

A productive and sustainable agricultural system, as well as the quality of human life, also depends on maintaining the integrity of the natural biodiversity that exists on earth. Diverse species, though most are small in size, serve as natural enemies to control pests, help degrade wastes, improve soil quality, fix nitrogen for plants, pollinate crops and other vegetation, and provide numerous other viral services for humans and their environment. Consider that one-third of all crops worldwide require insect pollination. Humans have no technology to substitute for this viral pollination task, or for many of the other contributions provided by the estimated 10 million species that inhabit the earth. Biodiversity has an economic value for the world as well. For instance, it is estimated that the benefits of natural species to the U.S. economy is more than $300 billion/year, and approximately $3 trillion/year for the world.

Many assumptions have been made as to how market mechanisms and international trade will function to effectively ensure against future food shortages. Unfortunately, the biological and physical limits of resources are typically overlooked in this equation. When these limits of resources are reached, food exports and imports will no longer be a viable options for countries. At that point, food importation for rich countries will only be sustained by starvation of the poor. In the final analysis, the existing biological and physical resource constraints regulate and limit all food production systems. These concerns about sustainable food sources for the future are supported by two observations.

First, most of the 183 nations of the world now are dependent on food imports. Most of these imports are cereal grain surpluses produced only in those countries that now have relatively low population densities, where intensive agriculture is practiced and where surpluses are common. For instance, the United States, Canada, Australia, France, and Argentina provide about 80% of the cereal exports on the world market. This situation is expected to change, if, the U.S. population doubles in the next 70 years as projected by the current population growth rate. Then, instead of exporting cereals and other food resources, these foods will have to be retained domestically to feed 540 million hungry Americans. The United States will no longer be able to serve as a primary food exporter.

In the future, when the four major food exporting countries retain surpluses for home use, Egypt, Jordan, and countless other countries in Africa and Asia will be without the food imports that are essential to their survival. China, which now imports many tons of food, illustrates the severity of this problem. If, as Brown (1995) predicts, China's population increases by 500 million beyond their present 1.2 billion and their soil erosion continues unabated, it will need to import 200-400 million tons of food grains each year starting in 2050. This minimal quantity is equal to more than the current grain exports of all the current exporting nations mentioned earlier. Based on realistic trends, by 2050, sufficient food supplies probably will not be available for import by China or any other nation on the international market.

TECHNOLOGY

Over time, technology has been instrumental in increasing industrial and agricultural production, improving transportation and communications, advancing human health care, and generally improving many aspects of human life. However, much of technology's success is based on the availability of the natural resources of the earth. In no area is this more evident than in agricultural production. No current or conceivable future technology will be able to double the world's arable land. Granted, technologically produced fertilizers are effective in enhancing the fertility of eroded croplands, but their production relies on the diminishing supply of fossil fuels. In fact, fertilizer use per capita during the past decade has decreased 23% and continues to decline, probably due to increasing economic costs.

The increase in the size and speed of fishing vessels has not resulted in increases in per capita fish catch. To the contrary, in regions like eastern Canada, over-fishing has become so severe that about 80,000 fisherman have no fish to catch, and the entire industry has been lost. Consider also that the available supplies of fresh water must be shared by more individuals, for the expanding agriculture and industry required to support an increasing population. No currently available technology can double the flow of the Colorado River; the shrinking ground water resources in vast aquifers cannot be refilled by human technology. Rainfall is the only legitimate supplier of water. Certainly improved technology can continue to help increase food production. Technology can result in more effective management and conservation of resources, but technology cannot produce an unlimited flow of those vital natural resources that are the raw material for sustained agricultural production. What technology can be used to stop the decline in per capita cereal grain production that has been diminishing since 1983 and continues to decline?

Biotechnology has the potential for some advances in agriculture, provided genetic modifications are cautiously and wisely used. However, the biotechnology developments from more than 20 years ago have not been able to stem the decline in per capita food production during the past 15 years. Currently, about 40% of the research effort in biotechnology is devoted to the development of herbicide resistance in crops. This technology will not achieve its promise to increase crop yields, but it will increase the use of chemical herbicides and the pollution of the environment.

We can no longer afford to ignore the fact that per capita food production has been declining for more than a decade, that now more than three billion people are malnourished. Related to this decline has been a per capita decrease in availability of the following resources: Fertilizers, 23%; cropland, 20%; irrigation, 12%; forest products and fish, 10%. Strategies for global food security must be based first and foremost on the conservation and ecological management of the land, water, energy, and all biological resources that are essential for a sustainable agricultural system. Our stewardship of world resources must change. The basic needs of all people must be brought into balance with the life sustaining natural resources.

The conservation of these resources will require the coordinated efforts of all individuals and all countries. Once these finite resources are exhausted they cannot be replaced by human technology. More efficient and environmentally sound agricultural technologies must be developed and put into practice to support the sustainability of agriculture and life on earth. Unfortunately, none of these ecologically sound conservation measures will be sufficient to ensure adequate food supplies for future generations unless the growth in the human population is simultaneously curtailed. Several studies have confirmed that to in order to enjoy a relatively high standard of living, the optimum human population should be less than 200 million for the United States and less than two billion for the world.

This seemingly harsh projection assumes, that from now until such an optimum population is achieved, all strategies for the conservation of soil, water, energy, and biological resources will be successfully implemented and an ecologically sound, productive environment will be maintained. The lives and livelihood of future generations depend on what the present generation is willing to do now to make agriculture sustainable and conserve the world's ecological resources.

POPULATION POLICIES - TEACHERS ROLE IN POPULATION EDUCATION

At the time of the World Population Conference in 1974, representatives from many countries argued that the best form of contraception was economic development. The conventional wisdom at the time assumed that once developing economies improved, the "demographic transition" would be automatic. Many countries have since modified their assumptions. One reason for this turnaround in thinking was the intrusion of reality: no such automatic process took place. In addition, information campaigns launched by UNFPA, NGOs and other development agencies demonstrated that population and development programmes, working in tandem, can provide the key to lower fertility rates. In this task, the media played, and will continue to play, a paramount role.

Although editors and writers have periodically rediscovered "population issues" over the last 25 years, they are still regarded as a "soft" topic. Nevertheless, the mass media are giving increased space to the connections linking population issues to environment and development concerns. One of the reasons for this is that the UNFPA annual *The State of World Population report* has received worldwide media attention. More than 1,000 publications around the world ran articles, features and editorials about the 1993 *The State of World Population report,* and 400 radio and television stations broadcast special programmes based on material from the report or interviews with population experts. Journalists and editors are becoming more sensitized to the subject of population growth and its relationship to the sustainable management of the planet.

Specialized coverage of population issues has also improved: a number of popular forums now exist through which population and family planning issues can be disseminated to a wider, non-specialized audience. The Fund's own monthly magazine *Populi,* with a readership estimated at more than 100,000 provides coverage of population and family planning issues to an international audience. Also, population issues are aired through the annual World Population Day, sponsored by UNFPA, which includes information and educational activities, including an international poster competition for schoolchildren. Recognizing that the media can either enhance or undermine public confidence in population programmes in general, and in family planning in particular, national and international population programmes are paying more attention to media needs for their converage of population issues.

Although information on population has improved significantly over the past two decades, many countrywide programmes have had limited success in getting their message out to rural areas. Persuading the electronic media, especially radio, to increase programming on population issues is one of the tasks facing planners during this decade. Radio, in fact, could be used far more effectively than it is. It has been estimated that there are more than 1.9 billion radios in the world, or one for every three people. Radio shows are relatively inexpensive to produce, compared with film or television, and radio does not require expensive hardware. Listening to the radio is convenient; people can listen while they work; it is entertaining; and radios are carried everywhere.

Sensitive television and radio programmes, which treat population and family planning topics in a no-nonsense fashion, can reach millions of people missed by the print media. Even the poorest, illiterate farmer can listen to a village radio set or watch television. India, the Philippines and the Republic of Korea were among the first countries to establish strong national family planning policies, and their government-owned radio and television stations have long been employed on behalf of their national population programmes.

As early as 1964, in Seoul, radio, home visits and other media were used to tell 45,000 women about contraceptive supplies and services. In Colombia, Costa Rica and the Dominican Republic, special radio programmes increased family planning acceptance rates. Community-based local radio stations have also begun to proliferate in some regions. In Peru, for instance, community-operated radio stations offer listeners topical, relevant commentary and information on a host of subjects, including immunizations for children, reproductive health and family planning.

Television has been used increasingly for informing the public about population and family planning issues. Some 20 countries have launched their own television programmes, usually in the form of educational spots of mini-dramas, to promote reproductive health and family planning. Mexico's family planning soap opera is exported to the rest of Spanish-speaking Latin America. Experience has shown that the most effective way to increase public awareness of population and health-related issues is to launch multimedia campaigns, employing television, radio, newspapers, magazines and specially prepared information booklets. A well-coordinated, comprehensive national strategy can reach millions of the uninformed.

The acceptance of population action plans is determined not only by the availability of services but also by the amount of interest in and demand for them. Population communication activities, such as promoting public support for census-taking operations, are essential ingredients of population programmes at both national and intercountry levels. To ensure success, communication planners must conceive, design and carefully implement a whole range of activities. Communication strategies need to be feasible, culturally acceptable and financially viable, facilitating programme acceptance within a specified time-frame. In addition, the results of those strategies should be measurable.

Today, more is being done in IEC programmatic areas, such as providing counselling for users of family planning services; preventing STDs (including HIV/AIDS); creating awareness of the linkages between resource use and population dynamics; social marketing of contraceptives; addressing adolescent reproductive health; and using entertainment to foster awareness. Because Governments decide on the objectives of national-level population programmes, communication activities vary from country to country, depending on the priority attached to population policies. Many countries have adopted as a basic principle the right of parents to decide in a responsible manner the number and spacing of their children. In such countries, communication complements other programme activities to ensure the provision of information and the availability of family planning services.

Well-directed communication campaigns also assist community workers in discharging their duties, enhancing the acceptance of clinic-based education programmes. In Egypt, for example, the state-controlled television network is running a highly successful series of family planning "mini-dramas". The scripts are well written and imaginative, and the characters are played by well-known actors and actresses. These mini-dramas run for up to 10 minutes and are so popular that a full 90 per cent of households surveyed after one year had seen the spots, could recall the characters and remembered the message. This communication campaign, among others, is one of the reasons why Egypt's contraceptive prevalence rate rose more than 10 percentage points in four years, one of the fastest rates of increase ever recorded.

The country's contraceptive prevalence rate is now nearly

50 per cent and rising. A UNFPA grant made the initial production of this series possible. Similar successes have been recorded in Mexico and Turkey. A Mexican television soap opera series is credited with bringing in thousands of women to family planning clinics. In Turkey, a special family planning programme aired weekly is watched by 55 per cent of all adult viewers. Television is also being used in Kenya and the United Republic of Tanzania. In the United Republic of Tanzania, for instance, modern research techniques are being applied to ensure the relevance of content and to measure the programme's impact on viewer attitudes towards family planning.

Population information centres now exist in almost every country whereas, 25 years ago, only a handful operated. Some are small libraries supporting a demographic training or research unit within a ministry, a university or a specialized agency. Others focus on a specific sector and are designed to support, for example, population education in schools, family planning programmes or national statistical data management. One of the most important developments in population information services is the growth of regional, subregional and international networks. These networks include the Association for Population/Family Planning Libraries and Information Centres (APLIC), with APLIC International being the first successful population information network servicing population libraries and information specialists.

The United Nations Population Information Network (POPIN), established in 1979, has a membership of institutions engaged in population information activities around the world. One of the largest regional networks is operated by the United Nations Economic and Social Commission for Asia and the Pacific (ESCAP), which has provided national population information centres with technical assistance, training and equipment. A subregional network—POPIN ASEAN—has been set up for members of the Association of South-East Asian Nations (ASEAN). In 1988, POPIN Africa was also launched. The Latin American Demographic Centre (CELADE), established in 1976, has set up a population documentation system, called DOCPAL, to help the countries of Latin America and the Caribbean collect, store, process and retrieve information on population. Another network, PROLAP, consisting of some 50 NGOs with an interest in population, is also operating in the region.

Population issues affect all aspects of life and must be treated as an integral part of school education. Children who grow up with an understanding of population and development issues and who learn about the importance of family planning and receive proper sex education become more responsible and informed adults, able to play active roles in social change and community development. There are four other reasons why school systems are important vehicles for population education. First, school systems reach the most children throughout any given country. Second, children who spend a number of years in school are likely to be the future leaders of their communities and countries.

By virtue of their formal education, they will be in a better position to hold important private-sector and government jobs. Third, retaining girls in school longer has a direct bearing on how employable they become and on the eventual size of their families. In addition, when both boys and girls are exposed to population education through the school curriculum, their knowledge, attitudes and decisions regarding other population issues can be influenced as well. Fourth, teachers — particularly those in rural areas — are often recognized community leaders. Their attitudes towards population issues and their own fertility behaviour add another dimension to the effects of population education in schools.

Since its first tentative introduction into school systems in the 1960s and 1970s, population education has expanded rapidly. El Salvador, India, Malaysia, the Philippines, Singapore, Sri Lanka and Thailand were among the first countries to introduce population education in their school curricula. Other areas quickly followed suit. By the mid-1980s, about 80 countries included population education in their schools. As of 1994, 100 countries were estimated to have such projects, with 41 in Africa, 26 in Asia and the Pacific, 13 in the

Arab States, 19 in Latin America and the Caribbean, and one interregional project. UNFPA has expanded its activities in formal population education, providing assistance to 98 new and ongoing projects in all regions in 1993.

These activities helped to initiate population education or consolidate its institutionalization in Benin, China, the Dominican Republic, Morocco, Nepal, Nigeria, Syrian Arab Republic, Togo and Yemen, among others. Furthermore, successful projects begun in the early 1980s took advantage of educational reforms in Nigeria and Morocco to complete the integration of population concepts into the general curricula and textbooks intended for both primary and secondary schools. Of course, the goals and content of population education differ among regions and countries. As a long-term policy goal, some countries aim at reducing the population growth rate. Others are concerned with improving family health and welfare, or with lowering the number of adolescent pregnancies.

Some countries, such as the Dominican Republic and Fiji, have also developed HIV/AIDS education information in school projects and have improved their sex education materials. Not only can population education help achieve such ends, but the nature of these aims helps determine the selection of content and approaches to population education. Now, more attention is being paid to family planning and to human sexuality, including gender issues, in the school systems of developing countries. Educating and empowering future mothers and fathers with decision-making information about contraception and smaller families will go a long way towards improving the quality of life for millions in the next century.

The importance of educating girls was highlighted during the Education for All Summit of Nine High Population Countries held in New Delhi, India, in December 1993, and amplified in the Programme of Action of the ICPD. Noting that "the eradication of illiteracy is one of the prerequisites of human development", the Programme of Action urges countries to take "steps to keep girls and adolescents in school". Increasingly, too, it is recognized that access to education alone is not sufficient to improve women's status, or to have an important impact on fertility. The quality of education — what girls learn and how they learn it - is a key factor in determining the eventual impact of education on behaviour patterns.

The main contribution of population education is in its impact on the overall quality of education that girls receive. If population education is timely and relevant to their lives, it strikes a positive chord in both teachers and pupils. Similarly, what boys learn about gender issues and how this influences their attitudes about women and the family is also vital to improving the status of women. In 1992, UNESCO compiles two books of examples of gender lessons from population education projects in Asia and Latin America. The results are being shared with developing countries around the world and serve as a basis for improving approaches to teaching about gender issues in the classroom.

Population education, although it is beginning to come of age in many countries, still needs to be institutionalized if it is to play its full role. Ways need to be found to ensure that population education continues to be a standard feature of both formal and non-formal educational systems. Key indicators that the institutionalization of population education programmes is under way are the following:

- Government commitment and support, which are reflected in, inter alia, the financial and human resources necessary for implementation, and the required policy and legislative changes.
- The creation of a central population education unit, usually within a ministry of education, with sufficient trained staff.
- The dedication, commitment and motivation of a "core team" — the central staff assigned to introduce population education — which are of paramount importance.
- The availability of high-quality technical assistance and back-up. Thus far, UNESCO, with UNFPA

funding, is the primary source of international expertise on population education for the formal sector.

- Sensitization and awareness creation at the national level among decision makers, programme implementors and the media, as well as on the local level with parents, religious leaders and the public.
- Adequate training for educators and production of quality teaching materials.
- The elaboration of a carefully worked-out planning document for introducing population education.

One way to tackle the problem of teenage pregnancies — on the rise in many regions — is to stress the family life and human sexuality components of population education in schools, combined with "youth-friendly" family planning programmes and access to contraceptives, where such activities would be culturally and socially acceptable. In some countries in Africa and Asia, teenagers below 18 years of age account for a full 50 per cent of all pregnancies.

Attitudes towards early sexual activity and child-bearing vary from country to country, as do the social consequences depending on whether a young mother is married. In all cases, however, the negative health consequences of many adolescent pregnancies are compounded by poor or non-existent prenatal care. In addition, most teenage women who bear children face limited educational and job opportunities. With limited prospects for the future and a high degree of dependency, it is too easy for teenage mothers to fall into a cruel cycle of more pregnancies. Education can break this cycle. But the programmes must be developed and launched.

Single-motherhood is not the only adolescent reproductive health issue. In countries where early marriage is prevalent, UNFPA has encouraged recognition of the health consequences of early pregnancies. The Fund has also studied and publicized the efforts of some countries — for example, Indonesia, Mexico and the Philippines — which have initiated educational activities for newly-wed couples, attempting to make this type of education more widespread. Reproductive health services for young people have been slow to emerge and are often controversial where they have taken form. Nevertheless, some excellent programmes have been developed to meet the reproductive and health needs of young people.

The Philippines has three centres especially designed for adolescents. Also, educational and clinic-based programmes in Antigua and Barbuda, Brazil, Chile, Ecuador, Guatemala, Indonesia, Jamaica, Mauritius, Montserrat, Nigeria and Peru focus on the needs of teenagers. The Adolescent Orientation Centres in Mexico City (CORA) and neighbouring areas go even further. Launched in 1978, these youth centres offer educational, medical, psychological and recreational activities for 11-19-year-olds. Family planning services, sex information and counselling are also available, and an outreach programme promotes the participation of young people in local community-development projects.

In Jamaica, the Women's Centre Programme for adolescent mothers displays an innovative participatory approach to meeting the health, education and family planning needs of young mothers. It was begun by the Jamaican Women's Bureau in an effort to permit the continued education of pregnant teenage girls (aged 12-16) who, because of social censure, had to withdraw from school. The programme has been a great success — nearly every teenage drop-out has gone back to school, and less than 5 per cent of the girls became pregnant again before finishing their secondary education.

Recently, the Fund provided assistance to the Mexican Family Planning Federation to develop and refine a sex education course addressing five closely related topics: communication within the family; puberty and reproduction; ethics of sexuality and youth; prevention of sexually transmitted diseases (STDs); and early pregnancy. The major stumbling-block to furthering sex education in many areas of the world is the simple fact that policy makers, opinion leaders and parents are either unaware of the benefits or oblivious to the problems. Educating these groups must also be given more priority by national population programmes.

To increase awareness of the support for population and family planning programmes, UNFPA has also supported projects outside the formal educational system. In Egypt, India, Indonesia, Malawi, Mali, Mexico, Mozambique, Nepal, Niger, Pakistan, the Philippines and Senegal, to name a few, family life education has been integrated into the general educational programmes of national cooperatives, workers' unions and adult literacy courses. Such projects have now been launched in all regions where UNFPA is active.

Unit VII

Recent Trends in Education

EDUCATION AND DEMOCRACY

The conventional wisdom, since at least the writings of John Dewey (1916), views high levels of educational attainment as a prerequisite for democracy. Education is argued to promote democracy both because it enables a "culture of democracy" to develop, and because it leads to greater prosperity, which is also thought to cause political development. The most celebrated version of this argument is modernization theory, popularized by Seymour Martin Lipset (1959), which emphasizes the role of education as well as economic growth in promoting political development in general and democracy in particular.

Lipset, for example, argues that "Education presumably broadens men's outlooks, enables them to under- stand the need for norms of tolerance, restrains them from adhering to extremist and monistic doctrinies, and increases their capacity to make rational electoral choices", and concludes "If we cannot say that a "high" level of education is a sufficient condition for democracy, the available evidence does suggest that it comes close to being a necessary condition".

Recent empirical work, for example, by Robert Barro (1999) and Adam Przeworski, Michael Alvarez, José A. Cheibub and Fernando Limongi (2000), provides evidence consistent with this view. Edward Glaeser, Rafael La Porta, Florencio Lopez-de-Silanes and Andrei Shleifer (2004) go further and argue that differences in schooling are a major causal factor explaining not only differences in democracy, but more generally in political institutions, and provide evidence consistent with this view. The high correlation between schooling and democracy is the cornerstone of this view.

This shows the most common measure of democracy, the Freedom House index of political rights, against the average years of schooling of the population in the 1990s. Correlation does not establish causation, however. Existing literature looks at the cross-sectional correlation between education and democracy rather than at the within variation. Hence existing inferences may be potentially driven by omitted factors influencing both education and democracy in the long run. A causal link between education and democracy suggests that we should also see a relationship between changes in education and changes in democracy. In other words, we should ask whether a given country (with its other characteristics held constant) is more likely to become more democratic as its population becomes more educated. We show that the answer to this question is no.

Countries that become more educated show no greater tendency to become more democratic. We further investigate these issues econometrically. We show that the cross-sectional relationship between schooling and democracy disappears when country fixed effects are included in the regression. Although fixed effects regressions are not a panacea against all biases arising in pooled OLS regressions, they are very useful in removing the potential long-run determinants of both education and democracy. We also document that the lack of a relationship between education and democracy is highly robust to different econometric techniques, to estimation in various different samples, and to the inclusion of different sets of covariates.

The recent paper Glaeser, et al. (2004) also exploits the time-series variation in democracy and education, and presents evidence that changes in schooling predict changes in democracy and other political institutions. However, we document below that this result stems from their omission of time effects in the regressions, so it reflects the over-time increase in education and democracy at the world level over the past 35 years. Once we include year dummies in their regressions, the impact of education on democracy disappears entirely. Motivated by the Glaeser, et al. (2004) paper, we also show that there is no effect of education on other measures of political institutions. In addition to the studies mentioned above, our paper is related to the large political economy literature on the creation and consolidation of democracy, which we do not have enough space to discuss here.

It is also related to our companion paper by Acemoglu, Simon Johnson, Robinson and Pierre Yared (2004), which investigates the other basic tenet of the modernization hypothesis, that income (and economic growth) causes democracy. In that paper, using both fixed effects OLS and instrumental variable regressions, we show that there is little evidence in favor of a causal effect from income to democracy either. We also offer a theory for the differences in long-run factors causing the joint evolution of education, income, and democracy, and we provide supporting evidence for this theory. The rest of the paper is organized as follows.

A country gets a score of 1 if political rights come closest to the ideals suggested by a checklist of questions, beginning with whether there are free and fair elections, whether those who are elected rule, whether there are competitive parties or other political groupings, whether the opposition plays an important role and has actual power, and whether minority groups have reasonable self-government or can participate in the government through informal consensus. Following Barro (1999), we supplement this index with the related variable from Kenneth Bollen (1990, 2001) for 1955, 1960, and 1965, and we transform both indices so that they lie between 0 and 1, with 1 corresponding to the most democratic set of institutions.

We also show that our results are robust to using the other two popular measures in the literature, the composite Polity index, and the dichotomous democracy index developed by Przeworski, et al. (2000) and extended by Carles Boix and Sebastian Rosato (2001) which are all normalized between 0 and 1 for comparison. Because of space restrictions, we do not describe these data here and refer the reader to Acemoglu et al. (2004) for details, and also for descriptive statistics on the key variables. Our main right-hand side variable, average years of schooling in the total population of age 25 and above, is from Barro and Jong-Wha Lee (2000) and is available in five year intervals between 1960 and 2000. The value of this variable in our base sample ranges from 0.04 to 12.18 years of schooling with a mean of 4.65. Our basic dataset is a five-yearly panel, where we take the democracy score for each country every fifth year.

This results in an unbalanced panel of 108 countries spanning the period between 1965 and 2000, with a total of 765 observations with countries included if they have been independent for at least five years, where independence year is determined using the CIA World Factbook (2004). We prefer using the observations every fifth year to averaging the five-yearly data, since averaging introduces additional serial correlation as we document below. Nevertheless, our results are robust to using five-year averages. We also report robustness checks using 10-year data between 1970 and 2000 and using subsamples that exclude former and current socialist countries, Sub-Saharan Africa, and predominantly Muslim countries.

CONCEPT OF SECULARISM AND ITS EDUCATIONAL IMPLICATIONS

The sense of belonging is a heady feeling. It anchors man in a social setting, feeding his vital need of self-recognition, which is a composite of both personal and social identities. Unlike other indices, religion's potency is not situational, but pervasive; it shapes both the personal and the social identities of an individual. As a belief and value system, religion has tremendous hold over a person's life. Its mores condition the individual's conduct in life and his manner of interaction with others. This identification with a community of believers helps a person understand himself and his place in the social environment. This is bedrock of the concept of positive communalism.

Yet, there is in this categorization, the possibility of

discrimination. One is favourably disposed to the "in-group" (the group to which he belongs) as compared to the "out-group" (the group of which he is not a member). In situations of heightened emotions engendered by an apparent insult or injustice, this "us" and "they" perceptions become adversarial. This is true of religion that has provided countless instances of acting as the great divider. Faith, regardless of the adjectives used to qualify it, implies an implicit acceptance of something or someone.

When religion is used interchangeably with faith, does it imply an uncritical reception and pursuance of its instructions? If so, therein lies the potential for inter-communal discord, where each community holds itself to be the possessor of truth and trapped in the fog of dogmatism, fails to see or even consider different view-points and respect the right of others to hold them. When taken to the extreme, this attitude may manifest in violent suppression of other creeds that are denounced as heterodoxy. Such religious bigotry has absolutely no place in a mixed society, where tolerance is the decree of existence.

Thus, we come to the concept of secularism in the context of a pluralist state. The orison of religious communities to bear indicators of their cultural identity and the festering discontent when denied the opportunity to do so by states, which claim to be liberal and tolerant, has highlighted the need to re-evaluate the concept of secularism as applied to state governments. Before going into an empirical reading of the current situation, a conceptual and normative analysis of the constitutive link of secularism with a democratic state is needed.

There is a wide misconception that secularism as enunciated by Western liberal tradition is uncontested, and that an uncomplicated separation of state and religion is an incontrovertible fact in these countries. As Scanlon puts it, each country in the West has worked out its own peculiar version, where the separation thesis means different things for the USA, France, Britain, etc. There is no trans-cultural ideal and this leads to the question: What values actually configure in the ideal of secularism?

To decouple religion from the policy and practice of the state is a very narrow way of viewing this concept. Secularism is a purposive concept and not just a dialectic outcome of Protestantism and Science. In its negative sense, it is a means by which the dominance of any one denomination is sought to be countered and religion and state are to be arrogated their own separate spheres of power and operation. In the positive sense, it seeks to promote a free and equal (at least, in the civil and political sense) society.In India, secularism implies a sense of tolerance and accommodation embodied in the concept of "sarva dharma sambhava". Here the state metes out equal treatment to all religions and embraces and supports all religions. The French laicite or the Turkish laiklik on the other hand, follows the separation theory to the letter and does not favour or support all or any one religion.

In the USA, as Sandel points out, the US Supreme Court, in 1947, upheld secular neutralism. The justification was that it would protect the church and the state and allow for the individual's right to choose. In practice, none of the cited examples have shown that the principle of equi-distance works. The head scarf and immigrant issues in France were a match in a tinderbox to the growing feelings of alienation among France's minority communities. In Turkey, the objective of secularism as formulated by Ataturk had to face innumerable challenges from 1972 onwards with the rise of the Islamic parties, which had the support of many who considered secularism as an elite objective. India too, with its great pluralist tradition, has seen a rise in negative communal feelings.

As a shibboleth of the Libertarians, secularism has been hyphenated with democracy and pluralism. Even the Communitarians like Taylor and Sandel, have found common grounds here. Secularism is seen as a condition of democracy and a decree of existence for a pluralist society. But how do Western liberal democratic states interpret secularism? The cases of the two women in Britain, one wanting to wear a cross and the other a burkha; instances of Sikhs being targeted for wearing turbans in the USA; Muslim men being discriminated because of their names itself; Netherlands banning the burkha, etc. show the low threshold of tolerance in these countries. Forget about it then being imposed in countries where the societies are in the grip of the theologians!

Vestigial dissent (for e.g., many young Muslim girls in the West wearing the hijab) is a visible manifestation of resentment. More and more youngsters are finding succour in their religion, an essential constituent of their self-identity and when it is denigrated, there is tremendous anger that simmers just below the surface and needs slight provocation to erupt and rip apart the fabric of the soi-disant multicultural society and state. As for secularism's relationship with democracy, only when the society (this is in reference to a pluralist society) is democratic, can the state become so. It means that in this context, no single ethnic or religious group can claim power and the individual has unmediated access to the polity.

I agree that a democratic state provides the most favourable environment for the growth of a secular (tolerant) outlook. Next is the purpose of secularism. If it is to foster social cohesion, then the complete separation thesis is otiose. Religion is configured in the human psyche and to relegate it to a matter of personal preference that has no influence in the public domain is impractical, as one cannot ask of an individual to efface the one aspect of his mental make-up that evokes such a strong a sense of attachment. Thus, we come to the crux of the issue: What form of secularism works in a pluralist state? Is it the one that bases itself in inclusiveness or that which is premised on insularity of state from religion? Bhargava makes an interesting suggestion. Instead of Political secularism, which has no conception of community, what might work is Ethical Secularism. It allows for different communities to reach an understanding that incommensurable objectives cannot always be realized in the same space and be tolerant of the limitations.

Today secularism has been transformed into an ideological instrument of the West, which spins the impression that its presence will automatically create a modern and more tolerant state. This is the version being peddled in Iraq. When a society is divided along religious lines and each follows its own agenda, the democratic polity that has been envisaged will be tenuous since it is imported and will negate any secularization of the society. So here the groundwork has to be done by generating an inclusive mentality that fosters feelings of accommodation and tolerance. The religious and political leaders have to be in accord regarding the basic framework of their state and how best to bring it out of the current crisis and make it a part of growth process that all countries of the world are going through.

In a heterogeneous society, secularism must fulfil the following conditions so that there is social cohesion and very little space for feelings of discrimination or appeasement:

- Procedural secularism
- Equitable resource allocation to all communities
- Prevent negative stereo-typing and bigotry
- Allow each community to promote its own culture as a "public good" where its promotion does not affect another community's practice of its own culture and religion
- Encourage and strengthen areas of cooperation between different faiths

What is needed is not an abdication of secular practice by the state, but a re-evaluation and if needed, a re-formulation of secularism that fits the needs of the state within which it operates and also the need of the individual to belong to a community. This is its true test.

EQUALITY OF EDUCATIONAL OPPORTUNITIES- WAYS AND MEANS

Democracy denotes not only freedom but equality as well. For democracy is a system that cares for all irrespective of their natural or other differences and henos, unless all are able to equally enjoy the fruits of democracy, the latter makes no sense. This is why Article 14 of the Indian Constitution guarantees to everyone the fundamental right to equality before the law and equal protection of the law. The implication of this provision is that no one in India is entitled to enjoy any special privilege and that laws of the country are applicable to all without discrimination. Article 14 is further supplemented by Article 15 that gives to every Indian citizen a fundamental right against discrimination.

Further, in order that the age-old prejudices may not inhibit ensuring equality at the social level, Article 17 abolishes untouchability and, again, in order to prevent the growth of any socially privileged class, as in the days of the British Raj, Article 18 prohibits conferment of title by the state on anyone. In addition to all this, Article 16 guarantees to every citizen equality of opportunity in government employment. Although the Constitution thus gives in the form of a fundamental right equality of opportunity in matters of public employment, it grants no fundamental right to equality of opportunity in other spheres. However, the Preamble to the Constitution assures equality of opportunity to every citizen.

Further, as Article 15 prohibits discrimination in all spheres, it may be logically derived that it indirectly recognizes a fundamental right to equality of opportunity. But guaranteeing equality of opportunity is not just enough. For a socially handicapped citizen, despite his best efforts and wishes, may not be able to avail of the opportunity available to others just because of his inclement conditions. This, no doubt, calls for a special arrangement on the part of the state in favour of backward sections of citizens for the purpose of bettering their conditions so that they are made capable of fully sharing equality of opportunity with others.

This is particularly important in a democracy. For, although, in actual practice, democracy is a majority rule, its primary task is to strive for the welfare of not alone the majority but of all and hence the disadvantaged among the people deserve a special treatment by the state. Seemingly, it is a violation of the principle of equality, but this violation or, what John Rawls has conceptualized as the 'difference principle' is acceptable in the interest of democratic justice. The framers of the Constitution, of course, were not unaware of it. But they identified only women and children as representing the weaker section of citizens and allowed the state to make special provisions for them by means of Article 15 (3).

But once the sovereign Indian Republic set out its journey, the powers that be began to realize that, besides women and children, socially and educationally backward classes of people together with scheduled castes and scheduled tribes also belonged to the weaker section, deserving extra care and attention from the state. Again, as education is one of the important indices of social betterment, it was also felt that in any programme for uplifting the backward sections the thrust should be on educational development.

Thus, immediately after the Constitution had became effective, the then Madras Government issued an order on reservation of seats for backward classes in the State Medical Colleges. But the order was struck down by the Supreme Court in State of Madras vs. Champkam Dorairajan on the ground that it was backed by no constitutional sanction. This was an eye-opener for the Union Government which lost no time in enacting the First Amendment in 1951 that inserted in the Constitution, among other things, Article 15(4), enabling the state to make special provisions for socially and educationally backward classes as well as scheduled castes and scheduled tribes.

This paved the way for reservation of seats for these categories of citizens in all government educational institutions. However, the Supreme Court in its judgment in Indra Sawhney vs. Union of India in 1992 directed that the total reservation for all categories of backward citizens in educational institutions must not exceed 50 per cent and that is being faithfully followed allover India till now. Meanwhile, in 2005, the Supreme Court stalled a move to make reservation for backward citizens in private educational institutions.

To overcome this bar by the apex court, the Government enacted 93rd Amendment that inserted in the Constitution Article 15(5), permitting this reservation. However, a law made under this constitutional provision has recently been challenged in the Supreme Court and the judgment of the

Court is still awaited. What will be the political decision after the judgment comes out may only be known in future. But what is beyond doubt is that the constitutional provisions on equality of educational opportunities in India are quite adequate.

WOMEN EDUCATION; GLOBALIZATION; PRIVATIZATION

From losing good government jobs, to less access to unionized jobs, to being left to pick up the slack when social services are no longer available, women are having a tough time coping with the reality of economic globalization. Women's experiences of both paid and unpaid work have been affected by this growing trend. More often than not economic globalization has led to increased workloads, lower pay, and more stress.

Economic globalization has meant that many companies are cutting costs. They are doing this by down-sizing. This means laying off staff, reducing salaries and benefits, hiring part-time staff as opposed to full-time, using home-based workers, laying off older staff about to receive pensions, and giving remaining staff increased workloads. Because women are more likely to be at the bottom of the rung, they are often most affected. The garment industry is one Canadian industry that has had to squeeze itself in order to compete in the global economy, an industry made up primarily of women. To read about one Manitoba woman's experiences in that industry visit Samantha's Story.

Downsizing affects women's home lives as well. Women experience increased stress when men lose employment, as they are forced to take on more of the financial responsibilities. In a world where men's self-worth is often tied up in their jobs, women with jobless husbands may well need to provide extra emotional support. During the Asian economic crash, "The Korean government promoted a national slogan 'Get your Husband Energized' that called on women to help offset the impact of the crisis on men, who on becoming unemployed or bankrupt were subject to depression."

The public sector has not been immune from the trend towards corporate downsizing. Women have worked hard for fair representation in government-funded jobs and are strongly represented in health care, teaching, and social work. These and other public sector jobs have long been a source of well-paying, quality jobs for women. As the Canadian Labour Congress reports that, "Women make up ¼ of the unionized work force in the private sector but 2/3 of the unionized workforce in public services." When these kinds of services are privatized or down-sized, a disproportionate number of women lose their jobs. For example, between 1986 and 1993, Canada Post down-sized and closed 1300 rural post offices, laying off 3000 people, 83% of whom were women. Public sector jobs also tend to be unionized. As well, affirmative action (equal representation of women and other minorities) is harder to achieve within the less-regulated private sector.

Reducing public services also affects women's unpaid work as they are forced to pick up the slack that the public sector leaves out. Women take care of patients sent home too early from the hospital, they find ways to teach their children things they're not learning in school because classrooms are overcrowded and special education services are gone, and they cook meals for older neighbours when funding for community food programs is cut. Women also keep families and communities stable through times of economic uncertainty. They improvise to feed their families when money becomes even more scarce.

Women also find jobs in an even tougher job market and are willing to work for lower pay when that's all they can find. As a result of corporate down-sizing and the reduction of the public sector, many women are finding themselves in non-standard jobs - the National Action Committee on the Status of Women reported in 1998 that 40% of women have non-standard jobs. At the same time public programs such as unemployment insurance have diminished. Those most affected by an increase in the number of qualifying hours are those in part-time or temporary work - in Canada women make up 70% of the part-time workforce. The number of work hours necessary to receive maternity benefits has also increased.

Globalization has greatly increased the flow of goods between countries. Many countries have reorganized their economies in favour of export production. In some countries, especially in Asia, Export Processing Zones have been created to house production facilities. Women make up much of the underpaid workforce in these areas where regulations and labour protection laws are relaxed or not enforced in order to attract foreign investors. Women's nimble fingers are in high demand as vegetable packers in Mexico, garment workers in China, and cotton harvesters in Egypt. These are all industries characterized by low wages, and poor working conditions including long hours, lack of safety standards, and barriers to workers organizing.

Unions have always worked hard to protect women in the workplace. Unionized women earn a wage much closer to that of their male counterparts than do non-unionized women. Unions also help workers who face sexual harassment and other workplace hazards and can bargain for benefits like child care. Many of the jobs lost in Canada have been unionized ones, while jobs created through economic globalization tend to be non-unionized. Home work and contract work is not usually unionized and few jobs in the boom industries in less-industrialized countries are unionized.

Education is one of the most crucial factors that allow women to compete as equals in the professional world and to earn an income of their own. Women with degrees earn significantly more than their counterparts without degrees. However, cuts to education and training have made education less accessible. Millions of dollars have been cut from education budgets in Canada over the past decade. The cost of tuition has risen and grant programs have been eliminated. As a result student debt loads have skyrocketed from an average of $8000 to $25,000. Because women still earn less, they pay back their debts more slowly. The Canadian government eliminated the National Training Act including training programs geared to women. Education and training are especially difficult for women with young children as child care services are often inadequate.

Globalization as a term and concept became popular by the end of the last century and the beginning of the new millennium. Some words and concepts such as 'nation', 'patriotism', 'swadeshi' and 'rural development' which gained more emphasis during the struggle for freedom of India are now sidelined by the popularity of globalization. Print media, television and other visual communications promote the idea of globalization with such captions as, 'Think globally and act locally', 'global village', 'global market', 'global banking', 'global society' and 'global communication'. However, there is a lot of confusion in using terms such as 'internationalization', 'westernization', 'modernization', 'christianization' and 'crossing the boundaries' that come with globalization.

Each of these terms has its own specific characteristics from economic, technological, cultural or religious point of view. Such characteristics of each term should not be diluted because each word carries a concept. We must be careful in using them synonymously or interchangeably. There are many voices of support for and critique of globalization. In India alone, many seminars and debates, both at national and regional levels, have been conducted on this topic between 1998 and 2001. Articles and books with data and analysis have been published on the merits and demerits of globalization. Not an expert in analyzing the concept or technicalities of globalization, I am using statistics from secondary sources rather than directly from reports and records of governments, World Trade Organization, World Bank or International Monetary Fund.

DEFINITIONS AND EXPERIENCES OF GLOBALIZATION

There is a wide range of definitions of globalization suggested by scholars. One definition is that "globalization is a process by which the economies of the world become increasingly integrated, leading to a global economy and, increasingly, global economic policymaking, e.g., through international agencies such as the World Trade Organization (WTO). Globalization also refers to an emerging 'global culture' in which people more often consume similar goods and services across countries and use a common language of business, e.g. English. These changes facilitate economic integration and in turn are further promoted by it. But in its core economic meaning globalization refers to the increased openness of economies to international trade, financial flows, and direct foreign investment."

Prof. M.A. Oommen says, "Broadly speaking, globalization may be considered a process of transnationalisation of capital, production and even consumer tastes and preferences on the logic of global exchange. There is, therefore, nothing amiss in characterising it as global capitalism." According to Ruigrah Van Tulder, globalization refers to "the multiplicity of linkages and interconnections between the state and societies which make up the present world system. It describes the process by which events, decisions and activities in one part of the world came to have significant consequences for individuals and communities in quite distant parts of the globe."

Various theoretical approaches to globalization are proposed by academics. Felix Wilfred lists various theories of globalization in his book and points out that "the options and interests of the theorists colour the way globalization is explained". Some have gone to the extent of believing that there is no salvation without globalization. Only economists, sociologists and scientists can understand the intricacies of the process of globalization. They have the skill and techniques to analyse its merits and demerits. One of the merits is that globalization presents new possibilities for eliminating global poverty and "can potentially benefit poor countries directly and indirectly through cultural, social, scientific and technological exchanges as well as through conventional trade and finance."

Moreover, developing the nations is possible since finance will be available. Goods will be freely available in good quality and people need not wait for long time or depend on the state to produce and distribute. Liberalization and privatization will bring healthy competition and improvement in quality and marketing. Such competition can bring down the prices. Another merit of globalization is that it can challenge some of the oppressive elements in our religions and cultures and lead to reform our society for better. On the other hand, poor countries could be locked into a pattern of dependency and may experience threats to their cultural identities. Felix Wilfred is highly critical of globalization that he discusses the deceptions of globalization in his book. Ordinary people on the road may not have the expertise to analyse the phenomena of globalization but they could feel and experience that something is happening in the world and their society is changing rapidly.

Their life is so closely linked to these changes whether they like it or not. Villagers who know the water of the wells or rivers see suddenly bottles filled with purified water and coloured water wrapped in attractive labels such as Coca-Cola, 7 Up, Pepsi, Aquafina Bisleri selling in the small shops in their villages. Ready-made garments of export brands such as Peter England, Louis Philippe, Van Hausen, Wrangler, Lee, Levi, Camel are sold in the shops in cities and towns. They see more global brands of drinks and clothes used by their favourite cinema stars and sports personalities on television and glittering billboards.

We notice that electronic goods sold abroad such as television, refrigerator, VCR, DVD, mobile phones, computers of many international companies like Sony, Panasonic, Samsung, Sharp, IBM, Hitachi, Thompson, BPL-Sanyo, Nokia and Siemens, Toshiba are now available in Indian market connecting the people of India with the global society. Even the cars of international brands like Ford, Suzuki, Mitsubushi, BMW, Benz, Hyundai, Daewoo and Chevrolet are sold in India. Millions of Indians understand that India has opened its door for multi-national corporations (MNCs) to import or produce for the huge market although they may not know the essential characteristics of 'globalization'.

They realize that the Indian government has liberalized the rules and opened the country for marketing the goods of international companies. Rich and middle class people who are attracted to modern technology and goods of international brands welcome globalization and enjoy the benefits of free market rather than getting the goods they wanted through smugglers. The lower middle class and poor are also getting influenced by the mass media to accept the process of globalization.

Unfortunately, they are unable to own such goods due to debts and poverty perpetuated by globalization, the very system influencing them. The poor people may not be aware of the characteristics of 'free market' and 'finance capitalism' of globalization but they experience the consequences of the free market due to loss of employment, degradation of environment, high cost of living, the marginalization of traditional skills, etc.

Many Indians have developed a fear of uncertainty about the future trend of their society. They have raised doubts about the ways and means to control the ongoing process of globalization. However, globalization has attracted many people whether they are educated or uneducated, rich or poor, white or black, upper caste or lower caste. Wesley Ariarajah points out four ways in which globalization is experienced, namely: a new consciousness of globalization, a new awareness of the gravity of the impact of globalization, a new realization of globalization as social and cultural and economic consequences, and a new level of comprehension that it can be directed to enrich human life.

It is difficult to measure fully the positive and negative consequences of globalization. However, evidences of the effect of globalization are seen in many parts of the world in terms of loss of jobs, bursting of financial institutions, and increasing debt of several nations, promoting western culture and habits, gradual disappearance of local skills and customs, and reaction towards western countries.

Often, by mistake, Christianity is regarded as the promoter of globalization. The fundamentalists in the Islamic and Hindu religions show their violence against Christian communities and work to develop tough resistance against Christianity rather than on the process of globalization itself. They may not be aware of the critical response raised by Christians on globalization. With the sense of inadequacy and incompetence on my side, I try to present this paper focusing my attention on surveying and listing the economic, social, political, religious and cultural issues and challenges of globalization, highlighting a theological response and suggesting changes in contemporary theological training in India.

GLOBALIZATION AND ITS ESSENTIAL FEATURES

Globalization is not a new phenomenon. Trade between nations and territorial expansion of political power across the oceans began a long time ago as the early history of Greeks and Romans shows. Evidences of global connections for trade are found in the Tamil Sangam literature. However, scholars try to trace the phases of the development of globalization from the time of the industrial revolution of the 15th century. Prof. T. K. Oommen speaks of three giant phases of globalization, with colonialism that began in the 16th century as the first phase.

He describes the emergence of two types of colonies viz., 'settler-majority countries' and 'ex-colonial countries', and the atrocities of colonialism in these two kinds of colonies. Both of them fought for freedom from their colonial masters and obtained it. But the 'settler-majority countries' such as USA, Canada and Australia joined with their European colonial powers after the freedom and worked together to become developed nations. Their relationship developed that they have become the First World which promote neo-colonialism today. Although the 'ex-colonial countries' of Africa and Asia have gained political freedom, they are left with impoverished economies, made to depend on their colonial masters for their various needs viz., getting technical knowledge and financial support for developing agriculture, industries and education.

As such, they had to continue to be politically

subordinated to the First World. The process of subordination is shifted from 'colonial mode of production' to 'subordination mode of unequal exchange' resulting in inequality as a major issue rather than differences. The second phase of globalization was the development of two ideologies viz., 'capitalist democracies' and 'socialist command economies' and promoting these ideologies to various countries. Such an effort on the side of North America and Europe for capitalist democracy and USSR and China for 'socialist one-party system' resulted in creating two blocks of nations following 'free market capitalism' on the one side and 'state controlled socialism' on the other side. Nations belonging to these two blocks involved in trade agreements, military expansion and propaganda war to globalize the world with their ideology and political system.

Cold War and polarization continued between these two blocks till the collapse of the Soviet Union. The third phase of globalization is the neo-liberalism and neo-colonialism with the economic features marked by the 'free market' and 'finance capitalism' and 'development'; political features of 'multi-party democracy' and 'insistence on observing human rights'; and cultural feature of homogenization. These economic, political and cultural features that characterize the modern process of globalization need a brief explanation before identifying and listing the issues of globalization. First, the policy of free market or trading enables one country to produce and market its goods in another country without any trade restriction and to transfer the profit back to its own country.

At the outset, it may look like an open policy and even poorer countries can take advantage of the policy of free trade. But the poorer countries do not have that much capital to invest in or develop sophisticated technology to produce goods that can withstand the international competition against the rich and well equipped MNCs of the First World. In order to stabilize international trade, exchange rate and the market after the World War II, the developed nations of the First World have created the General Agreement on Tariffs and Trade (GATT) in 1948 to their advantage. GATT was transformed into World Trade Organization (WTO) in 1995 to create a powerful centre of global economic governance.

While GATT deals primarily with trade, WTO's rules deal with agriculture, services, investments and intellectual property rights. The Third world nations need to sign the free-trade agreements if they want loans and technology for their development. WTO requires certain 'structural adjustment' in the economic and political policies of the developing and less developed nations and open their door for the flow of foreign capital to be invested by the MNCs, the construction of their industries for producing and marketing their branded goods. A MNC or Transnational Corporation (TNC) is a corporation or enterprise that conducts and controls productive activities in more than one country.

Multinationals bring not only capital but also 'carry with them technologies of production, tastes and styles of living, managerial philosophies, and diverse business practices including co-operative arrangements, marketing restrictions, advertising and the phenomenon of 'transfer pricing'. They engage in a range of activities, many of which have little to do with the development aspirations of the countries in which they operate'. Their worldwide operations and activities are primarily controlled by parent companies in the First World. The royalty on technology and patent rights is charged on the countries and transferred back to the First World. The sad part of the trend is that the nation-states are not playing the active role which they played in the earlier colonialism but are now controlled by the MNCs because of the power of the finance capitalism. The number of MNCs was 7000 in 1970.

This rose to 37,000 in 1991 and to 45,000 parent firms with 280,000 affiliates in 1995. All this shows the characteristics of their large size and worldwide control. 15 Out of this, 350 largest corporations control more than 40 per cent of the production and dominate the global trade. 16 The estimated sales of the MNCs in 1996 were over $7 trillion. UNO is also helpless except in certain political negotiations or applying the law of economic sanctions against a country. Second, free market and transfer of profits are possible only if the nation-states practice 'capitalist democracy'.

Under the 'socialist one party system', production and distribution are in the hands of the state.

It is very difficult for the MNCs to own resources of production, control the market, and transfer the profit in such a state-command political system. Globalization, therefore, promotes the political feature of 'capitalist democracy' throughout the world in order to facilitate the free flow of finance from country to country and growth of free market. One of the aims of globalization is to reduce the control of the nation-states on economic and political policies and force states to adapt capitalist democracy, implement SAP (Structural Adjustment Programmes) and promote liberalisation. Felix Wilfred points out the problems of SAP and writes, 'the state itself is dictated by the Structural Adjustment Programmes.

It is forced to deregulate or lose its control over market and economy which are to be handed over to private players operating internationally. And what is worse, the states are forced to cut the subsidies for food and other goods from which the poor benefit'. Third, globalization does not care about the originality and uniqueness of local cultures. It promotes homogenization of cultures through mass media making the people to believe that the world is coming closer and various communities and cultures are getting united and differences and clash of cultures in the world can be removed.

It promotes some sort of uniformity in production and consumerism for the branded goods of MNCs throughout the world. The culture of jeans, pop music, disco, fast-food like McDonald and KFC, soft drinks like Coca-cola and Pepsi, and mobile phone communication has taken the world. MNCs spend a lot of money on research to know the tastes and styles of different classes of people to suit their production and marketing. The process of globalization with these essential features has affected the lives of people in various countries including the First World. The following list shows the injustice and violation of human rights caused by globalization.

ISSUES OF JUSTICE AND INDIA RESPONSE

As a colony of the first phase of globalization, India has

historical experience of injustice done by colonizers and of liberating herself from their political, economic and social oppression. Struggle for justice is always set in a historical context reflecting on the past, evaluating the present situation, and drawing insights and strengths for the present struggle. I cannot, therefore, ignore the past experience of the struggles against colonialism in discussing liberation from the negative consequences of contemporary globalization. Such a comparison could serve as a methodology to understand and work out approaches for liberating ourselves from problems of globalization and to make use of it to enrich human life.

Gandhi had raised his voice against the evils of colonialism. His criticism and suggestions of alternative model of development against western capitalism, parliamentary system, cultural imperialism, homogenization and consumerism stand as valid insights to understand modern globalization. His teachings and actions are remembered as Indian heritage. However, Gandhi is not the only Indian response to globalization. A number of Indian economists, sociologists, scientists, religious scholars, Dalit, tribal and women leaders have responded in the past and are still responding to the problems created by globalization.

Economic exploitation of countries goes on since the time of territorial expansion of political power and colonizing the nations. Raw materials were taken from the colonies to the countries of the colonizers and the finished products were brought back to the colonies. The colonies supplied resources of production and functioned as the market. Producing similar goods by Indians in India itself was opposed by the British with a view to protect industries and the economic growth of Britain. Gandhi opposed this kind of exploitation of India and took bold experiments to produce clothes, salt and medicine in India itself defiling the laws and punishments of the British government. Robbing the poor and paying the rich was unacceptable to Gandhi.

The resistance to such kind of globalization of exploitation fueled the freedom struggle to become more intensive. Liberation from the British rule was achieved but within 55 years of independence, India is under the control of another phase of globalization. India has come under the power of neo-colonialism agreeing to the GATT agreements and opening the country for Foreign Direct Investment (FDI) and for free market. The estimated FDI to India is $3.2. billion in 1997 compared to $158 million in 1991- 92.

Many MNCs have come in since they see a vast market for their products as the population of India has crossed one billion. The major attractions for foreign investors in India are cheap labour, huge domestic market, lack of safety regulation and pollution control, and ineffective implementation of laws by the state. Their focus is on the consumerism of the rich and middle class Indians. They started controlling the resources of production and accumulating the profit. If they reinvest the profit to develop other Indian industries and create more jobs, then there is a recycling of the profit. But the major portion of the capital flows out of the country for further research and developing more sophisticated technology to reduce the work force and maximize their profit.

It seems that US firms alone received $27 billion in royalties and fees from all over the world in 1995 accounting for 56 per cent of global receipts. This kind of economic exploitation leads to the dominance of MNCs over Indian society. We are losing our freedom and authority and are reduced as objects of an economic system controlled by the MNCs. We can raise our voice and struggle against a nation dominating us but it is difficult to struggle against the economic system manipulated by giant financial corporations and international companies. The owners of these corporations are not nation-states but individuals and corporate shareholders living in different parts of the world. As Alvin Toffler points out, it is difficult to designate the nationality of these global corporations because 'they fly the flag of their customers, not their country'.

Investors receive their share in the profit of their investments. We need a new form of strategy to liberate us from the hands of the MNCs. Mere rhetoric against them is not enough. Working out concrete economic and political strategies only can liberate India from the injustices of modern globalization. Labour and Unemployment Both the earlier colonialism and neo-colonialism have done a lot of injustice to the work force. The British used the Indian work force in their steel and mining industries. They used them to develop roads and railways. They placed them on hills in cold climate to produce tea, coffee, pepper, fruits and vegetables. They were employed in plantations of rubber and sugarcane. The colonizers found Indians as hard working and could survive in odd situations and be paid low wages.

They transferred Indian labourers to their colonies of Sri Lanka, Malaysia, Fiji, Kenya and South Africa as indentured labourers to develop the plantations of tea, coffee, rubber, sugarcane and work in gold and coal mines. Indian labourers were kept in appalling conditions, paid low and separated from their families. Gandhi took up a long struggle against this injustice while he was in South Africa and worked for the rights of Indian labourers. The neo-colonialism of recent globalization continues to affect the work force in various ways. Regarding the wages, an Indian or Chinese worker costs $0.25 compared to $32 for a German and $24 for a Japanese worker per hour in 1995.

If the Unions demand more wages and benefits, MNCs either closed down their industries or ban the recruitment of unionized workers or give voluntary retirement as it happened in the Bombay-Pune-Thane region of Maharashtra accounting to 43 per cent of the job loss in 1990s. As the MNCs introduce hi-tech system of production more and more, thousands of people lose their jobs and have to migrate in search of jobs. They are not absorbed by the MNCs to be re-employed in their industries in another country. The trade restrictions of MNCs prohibit transfer of their labourers to another country or provide them job guarantee.

Many were forced to take voluntary retirement in industrial, banking sector, insurance corporations and postal service. Moreover, many small industries, banks and shops in local regions could not compete with MNCs and have closed down their businesses sending away their labourers. The redundant workers have no other option except to accept any job for daily wages, borrow money and live in poverty with the burden of debt.

DEVELOPMENT AND DEBT BURDEN

Development, soon after freedom from colonial rule, focused on improving the industries, agriculture, medical and educational facilities and eradicating poverty, pre-mature deaths, illiteracy and enhancing the standard of living. Rural development was given priority. 'Swadeshi' was one of the ideologies of the freedom struggle. The ways and means by which the ideology of swadeshi is to be continued according to Gandhi would have certainly left India behind in economic progress. But that ideology is a challenge to neo-colonialism too. 'Be Indian and Buy Indian' was the slogan during the period of Mrs. Indra Gandhi's rule.

India borrowed loans from WB and grants from developed nations to develop the industries and agriculture. Many Five-Year Plans were initiated with the help of these loans and financial grants. Our agricultural sector and industrial sector developed to make India a self-supporting nation. India achieved a lot in scientific and technological developments compared to other nations in Africa and South Asia. Modern globalization has shifted the focus of our development programmes. It has made us to shelf the ideology of 'swadeshi' to become self-reliant and depend on the MNCs.

The MNCs are telling us that they will provide all the goods we need including food, vegetables, fruits and seed for cultivation either by importing or producing in India itself with their patent rights and labour force. Globalization is pushing us to the stage that neither the state nor the local community is responsible anymore for production. The state is leaving the production and distribution in the hands of MNCs. The loans of WB and other financial corporations are not available to develop local industries and agriculture but are diverted for development projects such as expansion of road, airport, nuclear plants to produce power, and construction of dams to channel water for the industries of MNCs.

The development of these projects assist the development of production and marketing of MNCs. Developmental projects which could make India a self-reliant nation do not get priority in receiving external loans and subsidies. The trend of lending loans in the period of globalization is oppressive and making the Third world to depend continuously on MNCs as their colonies. These corporations are not willing to share the modern technology with the Third World but keep it within a few developed nations. Countries such as Cuba, China and North Korea which resist this kind of policy of development and granting loan are treated differently.

The debt crisis of Third World countries reached a breaking point between 1980 and 1990 because the rich countries had reduced the prices of goods exported from developing and less developed nations, forced the developing countries to devalue their currencies and increase trade imbalance. They are unable to settle the balance of payment. Kavaljit Singh says, 'In the wake of the balance of payment crisis in 1990, the Indian government was forced to take loans with harsh conditions from the World Bank and IMF. These loans were not just aimed at rescuing India from the balance of payment crisis. Instead, they served the wider agenda of these institutions to implement SAP and promote private foreign capital.

India's foreign debt has risen to $92.2 billion in 1996. Political Freedom Under Threat Trade leads the Flag' is the truth with the arrival of East India Company and colonizing of India by the British and ruling for about two hundred years. Any upsurge to question the authority of the colonizers or work for freedom was suppressed. The massacre of hundreds of innocent civilians assembled at the meeting in Jalian Wala Bagh stands still as an evidence for suppression of the British. The political freedom gained after a long struggle and suffering is under the threat of globalization.

Gandhi was in favour of freedom, democracy and united India but he was critical of the idea of governance following the British political party system and parliamentary structure. He accepted the idea of nation- state but promoted the ideology of 'trusteeship' through panchayat system of sharing of power, making decision, counting corporate accountability and governing the nation of India. He wanted the people at the grass root to have more power than the elected few at the top making decision for the entire nation. Any policy which threatens the political freedom and self-governance should be opposed by the people together and not left in the hands of the elected representatives in parliament. Gandhi might have suspected that the elected representatives could be influenced by the external forces or become corrupt for their own selfish gain and turn as oppressors of people. The ruling minority could join hands with external forces in the name of developing India at the expense of freedom and self-reliance.

This is what is happening today with our political leaders. They have signed agreements and surrendered the political sovereignty of India to a certain extent to the MNCs who dictate terms and conditions and demand structural adjustments in our political system. To whom should we direct our struggle for justice – against our political leaders or MNCs? Will the political leaders support the struggles of the affected communities or oppress them showing their solidarity with MNCs? James David narrates several oppositions of people of different countries against globalization including the nation-wide industrial strike by 15 million workers in 1992 protesting the New Economic Policy of Indian government. Political situation was changed in Venezuela due to anti-globalization movement but the change did not last long due to the interference of western countries in support of MNCs.

The MNCs have destabilized political governments if they oppose their policies and progress. This has happened to many countries which are politically and economically weak as Varghese George quotes the case of Chile, Haiti, Jamaica, Mexico and Peru. Alvin Toffler also points out that if the nation-state cannot bring law and order to protect the MNCs or control violence and terrorism against these corporations and their interests, then these corporations will 'put their own brigades into the field' and he quotes the example of the billionaire Ross Perot hiring ex-Green Berets to penetrate Iran and rescue his employees. Cultural Imperialism Territorial expansion of political power, commerce, or religions can easily promote cultural imperialism. The colonialism of the past brought the culture of the West to India. We still experience the hegemony of cultural imperialism of the West. Our habits, architecture, customs and education reveal the impact of western culture. Lord Macaulay said, 'to bring about a class of persons Indian in blood and colour but English in tastes, in opinions, in morals and in intellect' is an evidence of looking down upon the culture of India and of domination by the West. There arose a sharp reaction to the spread of western culture from different quarters of Indian society including Gandhi, Tagore and religious leaders.

The reaction fueled the growth of religious nationalism and fundamentalism. RSS, VHP and Islamic institutions regard western culture and Christianity as one and the same and so oppose Christianity. Using the free market finance capitalism and mass media, the new globalization promotes western culture particularly of American entertainment programmes as well as electronic entertainment goods. Western sports, cartoons, TV serial are telecast throughout the world that youth and children have accepted the values promoted through these programmes and entertainments. In order to reach the mass who cannot understand English, translations of the programmes in various Indian languages are made available. Indian folk stories of monkeys, fox and crow have been sidelined or even forgotten and replaced by Tom and Jerry, Flintstone, Bunny Rabbit, Popeye, etc.

A number of Indian games played in villages do not require sophisticated gadgets. They are not commercialized but played as a sport and good exercise. But the global media have promoted the commercialisation of sports, selling costly goods to be used for games. Old colonial games such as football, cricket, tennis and hockey have become the national sport of India. What makes us sad is that we are led to believe that our own culture is inferior to the culture promoted by the MNCs and mass media. Furthermore, the spread of western culture breeds culture of individualism. Individuals who adapt the culture of globalization promoted by consumerism are alienated gradually from the rest of the members of family and communities. Cultural imperialism leads the people to cultural alienation as it happened to Christians in India with the spread of Christianity and Muslims with the spread of Islam.

Cultural imperialism divided the families and communities rather than unites people. It is important to point out here that the spread of the culture of globalization is opposed by the Hindus and Muslims on the one hand since it affects the values and practices of these religions. It also creates identity crisis and thus leads them to be more communal conscious. On the other hand, the spread of Islamic fundamentalism and Hindutva of RSS is another sign of cultural imperialism over the rest of Indians.

The resistance and domination of these religious groups should take seriously the context of pluralism and value the way modernization and the influence of western culture and Christianity have contributed in reforming India. Envisaging the confrontations of different religions in India, Gandhi promoted the idea of 'Truth is God', a common ideology of 'satya' for all religions. He took effort to teach and educate people to be aware of the domination of one culture over another culture in India and hold on to good values useful to humanity. Liberating India from cultural imperialism promoted by the powerful communication media and MNCs is not easy but it is possible through teaching values and practicing them.

PRIVATIZATION – INDUSTRIES, EDUCATION AND HEALTH CARE

During colonialism, industries were owned by the British in their brand names like Lipton, Binny, Fenner, Harvey, Leyland, etc. As the freedom struggle gained momentum, the British were willing to include Indian businesspeople as partners and sold the industries to them after the freedom. British company names were changed to Indian names since indigenization was promoted. Many large scale industries such as railways and locomotives, iron and steel, telephone and mines were made public sector and controlled by the central government. Some industries were made a joint sector with the government holding more than 50 per cent of the share and management and leaving the rest of the shares for the public to own.

Many banks and insurance companies were nationalized and managed by the government. It is true that some of the industries and corporations in the PSE made losses due to outdated technology, lack of funds, interference of unions, inefficient management and rampant corruption. These problems should have been addressed and rectified rather than privatizing PSE. On the other hand, some of these industries are doing well even today. For example, the LIC which was nationalised with the initial investment of Rs. 5 crore is doing well. It has returned more than Rs. 1100 crore as tax and share profit to the government.

The General Insurance Company nationalized in 1992 paid back Rs. 275.94 crore as taxes and Rs. 26.87 crore as profit to the government. Some of the returns were used for the developmental projects by the government. 34 But modern globalization promotes privatization of industries, banking and insurance corporations. Agriculture, Education and Health Care are also included in the list of WTO for privatization in free market countries. If all the sectors of production and services are privatized, then, the country itself can become a private property of the rich business class. Through FDI scheme, the Indian government has allowed foreign financial corporations to invest in industries and banking and take over the industries.

More than 59 foreign banks have entered the country. Due to their role, the public sector banks have lost Rs. 5400 crore. MNCs are given license to produce telephones (Siemens, Sony, Sanyo), automobiles (Ford, GM, Hyundai, Honda, Toyota) and two wheelers (Suzuki, Yamaha, Honda) and to operate courier mailing services by DHL, Fed-Exp, TNT, UPS and domestic airlines. The present NDA government at the Centre is cutting down its investment in the public sector such as LIC, UTI,

Postal Service, Iron and Steel and Coal Mine and planning to sell some of the profitable industries like SAIL, Telecom and mobile phone service to MNCs.

The share of the India's best Public Sector Enterprise (PSE), SAIL was sold for a low price and traded at high as Rs. 212 per share after disinvestment. Other PSE such as ONGC, BHEL, Hindustan Latex are already on the list of sale. The disinvestment and privatization policy has already made many employees of the public sector to go on voluntary retirement. The job vacancies are not going to be filled by the government due to lack of funds for public sector. This is obvious again in the field of education and health care services.

Some of the state governments are giving license to families to establish schools, colleges, medical and engineering colleges and even Deemed Universities and poly-clinics, cancer and cardiac hospitals. The state is neglecting its responsibility to provide jobs, education and health care services to people in spite of the hike in taxes collected from the public and thus leaving the masses to the mercy of the MNCs. Privatization means paying a high cost for each service needed by the people.

Many will go without medical care and higher education in the future. Job losses will lead to debt and poverty. Liberation struggle should be directed against privatization of essential services and demand to protect our industries and banking from being taken over by MNCs.

ENVIRONMENTAL DEGRADATION

Gandhi opposed large scale industries and mass production mainly because they use a lot of natural resources, dehumanize people as labourers and pollute water and atmosphere. Work becomes a burden and people become slaves to machines and masters. He was in favour of cottage industries and developing agriculture and traditional skills of production. He promoted the economy of 'need-based' rather than 'want-based' production. His concern is to have sustainable development after seeing the effects of colonialism. But the present globalization makes room for MNCs to own land and other resources such as water, forests and power for their production. Furthermore, water, wood and marble stones are the commodities processed and marketed by MNCs.

Depletion of natural resources of the Third World and the environmental problems caused by the process of globalization are not the concerns of these giant corporations. Union Carbide incident in Bhopal stands as an example even today. Overseas project of Narmada Valley is another example for displacing thousands of tribals from their habitat. More than 15 MNCs including Uprohn, Monsantano, DuPont and Pioneer have monopoly over 122 genetically engineered products. Basmati rice and Neem products of India are coming under the patent rights of the MNCs. Moreover, MNCs are encouraging the commercial products like shrimp cultivation in Andhra Pradesh in the place of cultivating good quality rice.

Bibliography

Antler, J. & Biklen, Changing education: Women as radicals and conservators.

Apple, Michael W. Cultural politics and education. 1996.

Apple, Michael W. Ideology and curriculum. Boston: 1979.

Arnold, Matthew. Matthew Arnold and the education of the new order: a selection of arnold's writings on education. Bks demand umi london, Cambridge up, 1969. Lb 675 a76 1969 Arnstine, Donald. Democracy and the arts of schooling. Suny, 1995.

Arrowood, Charles T. Thomas Jefferson and education in a republic. Reprint of 1930 ed. Am biog. Serv. New york: 1930.

Augustine. Saint Augustine: on education. George Howie, ed. Chicago: 1969.

Augustine, Aurelius. The teacher. Washington, dc: Catholic univ. 1968.

Barber, Benjamin R. An Aristocracy of everyone. 1992.

Barrow, Robin. An introduction to philosophy of education. New york: 1988 lb 880 b34 barrow, Robin & White, Patricia, eds. 1994.

Barrow, Robin. Common sense and the curriculum. Boston: 1976 lb 1570 b328.

Belenky, Mary Field. Women's ways of knowing: the development of self, voice, and mind. New york: 1986.

Bellah, Robert *et.al*. Habits of the heart: Individualism and commitment in american life. Berkeley, ca: 1985.

Benne, Kenneth D. The task of post-contemporary education: essays in behalf of a human future. New york: 1990.

Bennett, John B. & Peltason, Contemporary issues in higher education: self-regulation and the ethical roles of the academy. New york: 1985.

Bennett, William J. To reclaim a legacy. Wash. 1984.

Berman, Hultgren, Toward a curriculum for being: voices for educators.

Beyer, Landon E. Creating democratic classrooms: the struggle to integrate theory and practice. 1996.

Beyer, Landon E. & Liston, Daniel p. (eds.). Curriculum in conflict: Social visions, educational agendas, and progressive school reform. 1996.

Biklen, Sari Knopp. School work: Gender and the cultural construction of teaching. 1995.

Bizzell, Patricia. Academic discourse and critical consciousness. 1992.

Bly, Robert. The sibling society. 1996.

Bok, Derek. Higher learning. Cambridge: 1986.

Boggs, Carl. Intellectuals and the crisis of modernity. 1995.

Bowers, C.A. Critical essays on education, modernity, and the recovery of the ecological imperative. 1993.

Bowers, C.A. Education, cultural myths, and the ecological crisis: 1992.

Bowers, c.a. Educating for an ecologically sustainable culture: Rethinking moral education, creativity, intelligence, and other modern orthodoxies. 1995.

Bowers, C.A. Elements of a post-liberal theory of education. 1987.

Boyd, William. The *emile* of Jean Jacques Rousseau: selections. 1962.

Broudy, Harry S. Enlightened Cherishing: An essay on aesthetic education. Univ. of Illinois Press, 1972.

Broudy, Harry S. "tacit knowing as a rationale for liberal education," teachers college record, 80(3) (feb., 1979), 446-462.

Brown, Les. Justice. Morality and Education: A new focus in ethics in education. New york: 1985.

Brumbaugh, Robert F. Whitehead. Process philosophy and education. Albany: 1982.

Buchman, Margret & Floden, Robert E. Detachment and

concern: Conversations in the philosophy of teaching and teacher education. New york: 1993.

Bull, B. L. "eminence and precocity: An examination of the justification of education for the gifted and talented," teachers college record, 87(1), (1985).

Burbules, Nicholas C. Continuity and diversity in philosophy of education: An introduction. 1991.

Cahn, Steven M. Classic & contemporary readings in the philosophy of education. 1996.

Callahan, Daniel. "ethics and value education," liberal education. 64, (1978).

Callaban, D. & Bok, S. "the role of applied ethics in learning," change, 11, (sept. 1979).

Callender, Willard D., Jr. The spirit of learning: philosophical reflections on learning & education. 1994.

Carnochan, W.B. The battleground of the curriculum. 1994.

Carr, Wilfred & Hartnett, Anthony. Education & the struggle for democracy: The politics of educational ideas. 1996.

Chazan, Barry. Contemporary approaches to moral education. New york: 1984.

Cherryholmcs, Cleo H. Power and criticism: Poststructural investigations in education. New york: 1988.

Cohen, Adir. Educational philosophy of martin bueber. Rutherford: 1983.

Cohen, Brenda. Education and the individual. Boston. 1981

Collins, P.M. "Newman and contemporary education," educational theory, 26(4), fall 1976.

Cooper, David Edward. Authenticity and learning: Nietzsche's educational philosophy. Boston: 1983.

Cooper, David E. Ed. Education, values, and mind. Boston: 1986.

Cox, H.G. "moral reasoning and the humanities," liberal education, 7(3) (1985).

Cremin, Lawrence A. The republic and the school: Horace Mann on the education of free men. 1957.

Crittenden, B. Education and social ideals. Canada: 1973.

Culler, A.D. The imperial intellect: A study of newman's educational ideal. New Haven: 1955.

Cultural Pluralism. Learning disabilities quarterly, (special issue), 6(4), (fall, 1983).

Dearden, R.F.; Hirst, P.H.; & Peters, Education and the development of reason. Routledge & K. Paul, 1972.

Denicolas, Antonio T. Habits of mind: An introduction to the philosophy of education. New york: 1989.

Devitis, Joseph L. Ed. Women, culture, and morality. New york: 1987.

Dewey, John. Democracy and education. 1966 (1916).

Donovan, Josephine. Feminist theory.

Dworkin, Martin S. Dewey on education: Selections. Teachers college press, 1959.

Eberle, Gary. The geography of nowhere: Finding one's self in the postmodern world. 1994.

Education, Ideology, and the hidden curriculum. Journal of education, (special issue), 162(1), (winter, 1980).

Egan, Kieran. Teaching as story telling. 1986.

Feinberg, Walter. Understanding education: Toward a reconstruction of educational inquiry. New york: 1983.

Feinberg, Walter & Soltis, and Jonas F. School and society. Ny: 1985.

Feinberg, Walter & Rosemont, and Henry Jr., eds. Work, technology, and education: dissenting essays in the intellectual foundations of american education. Urbana: 1975.

Furlong, J.J. & Carroll, and W.J. "teaching moral reasoning with classic texts," educational forum, 5(4) (1988).

Gadotti, Moacir. Pedagogy of praxis: A dialectical philosophy of education. 1996.

Garrison, James W. & Rud, Anthony G., Jr, eds. The educational conversation: Closing the gap. 1995.

Gaskell & Willinsky. Gender in/forms curriculum: From enrichment to transformation. 1995.

Getman, Julius G. In the company of scholars. 1993.

Gibson, Structuralism and education. New Jersey: 1984.

Giroux, Henry a. Border crossings. 1992.

Giroux, Henry A., Postmodernism, feminism, and cultural politics: Redrawing educational boundaries. Albany: 1991.

Giroux, Henry A. Schooling and the struggle for public life: Critical pedagogy in the modern age. Minnesota: 1988.

Goodlad, John I.; Soder, Roger; & Sirotnik, Kenneth A. The moral dimensions of teaching. San Francisco: 1990.

Gore, Jennifer. The struggle for pedagogies: Critical and Feminist discourses as regimes of truth. 1993.

Gouinlock, James. Excellence in public discourse: John stuart mill, john dewey, and social intelligence. New york: 1986.

Gowin, D. Bob. Educating. Ithaca, ny: 1987.

Greene, Maxine. The dialectic of freedom. New york: 1988.

Greene, Maxine. Landscapes of learning. New york: 1978.

Greene, Maxine. Teacher as stranger: Educational philosophy in the Modern age. 1973.

Gupta, Anil. The revision theory of truth. 1993.

Gutman, Amy. Democratic education. 1987.

Index

S

T

U

V

W